Your Brother's Keeper

Your Brother's Keeper

James R. Morrison, M.D.

Nelson-Hall nh **Chicago**

For Ted and Geoff,
and for Patricia

Library of Congress Cataloging in Publication Data

Morrison, James Roy, 1940–
　Your brother's keeper.

　Bibliography:　p.
　Includes index.
　1.　Psychology, Pathological.　2.　Psychotherapy.
3.　Consumer education.　I.　Title.
RC454.M678　　　　616.89　　　　79–27810
ISBN 0–88229–563–2

Copyright © 1981 by James R. Morrison, M.D.

Manufactured in the United States of America

10　9　8　7　6　5　4　3　2　1

Contents

Copy 1

Part III
Doing: Treatments and Management

Preface

I wrote this book to tell you about mental illness what many doctors do not—cannot, in fact, for it contains a lot of material that some psychiatrists, not to mention nonpsychiatric physicians, never learned in medical school. But the ten million or more Americans who at some time in their lives will have one of the major psychoses—manic-depressive disease or schizophrenia—have an enormous stake in this information, and it should be made available to them. For they can best be helped if their friends and relatives understand their conditions enough to assist them in seeking help and maintaining treatment.

Psychiatry, like no other field of medicine, seethes with controversy. Go to any bookstore and pick up titles at random from the "mental health" shelf, and you will find descriptions, theories and treatments of emotional disorder so varied as to confuse all but the trained professional. These presentations sound equally plausible on paper, but in the cold light of scientific scrutiny they span the spectrum of effectiveness from curative to fraudulent. To know what kind of care you have bargained for, you *must* be informed. Fortunately, you can learn more about psychiatry than about any other field of medicine. Although there is a great deal of material to cover, it is generally logical, largely commonsensical, and mostly nontechnical. But where can you learn these things? No textbook of psychiatry stresses the education of families, so many psychiatrists are not oriented to this task. And if no one will teach you to help, you must learn it on your own—which brings us back to this book.

I have presented a personal, but by no means exclusive, approach to diagnosis, treatment and management. In our group of "shrinks," we practice this brand of psychiatry, as do many other psychiatrists throughout the country. We have taught it to young doctors studying to become psychiatrists and family doctors, and with success, because we all have found that it helps deal rationally with patients and their families. Some psychiatrists and other mental health professionals who read this book (and I hope many will) will strongly disagree with the opinions I have expressed; a few may be downright insulted. But this volume was written neither to pan psychiatrists nor to pander to them. Any criticism I have stated or implied is for the sole purpose of more fully informing the nonprofessional about an area of life with which he has found himself vitally, often desperately, concerned.

I have tried to present this material in language as free of jargon as possible. I have written with a logical order in mind, but you may want to pick and choose. If you have begun reading in the back of an ambulance as you accompany your relative to the hospital, you may find the early chapters on symptoms and seeking treatment superfluous for now—skip to the section on illnesses, or treatment. Or you may want to skim over the details of treatment to learn what you need to do right now to help out (chapters 18 and 19). But I advise everyone to read about the illnesses themselves, for it is here, where you are least aware, that problems of diagnosis creep in to cause mischief. As you will learn, the theme of this book is that seeing a doctor is not enough to help your ill relative—you must also know enough about psychiatric illness to evaluate his progress, or lack of it. And you must get the doctor to see *you*.

To give you a better feel for the illnesses and problems described, I have included the case histories of a number of patients I have encountered over the years. These patients, and hundreds more like them, have served as a textbook for me, and I hope they will serve as such for you as well.

San Diego, Calif.
October 1979

Part I
Seeing: Identifying the Patient

1.
Hearing the Cry for Help

Roger Downing unlocked the front door and stepped into his living room, feeling vaguely uneasy. The house was quiet. Too quiet. Missing were the sounds of Lois clanking supper dishes in the kitchen, and the stampeding feet of the twins racing to greet him. No sound, save for somewhere the muffled chugging of an automobile engine.

For a moment he stood, uncertain, then strode to the mantle over the big stone fireplace, where he read the note taped to the mirror: "Kids arc at Mary's." The rhythmic throbbing tugged insistently at his consciousness until, forced to acknowledge its presence, he turned his head slowly back and forth to localize its direction. Down the street towards the highway . . . no, closer . . . the drive. Then—my God, the garage!

He bounded through the kitchen to throw open the door to the connecting garage. He staggered back, overtaken by the fumes and the sound of the station wagon chugging reliably away, belching forth its invisible clouds of poison.

He barely noticed the lipsticked message written backwards on the inside of the window: "I'm sorry." Like the title frame in a motion picture, the phrase partly obscured the scene behind the glass. Against the wheel, face turned toward him, slumped Lois, cherry red lips slightly parted in a phantom kiss, tears drying on pale cheeks. He jerked open the door and grabbed for the ignition key, and she fell heavily against him. As he supported her with his shoulder, an empty pill bottle bounced off her lap and onto the cement floor, drumming a hollow tattoo in the sudden, crashing silence.

Then sirens, shouted orders of doctors, rhythmically hissing respirator, quiet peep-peep of the cardiac monitor now barely

3

audible. And in the silence of the waiting room adjoining the intensive care unit Roger Downing sat, head down, hands half-clenched, half-praying. Waiting.

When he called Mary to ask her to keep the children, she cried, "I should have known!" And so should he, he supposed, but how? Known what? How do you know when someone you love is breaking down? How can you tell? His mind wandered back. . . .

When he first knew her, Lois had been witty and gay, a vivacious man-attracting coed bubbling with fun. Even then she had moments—well, days—when she seemed cross and out of sorts. Those times when she was cranky and irritable, unreasonable (weren't all women?), even tearful, occurred infrequently, inconveniencing but not alarming him. He had called it "premenstrual tension" early in their relationship, and they even talked about it once or twice—between times. Then she laughingly agreed with him that she had her moments of bitchiness, and he accommodated himself to them and to her, and they were happy.

The arrival of the children was a time of joy compounded with some anxiety, for twins had not been suspected until late in her pregnancy. Although the delivery was easy and the babies healthy from the start, for several months afterwards Lois had been more prone to spells of moodiness than before. But by the time their son and daughter could sit alone she had recovered fully and enthusiastically assumed the duties of motherhood.

It had been several months before that he first noticed anything really wrong, and then it was only a subtle, quiet shadow which occasionally darkened their lives. When he called from work in the afternoon she might assume a distant coolness which they both would recognize and later explain as the natural tiredness resulting from the unrelenting demands of two healthy children. If the dishes more often soaked in the sink until he did them himself before work the next day, he regarded it a small price to pay for his wife's happiness.

But he wondered, too, at the bone-deep weariness which more and more often sent her to bed exhausted soon after the children were tucked in. And it had begun to affect her life in other ways. Upon completing the first semester of her Spanish class at the night college, she did not go back for the second. Formerly a fervid local politicker, she let the town fend for itself as she stopped attending council meetings. Her weekly phone calls to her mother became sporadic, then ceased altogether.

Her mood changed. The good, high periods had disappeared, leaving at best a flat calm which registered neither offense nor delight. Brief crying spells punctuated the sadness which settled in her features like a fog; in response to her growing irritability his daily lunchtime phone calls stopped.

About two months before, Lois had finally visited Dr. Fiddler, physician to the family since Roger's childhood. Apart from a five-pound weight loss she was pronounced to be in perfect health. The headaches, fatigue and loss of appetite of which she complained were "just nerves"; she returned with a bottle of sleeping pills, and for a few days felt better.

But the depression resumed, to Roger's annoyance.

"My God, Lois, pull yourself together! You've been dragging around here like a limp washrag for months now. Why can't you get your head on straight?"

She had refused him in bed more often of late, and he had tried to be understanding, but even patient husbands have limits to their tolerance. A few times she had tried to explain to him how she felt, but he had either not understood or not listened. More and more now she spent day and night alike in silence.

He noticed that she seemed at her worst in the morning, frequently awakening several hours before he did. A few times he had arisen at five or earlier to find her sitting in the kitchen smoking cigarettes, a habit which she had given up years before at his request, and drinking black coffee. Coffee and cigarettes—the only "food" she claimed she could tolerate before noon. By nightfall her appetite usually improved, but still she must have lost fifteen or twenty pounds in all. Her clothes hung loosely on her never ample frame, and he kiddingly offered to send her CARE packages.

At his insistence, she had finally consulted Dr. Fiddler again, two days before. She returned with tranquilizers, a new bottle of sleeping pills, and some advice: "You have a great deal to be grateful for, young lady—two fine, healthy children, a husband who loves you very much, and a lovely home. You'll just have to get busy and pull yourself together."

She had put the bottles carefully away in her dresser drawer; he had not seen her take the medicine. Could she have been saving the pills for this? Guilt and remorse swept over him in a rush; he closed his eyes and leaned far back on the greasy plastic upholstery of the waiting room sofa.

He must have slept, for he awoke to sunlight shining through the venetian blinds covering the small window, creating a barred pattern on the highly buffed tile floor. The doctor in charge of the intensive care unit stood over him, waiting.

This scene—a patient comatose, a spouse brooding on the past, wondering what might have been done differently—can be found in any hospital emergency or admitting department. Throughout the country, it is replayed hundreds, perhaps thousands of times weekly. Yet the drama of suicide, completed or attempted, represents only the tip of the iceberg which is major mental illness, a problem so prevalent as to touch the lives of nearly everyone at some point. One out of ten persons will be admitted to a psychiatric hospital at some time during his or her life; eight million of us will have at least one attack of depression similar to Lois Downing's, and two million more will be affected by schizophrenia. Twenty thousand suicides are reported in this country each year—a death every twenty-six minutes—but tens of thousands more go unreported. And for each person who successfully completes suicide, several others mutilate themselves in attempts which, though unsuccessful, often result in an agony of physical and mental suffering, loss of time from work, and hospitalization.

The tragedy, of course, is that most of these dramas need never be played. Modern psychiatric treatment may not offer the assurance of recovery in every case, but in the last three decades we have come so far with treatment that most patients recover, and most others improve markedly. Although even someone as severely ill as Lois can be treated successfully, depression which has progressed as far as hers requires the intensive care afforded by hospitalization. But illness caught earlier in its course can usually be treated on an outpatient basis, at an incalculable saving of time, money, and human distress. Obviously, the trick is to identify the illness in its early stages, a feat to which Roger Downing found himself unequal.

Of course, he had had no formal training in detecting psychiatric illness; but then, he did not really need any. Once they have lived through an episode or two of illness, relatives of psychiatric patients usually become excellent observers and recorders of behavior. They learn to look for early symptoms which may indicate a recurrence, and because they see the patient every day, they can often predict relapses even before the psychiatrist can. Through readings or talks with the doctor, they understand the quirks of the illness, and they come to know, often better than the physician, the course it will take. They are then able to steer their relative to the proper professional resource early enough to save months of misery, thousands of dollars, and perhaps life itself. All they need is sufficient familiarity with the condition to avoid the terrified paralysis that comes of not knowing what to do.

In the case of Lois, the warning flags flew early. Roger recalled them clearly once he paused to review the events of the past few months. Had he been better informed, he might have sought help shortly after her difficulties began. In the next two chapters we will reexamine the course of her illness to see what signals of ensuing illness she emitted almost from the beginning, and how her husband, with some understanding of psychiatric symptoms, might have saved her the months of anguish which culminated in a gas-filled garage.

2.
Signals of Mental Distress: Social Functioning

When a psychiatrist makes his initial examination, he enquires into many areas of the patient's life. While some of the effects of mental illness are so obvious that anyone can see them, other subtle symptoms are revealed only by careful questioning. But there is nothing mysterious about these indications of illness, and the psychiatrist is no magician. He only asks questions and makes simple observations which he knows will lead him to a diagnosis. As we will see, any thoughtful person can learn to observe and understand most of these early signals of mental illness. In the following pages you will find illustrations of many of these symptoms, as well as definitions of some of the confusing terms psychiatrists use as we discuss the effects of mental illness on the lives of the patient and his family.

Early on, Lois's depression cut into the day-to-day activities she had formerly enjoyed. Begun with enthusiasm, her Spanish class and her attendance at the town council meetings became a burden, and she dropped them. Falling out of the telephone habit could have provided a warning to her mother, had she known that depressed people often choose to be alone, avoiding even church functions which they once attended "religiously." Formerly enjoyed sports, like bowling leagues, bridge clubs or TV no longer arouse the patient's interest. "I'm just not interested anymore," he may state. He rationalizes this lack of drive by stating that he is too busy or too tired. If his wife tries to encourage greater participation, he ignores her, or irritably complains that she nags him.

8

Not everyone shows social difficulties by withdrawing from other people, however. Under the influence of psychiatric illness, some people interact entirely too much and too well, becoming excessively outgoing, annoyingly jovial, or spontaneous to the point they will not be quiet.

The door of the College Corner Tavern flew open with a crash which set glasses rattling on the shelf behind the bar. Fred and Ivan, seated at a small table behind the pinball machines, turned around in their chairs to get a better view of the disturbance. What they saw was Gilbert Grand standing in the open doorway wearing a red hunting cap, arms akimbo, laughing uproariously at their surprise. He strode to the table, turned a chair around and straddled it.

"Hi, guys! Been waiting long? I'd've been along sooner but I had to get some things straightened out with my lawyer." He turned to the bar. "Give me a lawyer's on the rocks—I mean a Teacher's on the rocks—better make it a double!" Gilbert almost immediately resumed his conversation.

"Wait'll you see the plans I've been working on," he said, unfolding several pieces of smudged drafting paper. "This idea's going to turn plenty of people on, you better believe me. I spent all day at the library checking out some of the technical problems, and working out the solutions. *Nothing* can stand in my way now!" He shuffled the pages back and forth excitedly, then demanded, "Well, what do you think?"

Fred and Ivan shifted uneasily in their chairs. They had all been close friends since entering engineering graduate school two years before. They had stood up for him when he married Eileen the first winter, and one or two days a week they had been together after classes. He had always appeared modest, hard working and rather unassuming, earning him the affectionate nickname of "Clark Kent."

Gilbert's drink arrived. He drained it off at once, then handed the glass back to the bartender. "Make me another one of those," he said, "and set 'em up. Drinks for the house, I'm buying."

He stood and gazed about the mostly empty room, bowing slightly when he appeared to catch someone's eye. Abruptly he sat down and turned once again to his plans.

"This is the Grand Gauge Monorail," he said, pointing to one sheet of paper. "Tremendous success with these things in Japan, but we won't use cheap foreign parts, no sir! Nothing but good old U.S. made-in-America machinery for the Grand Gauge Monorail. Seattle to Miami in twenty-four hours. Top speed of over two hundred miles an hour. I've got the route all laid out here on this piece of paper. Straight as a string."

"Gosh Gilbert," Ivan ventured, "it seems kind of impractical. Do you think . . ."

Gilbert seemed not to hear, and hurried on. "This will make Amtrak look like model railroading," he said. He jumped up from the table, took a roll of nickels from his jacket pocket and began to play two pinball machines simultaneously. After a few moments of play, he returned to the table and scooped up his papers, tossing a wadded twenty-dollar bill onto the table.

"Drinks are on me. *Everybody's* drinks are on me." He exploded through the door, slamming it with another terrific crash.

His dinner was ready a little before he came home that evening, and Eileen moved slowly about the kitchen putting the finishing touches on the meal. Eight months pregnant, she worried about Gilbert. He had seemed rather blue about job prospects for the past few days, and had complained of some difficulty sleeping. But he was in good spirits when he left for school that morning, rather earlier than usual, and he sounded almost elated when he telephoned her at noon to tell her about the new project in which he was engaged.

At length he arrived, bounding through the living room to the kitchen. From the doorway he sailed his hat through the air like a Frisbee, landing it squarely in a pan of mixed vegetables simmering on the stove. He laughed as he fished it out, licked the sauce from his fingers and set the hat back on his head.

"Hi ya, Baby," he bellowed. "How's my favorite little stewed tomato?" He clasped his arms around her and lingeringly kissed her, his hands wandering over her backside. He turned off the burners on the stove, picked her up and carried her into the bedroom.

"Dessert first," he chuckled. She objected faintly, but the novelty made it seem refreshing.

Later, he only picked at his dinner, showed her some papers, and explained his project.

"I've already taken out options on some of the property along the right of way," he said. "This will make us millions— millions! I've already spoken to the President about it!" He spoke hurriedly, and she had some difficulty in following him as he jumped from point to point in his hurried discourse.

At last, unable to get him to answer some of the questions which were troubling her, she arose and went into the bedroom.

He jumped up from the table, and started after her, anticipation again showing on his face. . . .

"He's supposed to meet me here at four," she told the doctor several days later. It was a quarter past. "I told him I was feeling nervous—he'd never come for himself. He doesn't think there's anything wrong with him."

She stared at the Kleenex box which he had offered her, took one, crushed it in her hands, and pleaded, "Isn't there anything you can do?"

"I'm afraid I really don't know enough about your husband yet to do anything," the psychiatrist responded. He tapped his pencil on the polished mahogany desk-top. "Tell me about the televisions."

"Well, we had talked about getting a new TV—even picked out a color portable. So I wasn't *too* surprised when they delivered one from the store, even though it was a 23-inch model. But two more came the next day. And then there came all sorts of weird things he'd bought on our Mastercharge. An electronic organ—he can't play a note—and six pairs of tennis shoes, and a stuffed alligator. My God, doctor, a six-foot stuffed alligator in our living room!" She needed another Kleenex, and took it.

"And the talking. Doctor, he talks twenty hours a day, about anything. Everything! You can't get him to shut up for five seconds. You'll see."

More Kleenex. And loud voices in the outer office, followed by a louder tattoo drummed upon the door. And Gilbert Grand, standing in the now-open doorway, dressed in his underwear and engineer's boots, a black cape flung about his shoulders, eyes staring far away, beatific smile on his face. . . .

Clutching her swollen abdomen, his wife wept.

People with outrageous symptoms like Gilbert Grand's demand (and receive) attention. Lois Downing's symptoms were no less spectacular, but they developed so gradually that they blended with her normal personality. This gradual onset of her illness prevented it from coming to medical attention more quickly. From the two patients we can derive a basic principle which will guide us in identifying emotional problems: a *change* from the previous personality frequently heralds mental illness.

The fundamental building blocks of personality—temperamental attributes such as activity level, quality of mood, persistence, adaptability to new situations as well as other features—are present almost from birth, and recent research by child psychiatrists suggests that these traits remain relatively unchanged throughout life. The behavior and attitudes he sees in others throughout his childhood also influence the child's developing personality, which by adolescence is generally recognizable as that which he will carry, more or less fixed, into adult life. Marked personality changes usually do not occur after adolescence, so, from mid-teens on, careful attention should be paid to any striking modification. Common warning signals include altered life goals (sudden shifts in career plans, decisions to marry or divorce) and approach to (or avoidance of) other people. If you find yourself saying, "She just doesn't seem like her old self," your relative may be showing signs of developing emotional illness.

SEXUAL AND MARITAL FUNCTIONING

Both patients we have encountered so far had difficulties in their sexual adaptation, but sex represented a different sort of hardship for the family of each. Gilbert Grand's frequent demands for sex proved more than his wife's delicate condition could fully accommodate. At that, they were lucky, for sometimes a heightened sex drive (*libido*) takes a decidedly inappropriate direction, causing the patient to approach relatives, casual friends, total strangers, children, or even animals. Venereal disease and remorse may be all the patient has to suffer after an illness-induced fling, but a woman who awakens from a siege of psychiatric illness may find herself pregnant. Recovering from a manic state during which she had entertained a succession of boyfriends, one college girl sheepishly admitted that she "must have been bitten by the bed bug."

Fortunately, dalliances such as these are the exception rather than the rule. Rather more frequently, decreased interest in sex attends the onset of psychiatric illness. Lois Downing became so occupied with her troubles that she couldn't have cared less about sex. But because depressed women are still physically capable of sex, depression in the accommodating wife may be noticed less than in her husband, who may be affected also by a physiological inability to achieve or maintain erection (*impotence*), usually to his considerable distress. And both men and women may lose their ability to have an orgasm.

In the midst of all this psychological and physical sexual turmoil, enter the spouse—with complications. Disappointed by her husband's lagging libido, a wife may seek sexual fulfillment outside the marriage. The patient, even more troubled by his flagging amatory zeal than he can admit, may also wander from the nuptial bed, hoping thereby to stimulate himself into a better performance. The chaos which results when these events come to light, as events are wont to do, may provide the stimulus for the initial psychiatric consultation.

But matrimonial bickering and backbiting may be caused by problems other than sexual dysfunction (sex in some cases becoming "the only good part of our marriage we have left"). The patient-to-be finds it hard to appear interested in his spouse, so preoccupied is he with his own problems. A healthy marriage, like a healthy puppy, must be fed, watered, and petted daily, obligations which the patient can no longer meet. And as he becomes less responsive to his spouse's needs for compassion and communication, he finds himself increasingly in the doghouse. He sees life "through a glass darkly," as the black fog which hangs over him changes his perspective toward his family. He is swept up by anger over which he has no control. Sometimes he reads hostility into the attitudes of others, and comes to believe they persecute him. Because you see only the behavior produced by these changes in mood and thought and can neither experience nor comprehend the anguish concealed by the anger, the irritability, or the silence, you keep playing the game of life as it was before, expecting that your relative will do the same.

But for him the rules have changed; now he plays at a considerable disadvantage. Not only can he not communicate, he cannot even comprehend that his own point of view has altered. Because he does not realize he is ill, he cannot justify his actions and attitudes, which only confirm his increasingly low opinion of himself. Because he, too, continues to judge himself by "normal" standards, everyday social interchanges leave him, like Lois, increasingly anxious, guilt-ridden, and depressed. And, because so much of his trouble seems to occur at home, he begins to blame his low moods on "marital discord" and may seek relief in separation or divorce. Because of the confusion of cause and effect typical of mental illness, he does not understand that his connubial conflicts *result from* his emotional disturbance, and not the reverse. Of course, the situation sometimes is reversed, as even the most tolerant husbands and wives have their limits. When confronted daily with the supposedly perverse attitudes of the patient, his spouse may eventually tire of being abused and may decide to throw in the sponge. The divorce which sometimes results is a twofold tragedy. Not only could it be prevented by early recognition of the symptoms of illness, but breakup of the marriage may render the patient more despondent than ever, and less accessible to treatment. Or convalescence may be prolonged by the patient's impression that he now has "nothing to live for."

The physician can only treat the illness—the family remains the actual mainstay of the patient, representing the most important reason he has for wanting to recover. And in the hands of a skillful physician, the family can also be a valuable instrument for administering therapy and evaluating its progress. To provide help like this, it is vital that the family learn to swallow pride and put aside feelings of injury and neglect and to view the patient's attitudes and behavior as symptoms of illness. This done, the battle for the psychiatric patient's mind has been half won.

ALCOHOL

Many a man (and woman, too) has turned to drink as the early symptoms of psychiatric illness begin to take their toll. When excited, a Gilbert Grand feels he can "hold his liquor" better than usual, and he may imbibe prodigious quantities of beer or hard liquor as he unfolds his grandiose schemes. The reason is simple: through trial and error he has learned the power of alcohol to depress, or slow down the brain. Why he would want to slow down is a point that often puzzles those who see him in action; apparently he is having the time of his life. But people often feel quite uncomfortable when "speeding up" like this; their thoughts race so fast, their tongues must struggle to keep up; they complain of the "jitters"; they cannot sleep. So they drink just to unwind enough to sleep. This type of drinking can lead to alcoholism when kept up long enough, but this usually takes years. In the short course of his illness, Gilbert Grand had no chance to become even suggestively alcoholic.

The common expression "drown your sorrows in beer" has a special meaning in psychiatry. When depression becomes intolerable, some people seek relief in alcohol from their morbid thoughts. Time and again psychiatrists see patients who at first appear to be simply alcoholic, but who later prove to have disorders of mood (depressions or manias) which require vigorous treatment. Unfortunately, some psychiatrists do not always recognize what they see; their patients may limp along for months or years, treated for one illness but suffering two. In any area of medicine, "symptomatic treatment" like this is usually doomed to failure at best and at worst, to disaster.

Although estimates vary depending upon the definition of "alcoholism" used, between five and nine million Americans drink enough to be classified as alcoholics. How many people drink because of a preexisting psychiatric illness we cannot even guess; undoubtedly, a substantial number do. For them the feelings of remorse and the inability to cope with life resulting from heavy alcohol abuse add to the already overwhelming burden of psychiatric illness. So guilt augments depression, which in turn leads to more drinking. Our general rule for recognizing illness might be paraphrased: anyone whose drinking behavior changes may be having a mental problem.

When you hear of "alcohol problems," you think of delirium tremens and bleeding ulcers. But few alcoholics ever have such severe health complications. The difficulties of the average alcoholic will more likely be social in nature. He fights with family and friends who tell him he drinks too much, at the same time feeling secretly guilty about his drinking. Absenteeism or chronic tardiness leads to dismissal from work; he piles up traffic accidents and tickets until he loses his license. Unable to stop drinking, he desperately sets rules to try to regain his lost control—the old "I won't drink before 5:00 P.M." ploy. Other early symptoms of problem drinking include "blackouts," in which the patient cannot remember what he did the day before when drinking ("You were

really a riot at the party last night, Harry—don't you remember?");
preoccupation with alcohol ("I won't go to Tito Taylor's party—he
never serves anything but fruit punch"); gulping the first one or
two drinks; sneaking additional drinks in the kitchen ("I don't
have to have it, but rich Aunt Minnie might not understand"). One
swallow makes neither a summer nor an alcoholic, but any one of
these symptoms should put you on the alert for the possibility of
an alcohol-related illness.

DRUG ABUSE

Too heavy or nonmedical uses of other substances serve as a
similar warning of ensuing illness. The salesman struggling to fill
his week's quota may smoke more cigarettes as his anxiety mounts.
The housewife under tension from demands of husband, children
and volunteer activities drinks coffee throughout the day until by
nightfall she is a walking, shaking advertisement for Postum. Just
as overuse of these conventional drugs—alcohol, tobacco and coffee—may warn of oncoming illness, so may abuse of "street drugs"
like marijuana, LSD, amphetamines, barbiturates, and even narcotics. Young people are particularly likely to resort to drugs in an
effort to escape the feelings of depression and boredom which they
themselves may not even recognize.

Although Benny's father had been the black sheep of the
family, the name he left his son was that of a department store
chain in a large midwestern city. His mother lived with him
five thankless years without benefit of clergy, finally tired of
his drinking and moved with Benny into a squalid ghetto tene-
ment. There she supplemented her relief checks by occasionally
purveying her body to those with a taste for shopworn goods.

As he grew into his teen years, Benny improved little upon
his circumstances. His school performance desultory and his
friends few, he began at age fifteen to "blow grass" to relieve
the boredom of unrelenting idleness and the anxieties of con-
summate poverty. Dropping out of school in his sophomore
year, he assumed a hippie lifestyle in a communal house near
the center of the city. During the next three years, while most
of his young cousins attended private schools and took riding
lessons, Benny lived on the charity of his friends, devoted to
acid rock and hard drugs.

Eventually he found his way to the reclining chair in a psychiatrist's office. "I was never much into smack (heroin)," he said, his long blonde hair flowing over a "keep on trucking" tee shirt, "but I did everything else. Man, I'd drop acid, smoke weed, shoot up speed and drink half a gallon of Thunderbird, all at the same time. I wanted a total wipeout. I didn't want to feel a thing."

Gaunt, thin, and disheveled, Benny did not recognize his mood as depression, but when treated with antidepressant medication, he rapidly gained weight. His interest in outside activities improved; he found a job, bought a motorcycle, and acquired an "old woman," the first time in his life he ever felt like loving.

Although he still smokes marijuana, he now has no desire to take other drugs; his spirits, he says, are no longer depressed. Although somewhat unusual (but true), Benny's case suggests that at least some teenagers and young adults begin to abuse drugs to relieve symptoms resulting from treatable mental illness.

WORK

At work the mentally ill are particularly vulnerable; high job performance demands adequate interest, concentration, and energy. The patient himself may notice a decline in the quality of his work, a decreased capacity for prolonged concentration, or excessive fatigue after a short time on the job. He begins to think of quitting or changing a job he used to enjoy, believing (after twenty years) that he is "in the wrong line of work." The salesman lies in bed until noon rather than hurrying out early in the morning to solicit new orders. The meticulous housewife allows dirty dishes to pile up in the sink and the beds to go unchanged for weeks.

Performance of schoolwork, the job of children, adolescents, and many young adults may suffer, too. Under emotional stress, even the young child may bring home a failing report card covered with those old-standby teachers' comments, "does not work up to capacity," "needs further improvement." Older students find they cannot concentrate on examinations or complete term papers; college students experience Brobdingnagian indecision as to which courses to take, and flit from one major to another.

The child younger than twelve may become hyperactive in the classroom. Utterly unable to sit still, he repeatedly jumps from his seat to sharpen a pencil, to drink from the fountain, or to visit with his neighbors. His attention span plummets, followed by his grades, and even story time may not sustain his interest. Sent to principal or counselor as behavior problems, the emotional base for over-activity passes unnoticed in many of these young students. Physicians may mistakenly diagnose these children as having minimal brain dysfunction and treat them with stimulant medication such as Dexedrine or Ritalin. This treatment succeeds quite well in many hyperactive children, but when applied in a misdiagnosed case can lead to chaos. In any child whose hyperactivity has not been clearly present from the earliest years, depression or other emotional problems should be suspected until proven otherwise.

Tattling, tantrums, and tears in a child are often explained as "just going through a phase," but no one really knows what this means. Most "phases" are short-lived and benign, so an extended period of altered relationships with peers and parents suggests more serious problems which should be investigated. One couple put up with two years of crying, irritability, and poor grades before seeking help for their nine-year-old son. On the first visit, the diagnosis of depression led to antidepressant therapy, relieving his symptoms within a month. But no one could wipe away the two years of frustration and self-criticism which must have left their indelible mark on his personality.

In an older age group, persistent change of personality is sometimes referred to as "adolescent turmoil," a term implying that unpredictable teen-age behavior results from problems due to the trauma associated with growing up. Actually, many young people sufficiently troubled to come to the attention of their teachers have genuine mental illness—something more than just a hard time growing up. All should be carefully evaluated, and some will need treatment.

Many students who complain of an "identity crisis" actually suffer from depression. Just as in older patients, poor concentration and feelings of worthlessness lead to the desire to escape to a less demanding environment. And, being more mobile, many do drop out of high school or college to "find themselves," and do not receive the medical attention they deserve.

The military, ministering as it does to a "captive" population, presents special social difficulties to patients and to their families.

Although the uniformed services try hard to screen out men and women who are psychiatrically ill, many unfit inductees sift through simply because they were too young to show symptoms at the time they joined up. Consequently, a fair number fall ill while on active duty, some coincidentally, some stressed by the need to conform or by the injudicious use of alcohol which is, if not freely, at least cheaply available to service people. Were psychiatric care only as readily obtainable, the plight of the military patient would seem less poignant. To be sure, some with less severe emotional illnesses are treated and returned to duty. But the traditional service approach to psychiatric problems has been an administrative one, emphasizing speedy discharge for the "offender" (not patient) who appears unable to conform to military life. Substantial numbers of veterans are discharged with inadequate evaluations and/or incorrect diagnoses and return to society, sometimes with no treatment at all. On the other hand, some individuals continue on active duty for years despite low-grade psychiatric illnesses which, though serious enough to occasionally impair work performance, do not render them totally unsuitable for the service. When finally discharged from active duty, these people may be unable to compete in the more demanding civilian labor market, become increasingly ill or drink excessively, only then seeking treatment.

We have seen that social symptoms often define mental illness early in its course. You may have trouble learning to regard difficulties in getting along at home and at work as indicating illness, but once you do, you will be better prepared to recognize trouble early and to move your relative toward help. The mental symptoms discussed in the next chapter may not be obvious so soon, because they exist entirely in the patient's mind until he chooses to talk about them.

3.
More Signals:
Physical and Mental

Although social difficulties certainly can suggest mental illness, what we usually mean by "symptoms" are the psychological and physical changes which the patient experiences. Often, he cannot identify these symptoms in himself: relatives or friends may notice some, but others remain in hiding until medical examination. But you can learn to recognize nearly all, even before noticed by the doctor, if you have a "map" to guide you along the path taken by the psychiatrist as he ferrets out psychopathology. But while reading about low moods and high, delusions and hallucinations, keep in mind that nearly any "symptom" can occur in a normal individual, and that all well people have occasional "symptoms." Medical students who forget this diagnose pneumonia whenever someone coughs, or imagine that they themselves suffer from every disease they study. And as is true for any illness, it is better to avoid "medical students' disease" than to cure it.

In somewhat simplified form, then, what follows is a discussion of the characteristics a psychiatrist turns over in his mind each time he evaluates the emotional condition (he calls it the "mental status") of a new patient.

CHANGES IN APPEARANCE

A psychiatrist begins to assess his patient from the moment he sets foot inside the office. Although sometimes hard to detect in teen-age and college students, changes in personal habits, body cleanliness, dress, and mannerisms can mean mental distress. The depressed patient wears the same clothes day in and day out, or he chooses colors as drab as his mood. Like Gilbert Grand, the excited, grandiose patient puts on loud, garish colors or bizarre combinations of clothing which fit his mood but not the occasion. One psychotic lady came to her appointment with dozens of paper tags and bits of tinfoil dangled by strings from her dress. The person gradually withdrawing from reality stays more and more to himself, isolated in his room, paying little attention to his personal habits. He forgets to shave, to wash, or to change his underwear for weeks at a time, until he has quite literally an air (but not of mystery) about him.

The patient's mental state may be revealed by his "body language": Gilbert Grand's sudden bursts of energy clearly showed his agitation, but more usually you will find subtler signs such as knuckle-cracking, finger-drumming, and seat-squirming. Tearfulness, trembling lips, or forced smiles reveal the tension felt by an anxious patient who in an advanced stage of illness may become immobile, mute, or assume bizarre (catatonic) positions. All in all, only the exceptional patient appears at the psychiatric emergency ward clean-shaven and dapper—and well-behaved.

SPEECH

Gilbert Grand talked torrentially. His friends tried to interrupt his loud, rapid speech, but gave it up as a bad business; he overwhelmed them with his verbal diarrhea. This well-known pattern of talking, called *push of speech,* typifies elated patients who may also complain (or brag) that ideas come so rapidly to them they must jump quickly from one thought to the next. Asked what day he entered the hospital, one man responded:

"I came in on a Tuesday/today is Friday/we have fish in the stream by our house—
Tomorrow is Saturday/the next day is Sunday/you're spoiling my fun day, you louse."

Once you make the connection between Friday and fish, you can see a certain curious logic to his statement. But this flow of thought was determined not by the needs of the occasion, but by the sound of his words—rhyme, but no reason. Such a *flight of ideas* often accompanies push of speech in excited patients and is quite typical of mania. "Loose" associations of thought like these may also be influenced by puns and other similarities in word sounds.

Depressed patients often speak abnormally, also, in a most distinctive manner. Had we interviewed Lois Downing, we might have noticed her slow, retarded cadences with long pauses between words, phrases, and sentences, every utterance seeming to require tremendous effort. She might also have complained that her thinking had slowed down, that she could not concentrate, or that her mind was a blank. The severely depressed offer few spontaneous comments, only replying yes or no to questions when they answer at all. Should the depression advance still further, speech may grind to a complete halt as the patient retreats into a shell of muteness, merely turning quietly away from any intruder upon his solitude.

Some other patients speak quite irrelevantly, their responses logically unrelated to the question asked. A nineteen-year-old girl, ill for many months, was asked by a young and rather impressionable medical student why she had been admitted to the hospital. Her reply, accompanied by a hawk-like gaze and firm pressure on his arm, took him somewhat aback; she queried, "How many hairs does a man have around his penis?" The friend of someone given to such *tangential speech* will volunteer that he "cannot understand what he is trying to tell me." This type of speech pathology (yet another loose association) suggests severe illness and requires immediate attention.

ALTERATIONS OF MOOD

Mood, our state of mind (how we feel at any given time), is one of the most important features which a psychiatrist assesses, and the most commonly encountered abnormal mood state is depression. Lois Downing actually told her doctor that she felt sad, but other depressed patients may express this mood by a variety of equivalent statements: blue, nervous, lonely, depressed, down in the dumps, anxious—these are only a few of the expressions which people use to describe their low spirits. The mood of depression is pervasive and often infectious, causing those around to feel depressed, too.

Everything about Lois advertised her misery. With the corners of her mouth turned down and her eyes lackluster, she would sit quietly, shoulders sagging, seeming ready to burst into tears at any moment. Not only did Lois *feel* sad, she also *looked* depressed. Our actions and appearance express the mood we feel and play an important part in conveying how we feel to others. It often happens that someone will communicate the *affect,* or feeling tone, accompanying his thoughts better by these nonverbal means than by direct statements—who has not at some time said that he feels "fine," only to be given away by his expression or the slope of his shoulders?

Depressed mood may not be present all the time. Early in the course of illness, especially, some days are good, some bad. Certain times of the day may be better than others for some, and many patients improve temporarily when distracted by the presence of friends or relatives, or when engaged in pleasurable activities. But the more severely depressed they become, the less likely they are to be buoyed up by environmental circumstances.

Crying spells often, but not invariably, accompany depression—some patients lament that if only they *could* cry, they would feel better. Crying spells can occur suddenly, without warning; the patient cannot explain them, and they embarrass him because they show his lack of control.

Many very severely ill people will have persistent gloomy thoughts of death; some even wish to die. Suicidal ideas, which can occur in a number of different psychiatric illnesses, may be acted upon by the patient who, in desperation, sees no other way out of his misery. Some people make only veiled hints at suicide ("You'd be better off without me") and others may say nothing, but quietly go about arranging their affairs, willing their bodies to a medical school. Most who eventually try it do communicate their ideas to someone, however, and these expressions of the wish for death must be heeded, no matter how trivial they may seem. Because of the importance of suicide as a symptom, we will devote an entire chapter (chapter 13) to it later.

We encounter a euphoric (high) affect like Gilbert Grand's much less frequently than we do depression, but when present it is hard to miss. Periods of mild elation or "high spirits" can occur briefly in almost anyone whose day is sunny and whose life is untroubled, but an abnormally high mood which lasts longer than a few hours indicates the need for immediate consultation. Other types of abnormal mood and affect which hint at the need for psychiatric evaluation include persistent irritability, anxiety, hostility or anger in a formerly pleasant, easygoing person. Benny felt only profound boredom until he received treatment—only then did he recognize the depressive quality to his mood. In fact, patients quite often do not recognize these altered mood states in themselves, complaining only of feeling "nervous," "uptight," or "close to a nervous breakdown."

Because most people can usually control the expression of their emotions, we often find it hard to realize that someone in the throes of a psychiatric illness cannot regulate his feelings, and this results in inappropriate, even harmful advice given by well-meaning friends: "You'll be all right if you just snap out of it. Raise your chin and start acting like a man." Were this always possible, there would be no need for psychiatrists, or books of advice (or, for that matter, relatives). But all are needed, and sometimes urgently, for only the rare (and only mildly disturbed) patient can, so to speak, pull himself up by his mental bootstraps.

A psychiatrist examines his patient not only for the type of affect, but for variation (lability) of affect. An abnormally elated patient may laugh uproariously only to break down into tears seconds later. Because similar shifts from tears of joy to tears of sorrow can result from head injuries and brain tumors, affective lability may require complete physical and neurological evaluation. At the opposite extreme is the marked loss in the range of affect, commonly called "blunting" or "flattening." Those so affected seem to regard all matters with approximately equal interest, responding neither with the smiles nor frowns that the occasion would seem to dictate.

Finally, the psychiatrist assesses appropriateness of affect. Does the patient laugh or appear sad at the right times? Both Lois and Gilbert showed affect appropriate to what they talked about, even though each had abnormal *type* of mood. But patients with inappropriate affect giggle to themselves when describing events we would consider sad, such as a friend's death, or they cheerfully discuss perfectly frightening experiences, such as the paralysis of a leg or sudden blindness, with an enthusiasm usually reserved for Christmas and X-rated movies. This lack of concern, called "la belle indifférence" (lofty indifference) is usually associated with neurosis and personality disorder. Laughing at tales of sorrow or sniggering when nothing has been said at all often indicates serious psychiatric illness.

Still, because laughing and giggling form a natural part of everyday life, we tend to explain it on the basis of embarrassment. If you have lived close to a friend or relative whose life is being affected by mental illness, you have experienced the frightening, sinking sensation of knowing something is wrong, but not wanting to believe it. Not only will you believe any reason he gives for his behavior, but you yourself make excuses for all sorts of peculiar actions. You naturally tend to explain the progression of symptoms in readily understandable terms, usually as an effect of the environment upon the patient, even though you must strain your credulity to the breaking point to do so. Examples: she became depressed because her mother died (six years ago); he drinks because his father beat him (when he was a lad); he laughs a lot because he has a new money-making scheme (actually a symptom of his illness, not the cause). Rationalizations like these are perfectly understandable, but try to resist the temptation to swallow them whole; to give in may delay psychiatric evaluation and treatment.

Body Function

Disruption in the normal rhythms of body functioning frequently accompany psychiatric illness. Rather early in the course of her illness, Lois Downing experienced mild difficulty in falling asleep (initial insomnia), for which she obtained sleeping medication. Later, she developed a classical symptom of severe depression: awakening long before the alarm, then lying awake until morning, unable to fall asleep again (terminal insomnia). Occasionally the opposite of insomnia *(hypersomnia)* will occur, particularly in adolescents and young adults who state that they cannot stay awake in class or whose parents complain that they cannot be routed from bed, even if they have slept until noon. Unfortunately, doctors sometimes yield to the temptation to treat the symptom of sleep disturbance with pills, rather than attacking the underlying illness. This is just more symptomatic treatment. Although disturbance of sleep can occur as an isolated symptom of no great import, it often means mental illness of a greater or lesser degree. It is only one of the many symptoms which the psychiatrist tries to put into perspective before he starts treatment.

Both Lois and Gilbert ate less when they became ill. Appetite disturbances indicate stress, and often provide early signals of illness. The psychiatric patient who loses his appetite for an extended period may experience profound, though rarely life-threatening weight loss. Food nauseates him; he feels full, gaseous, or bloated. He arises from the table after a few bites, and his relatives complain that he eats like a canary. Clothing hangs as he loses weight, and he may become weak or anemic from hunger and malnutrition. But for nearly every "black" psychiatric symptom there is a "white" one; in the grip of a mental disturbance, some people begin to eat compulsively, perhaps out of boredom or loneliness, even though they do not feel particularly hungry. Although less common than weight loss, profound increase in weight can also herald the onset of psychiatric illness.

Roger Downing recalled that his wife often seemed extra irritable and depressed in the morning, yet had nearly returned to her usual self when he arrived home at night. This characteristic of illness we call "diurnal (daily) variation" of mood, a behavior pattern probably related to disturbances in the inherent rhythms of the nervous system (the so-called biological clock). Like Lois, the patient typically feels worse in the morning but improves as the day progresses. But some people, usually those who are less severely ill, begin the day feeling relatively well, then become more and more depressed, tired and irritable as the day wears on.

Physical symptoms are seen quite commonly, and may be the only problem the patient complains of initially. With emotional problems occupying an increasing amount of the patient's energy, he may complain that he feels "tired all the time" or "has no pep." Persistent anxiety can lead to typical tension headaches (pain at the base of the skull radiating down the neck) or to back pain and a variety of other musculoskeletal complaints. Like most physical symptoms, constipation may start out mild, but worsen as the illness progresses until the patient delusionally believes that his "bowels have turned to cement." One physician became so agitated and delusional that he thought his heart would stop, and he required his nurse to take his blood pressure every five minutes to prove he was still alive. Another patient suffered the ultimate in anxiety-provoking physical symptoms—he believed his penis was shrinking, and would continue to shrivel right up into his abdomen!

CONTENT OF THOUGHT

By this phrase we mean all of a person's ideas, beliefs, attitudes, and mental images. We associate severe abnormalities of thought content with "craziness" or "insanity." Those people who do not recognize the unreal quality of their thoughts have a condition we term "psychotic."

When Gilbert Grand began to explain his plans for a coast-to-coast monorail, his friends first considered it a joke, then tried to argue him out of it. They could not, and we therefore conclude that he was delusional: a *delusion* is a fixed (unshakable), false belief. Gilbert's delusions were of a grandiose or expansive nature, but other types of delusion also occur: delusions of jealousy (that a spouse has been unfaithful), of guilt (sinfulness), of ill health (believing, for example, that one's body is infested with cancer). One man hospitalized for depression believed that he would be wiped out by imminent poverty, despite the fact that his sick leave and disability insurance left him financially better off sick than well. Some patients imagine themselves the victims of plots by foreign spies, the CIA, or Senate investigating committees. These persecutory delusions we call *paranoid,* a term which unfortunately has been used quite loosely of late, particularly by the drug and youth cultures, to mean feeling fearful or harassed ("hassled") without necessarily being delusional at all.

Determined largely by the culture in which we live, the content of delusions has changed with the times. The Gestapo, FBI, and KGB have all had their vogue, and as science has advanced, so has the technology inherent in delusions. Marconi not only invented the radio, but he inspired countless patients to believe in mind control by "the wireless." Television and radar influenced psychotics of the 1940s and 1950s, to be superseded by satellites in 1958 when women reported that they could receive messages from Sputnik on their hair curlers. Patients often retain enough insight to realize that their ideas fall a bit outside the mainstream, and they believe (not unreasonably) they will be laughed at, or taken for mad. Consequently, many maintain a fearful silence so complete that even close friends remain unaware of the truth until after hospitalization occurs.

Hallucinations, further symptoms of psychosis, occur when a person believes he hears, sees, smells, tastes, or feels something in the absence of an actual sensory stimulus; the girl who hears voices coming to her through the wall calling her a lesbian experiences auditory hallucinations. Like delusions, hallucinations usually indicate serious or more advanced psychiatric illness, but they may also be seen in cases of brain injury or toxicity. Although delusions and hallucinations generally indicate severe pathology, they do not necessarily mean a more protracted course or worse prognosis. In fact, the patient with sudden onset of severe symptoms may even have an advantage, in that he is more likely to be seen and treated early.

Some people with developing illness spend much time worrying or ruminating about things they have forgotten to do, or they incessantly berate themselves for supposed indiscretions of conversation or manners. They express unreasonable fears (*phobias*) of animals or of situations such as thunderstorms, traveling away from home, heights, and nearly every other conceivable life situation.

Most of us have experienced awakening early in the morning and imagining we have seen someone in the room, bugs on the wall or animals prowling around outside. These misinterpretations of an actual sensory stimulus (*illusions*) commonly occur in normal people and by themselves carry no implication of developing mental illness. You may have experienced another peculiar sensation often reported by normal people; suddenly, while minding your own business, you feel that you have been in that same situation before, even though you know you have not. This type of "déjà vu" (already seen) experience has no particular psychiatric importance either, although it can worry the dickens out of someone who does not know what it means.

SENSORIUM

The psychiatrist also always evaluates the patient's ability to think and remember, the sensorium. The patient himself may realize that he "cannot think as clearly" as he used to, or more typically, he does not understand that his thinking has become impaired. Whether mentioned spontaneously by the patient or complained of by relatives, memory for recent events usually becomes impaired first. He misses appointments or forgets birthdays; he repeats questions several times, despite the fact that he has already been answered. He may feel confused or lost, and in severe cases becomes disoriented, not knowing the day, the date, or even where he is. One husband, complaining that his wife had forgotten their luncheon date on six successive days, decided that *he* must be losing his grip because he kept agreeing to meet her.

The psychiatrist further evaluates mental functioning by asking the patient to name the past five presidents in order, to recall current events ("Who won the World Series last week?"), and to perform simple arithmetic—subtracting of multiples of seven from one hundred is a favorite, if annoying, task imposed by the headshrinker. He tests abstract reasoning when he asks the patient to explain in his own words the meaning of a familiar proverb (for example, "Don't cry over spilt milk"). People with reduced mental capacity will give a "concrete" interpretation ("If you spill it, you shouldn't cry").

JUDGMENT AND INSIGHT

Judgment, the ability to make an appropriate decision in a given situation, is inferred by the psychiatrist from the patient's history. Clearly, when Gilbert tried to set up a huge corporation to build a monorail, made excessive demands of his pregnant wife, and appeared in public dressed only in his underpants, he showed markedly defective judgment. We would also say that Lois used poor judgment when she decided to kill herself, although from her perspective of hopelessness the decision must have seemed reasonable. Fortunately, we judge by the standards of the healthy world, not by those of the sick patient. Otherwise the entire evaluation system would bog down in a sea of philosophical quicksand.

Insight indicates the patient's capacity to understand his present situation; for the purposes of the psychiatric examination, it means his ability to understand that he is ill (if he is). Poor insight and judgment frequently go hand-in-glove, but not always. Although she might not have been able to pinpoint it, Lois understood that something had gone very greatly wrong with her; thus we would say that her insight remained fairly good. But her judgment as to an appropriate solution to her problem ultimately failed her completely.

Listening for Symptoms

In these two chapters we have described and illustrated the most important symptoms of psychiatric illness. Many patients will show only the mildest of symptoms, which disappear either spontaneously or after a short period of treatment. Others progress sooner or later to the more severe symptoms, eventually needing hospitalization and vigorous psychiatric intervention.

But bear in mind that one or two symptoms do not constitute a psychiatric illness. At one time or another everyone has had one or more of the "symptoms" we have mentioned in this chapter. For example, although most people have had periods of gloom at some time in their lives, most do not go on to a depression severe enough to require treatment. So try to avoid the trap so many medical students fall into when they "find" they have fallen prey to every disease they study. However, even if you manage to avoid the sophomoric conclusion that *you* are sick, you will still be in danger of the more sophisticated pitfall, the Waterloo of many a psychiatrist; diagnosing psychiatric illness in the rest of the world. In one study of a lower socioeconomic group of *people* (not patients) picked at random in Manhattan, the researchers found only five percent of those interviewed to be psychiatrically well; nearly half had mild to moderate symptoms, and the rest were worse! Apparently, sickness, like beauty, lies in the eye of the beholder.

When someone you know does appear emotionally troubled, it often helps to sit down with him and "be a good listener," occasionally asking questions to further draw out his feelings. Although he will need encouragement, for he may feel ashamed and guilt-ridden, he will probably respond with surprising candor to a sympathetic and noncriticizing listener. The anxiety, agitation or crying spell that precipitated the "talking out" session may represent only the top of a rather considerable iceberg, but problems which seemed insoluble at first will be found soluble in conversation. Simply having another human being to "bounce ideas off" may prove all that is needed for resolution of the problem.

Constructive listening usually proves more difficult than you might think at first. If you are like most people, you will feel embarrassed or uncomfortable at hearing the problems of others. What you hear may remind you of your own problems, or you will feel unsure how to respond, finding it easier to "tune-out," make jokes, or trot out clichés like, "Just pull yourself out of it," or, "Things could be a lot worse." Platitudes like these are usually worse than useless; his inability to follow your advice only adds to the patient's already considerable stockpile of guilt. You might just as well tell a victim of arthritis, "See here, just straighten up and stop this pain nonsense!"

You will find it easier to fulfill the role of the sympathetic listener if you remember that you do not have to correct the problem to help your friend with it. Had he complained of chest pain, you certainly would not feel constrained to treat him for heart disease, but you would see to it that he obtained proper care. Your obligation to him with mental pain is no less than this—and your responsibility no greater. You do not have to accept the blame for his problem, to persuade him that he has assessed it incorrectly, or even to agree with him that he has one. All you really need to give is what *he* needs: quiet listening and sincere indication of concern. With this approach the presumptive patient, reassured that someone cares, will usually unburden himself of his trouble, and you will identify as many warning flags as may be found. In later chapters, we will see how psychiatrists use these signals to identify illness, and how diagnosis then leads to treatment.

4.
When Symptoms Spell Sickness

We have learned that normal people can have symptoms without being mentally ill. So how do you know which symptom is really important—which sign means that someone close to you needs help? Because psychiatrists do not usually see "nonpatients," in order to examine the case history of someone who is not sick, but who does have symptoms, let us consider a hypothetical situation, one which might happen to almost anyone.

The day Silas Curmudgeon retires as sales manager for the Whiplash Manufacturing Company, Gary Grindstone, twenty-year veteran of the sales department is elated, for he is next in line for the job. Imagine his chagrin when Wesley Whiplash, the boss' nephew, is instead promoted from junior assistant stock boy to the position Gary covets.

He arrives at home that evening fuming with anger. First he complains that dinner is late, then picks at his food. He berates his wife when she observes that he is not eating, and yells at his teen-age son who has cut neither the grass nor his hair. Perplexed and hurt, he stalks off to bed where he tosses for hours before falling into a restless sleep. More than once he awakens, eyes filling with tears of frustration, to the realization of his loss.

The following day he finds it hard to concentrate on his work as he fantasises scenes in which he slowly crushes Wesley Whiplash beneath a mounting stack of order books. Several times he begins to pen his resignation, but each time crumples the paper in disgust. More than once he catches himself thinking "What's the use?"—and wonders what he means by this. As the weary day drags by he feels worse and worse, and that evening a towering headache does little to improve his temper. But he sleeps better that night, eats a good breakfast the next morning, and speaks civilly to his family, much to everyone's relief. In the succeeding days his anger subsides and he begins to examine his job performance, searching for reasons he was not promoted. Could Wesley's master's degree from the Harvard Business School have influenced the decision? With increasing enthusiasm, he makes plans for furthering his own education, and within two weeks he has returned to his usual self.

We have just encountered several characteristics which can indicate a need for psychiatric evaluation: persistence of symptoms, severity of symptoms, combinations of symptoms and the progression of symptoms. We will now discuss these factors to see how they allow us to recognize the need for help.

PERSISTENCE OF SYMPTOMS

When Gary lost the promotion he thought he deserved, he experienced emotions which could be normal, or could indicate a developing mental disorder. He felt sad, he wept, he lashed out angrily at his wife and son; both sleep and appetite suffered. But the amazing resiliency of the normal human mind asserted itself, and within a few days, his mood stabilized, and he began to think rationally once again—of new, more effective solutions to his problem.

Short-lived "mini-depressions" like his will hit almost any one of us from time to time. We feel sad at any loss, whether of a promotion or a loved one. Indeed, the "grief reaction" which settles in at the death of a parent, a child, a husband or wife, has served for years as the model of "normal" (healthy) depression. During these times, the bereaved may briefly experience some of the more common symptoms mentioned in the previous chapters: lowered energy, poor concentration, loss of sexual interest, decreased work performance, ruminations about the past. He may even feel quite guilty, condemning himself with recriminations such as, "If only *I* had been driving . . . ," or "I shouldn't have let him get so overweight." Thoughts like these rarely, if ever, become delusional, however. The sufferer continues to recognize the "as if" quality of his ideas, which little affect his behavior. If he seems to hear a voice calling his name, he recognizes it as his imagination; it does not have the quality of an hallucination. If he awakens at night to the apparition of his dead relative seated at the foot of the bed, he quickly recognizes the experience for the illusion it is, caused by a dimly lighted pile of clothes thrown over a chair.

The duration of a grief reaction depends upon the severity of the loss and the personality of the bereaved. Generally, the more severe symptoms gradually begin to abate after a few days, disappearing within a month or two at most. If symptoms persist undiminished past the normal grieving period—or if they worsen—a physician becomes suspicious that a depressive disease which requires treatment has supervened.

Similarly, our suspicions should be aroused when normally transitory symptoms such as marked hostility, suspiciousness, anxiety, or seclusive behavior settle in and stay. Alterations of mood or behavior identified by friends, relatives, or the patient as "different from his usual self" and which persist over a period of weeks or recur episodically may indicate mental illness.

SEVERITY OF SYMPTOMS

Some symptoms clearly demand more immediate attention than others. Fixed, false beliefs (delusions) and false perception of the senses (hallucinations) indicate severe psychopathology; these urge immediate treatment. But because they occur within the patient's mind and cannot be observed directly, we must depend upon the patient to tell us about them. Often he is reluctant to do so, fearing that he will be regarded as mentally ill, or will be hospitalized—fears which may be quite realistic!

When a psychiatrist goes fishing for these symptoms of psychosis, he leads gradually into the subject by asking the patient if he has had unusual experiences, "things which happen to you that you cannot explain." If his only reply is a blank stare, he may explain, "Sometimes when people are disturbed or unhappy they have experiences which are difficult for them to understand. They imagine that they hear things or see things, or they have ideas which are troublesome to them. Has anything of this nature happened to you?" Such gentle questioning, with the implied reassurance that the examiner understands and will not censure a patient for having bizarre ideas, frequently coaxes forth material which he previously has kept to himself.

Although you might feel uncomfortable at directly enquiring about hallucinations or delusions, you can certainly, in a sympathetic way, ask a troubled relative if he has had any bothersome thoughts or ideas. A positive response might lead you to further draw him out, just as a psychiatrist would do: "I'd like to hear some more about that." Sympathetic, open-ended questions like, "Tell me more," or "And then what happened?" will encourage him gradually to unburden himself of his worrisome ideas and feelings.

Of all the severe psychiatric symptoms, that most commonly encountered is suicide. Suicidal ideas and attempts commonly occur in a number of psychiatric illnesses in which intolerable anguish leads the sufferer to seek any means of escape, including death. Although an entire chapter (chapter 13) will be devoted to this subject later, the potentially serious consequences of a suicide attempt prompt a discussion now of suicidal ideas as symptoms.

You sometimes hear that "those who talk about suicide never do it," but nothing could be further from the truth. The majority of those who successfully commit suicide do warn others of their intentions, either through previous suicide attempts or by more or less direct statements. In many cases, they have recently visited a doctor who should be alert to this danger (but often is not), but sometimes only close relatives or friends know of their intentions prior to the attempt.

Some severely ill people make direct statements: "I have been thinking about killing myself," but more commonly one hears comments indicating a general dissatisfaction with life, or lack of hope for improvement. "My life seems empty and useless," "Sometimes I think all of you would be better off if I were dead," or "I don't see any hope for the future" all express the self-destructive feelings of these severely ill people. Unfortunately, friends and relatives sometimes become so used to hearing such talk that they "tune it out," no longer responding even to increasingly desperate cries for help. Our human ability to adapt to nearly any repeated stimulus does not always work in our best interest.

A psychiatrist takes any communication of suicide idea or attempt seriously. Until he knows the patient well, has made a diagnosis, and can state reliably whether an actual attempt is likely, he assumes that the patient's intention is genuine. You should regard suicidal ideas at least as seriously, and seek advice from a competent psychiatrist whether or not there seems to be any doubt as to your relative's real plans.

Similar considerations should apply to those who have expressed homicidal ideas, but unfortunately this type of behavior is less predictable, more likely to be impulsive (and perhaps less treatable) than suicide. Murder is most often a crime of passion; those who kill seldom speak of it beforehand, either because they did not plan it or because they *did*—and are understandably shy about broadcasting their intent. Mental patients only rarely commit homicide, but those who do usually are driven by one of two symptoms: delusions and depression. Individuals who believe they are being watched or persecuted sometimes act violently and unexpectedly on their delusions. One elderly man with a brain tumor suddenly developed the delusion that his landlady was trying to poison him. He shot her through the chest as she brought him a tray of food, after which he blandly remarked to the police, "Well, I *had* to—it was her or me." He died of his disease before he could be brought to trial.

Occasionally a suicidally depressed person will kill his family as well as himself, believing that his loved ones will be better off permanently removed from this mortal coil. Whenever they occur, statements of homicidal desire or intent should be taken extremely seriously, particularly when the patient has ready access to lethal weapons like guns or knives. And you should also bear in mind that risk for homicide and suicide increases in anyone who loses firm control of his impulses, as when under the influence of drugs or alcohol.

Combinations of Symptoms

Suicide attempts, reckless spending, hallucinations and homicidal threats are the chicken-pox of psychiatry—they stand out so clearly that even the untrained observer knows they mean trouble. But many patients, perhaps the majority of those needing treatment, never develop such obvious warning signs. Then the psychiatrist must enquire about a wide variety of possible symptoms as he attempts to find a pattern which will allow him to make a diagnosis.

For example, if you complain to your doctor of pain in your arm, it may excite little interest—only a bruise, perhaps. But a tender spot demands further investigation, and if he finds heat and redness as well, he knows from these classic symptoms that you have an infection. Had Lois Downing felt sad but never lost her appetite or her ability to work, and had she not developed the other accessory symptoms mentioned in the previous chapters, any physician would likely (and rightly) have discounted the severity of her depression. Thus, doctors use the number of symptoms and the manner in which they combine with one another to determine not only that illness exists, but to gauge its severity and even to suggest which treatment he should prescribe.

PROGRESSION OF SYMPTOMS

When Roger Downing thought back over the early course of his wife's illness, he decided that the first identifiable change occurred when she stopped having her "high," or mildly elated periods. In this case, then, the first indication of advancing illness was the *absence* of something which had been present before. She then went on through successive stages of increasingly troublesome symptoms: occasional crying spells, difficulty falling asleep, irritability in the mornings, all of which became more pronounced with the passing days.

As her illness progressed, new symptoms developed. Not only did she lose her appetite, but her weight dropped noticeably. Whereas at first she could not fall asleep, now she would also awaken in the small hours of the morning, unable to return to sleep—a typical finding in severe depression. Later, more frightening symptoms such as guilty ruminations about suicidal ideas appeared, but because of their gradual onset those who saw her every day hardly noticed. Such "blocking out" of the evidence of increasing illness by her relatives in no way meant that they did not care. It is the same with anything that happens gradually; you do not notice the growth day-by-day of your own child—it is when he tries on an old pair of trousers that you suddenly realize he has grown two inches. In the same way your mind naturally rationalizes, or accommodates to, gradual changes in the actions or attitudes of those you see every day. This flexibility normally helps you to adapt comfortably to our ever-changing world, but it can also cause you to be too accepting of abnormal behavior. When you think back over changes which have occurred, as Roger Downing did, the number of warning signs which you have completely overlooked may surprise you. But if a long time has passed since the first symptom, try not to let guilt feelings keep you from going for help; the doctor understands perfectly well how illness can sneak up upon a person, and he will not hold the delay against you. You have only responded to change in a human way.

POINTS OF VIEW

Before actually consulting a professional, it may help you to speak with other relatives and friends to learn whether they, too, have noted symptoms. The advantages of obtaining this kind of corroboration in advance are several.

Usually you see only one or two sides of a friend's life; one person cannot be as well acquainted with the details as several informants can be. With historical information available from more than one source, the doctor can more easily piece together a story recognizable as a known psychiatric illness. These additional views of, say, the patient's work habits, his performance in school, his hobbies, and his relationships with friends may well provide the information necessary for diagnosis, paving the way for rapid treatment.

On the other hand, a second viewpoint may so satisfactorily explain the presumptive patient's behavior that you now realize he is perfectly well after all. For example, during the past semester in college Joe has seemed tired, and his grades have fallen. When his worried parents question him, he irritably responds that he feels "fine, so quit hassling me!" So they ask his roommate, who tells them that Joe works at night to earn money for the car his parents said he could not have until graduation. Relieved, they agree to help with the car now if he will give up his night job. By obtaining more information, Joe's parents may have saved unnecessary and expensive psychiatric consultation.

Assuming that the illness you have suspected really exists, talking over the situation helps to unite friends and relatives to deal more effectively with the patient. The problem can be particularly acute when he has been an authority figure like a parent or spouse who is used to giving orders, not taking them. And, if he does not recognize his own illness, he may show a surprising degree of ingenuity in avoiding the "embarrassment" or "unnecessary step" of seeing a psychiatrist. But if the family has already caucused and agreed on a course of action, you will know (if you have been delegated the direct responsibility) that when the patient tries to refuse treatment or hospitalization, the others will stand behind your request for treatment. Many a well-meaning friend has been deterred from carrying through with the agreed-upon appointment by a persuasive patient, and more than one has arrived there only to find that the doctor regards *him* as the patient—physicians can be persuaded as well as anyone else. The general discomfort of this situation can be avoided by first obtaining the cooperation of the rest of the family.

Of course, it is neither necessary nor wise to run about willy-nilly asking if employers, friends, or ministers have noticed "how peculiar old Silas has been acting recently." Old Silas may be plenty sick indeed, but many people still harbor suspicions about those afflicted with a mental illness, prejudice due largely to ignorance of its types, causes, treatment, and outlook. But now, when you are trying to help your ill relative, is hardly the time to try to convert the heathen by foolishly exposing him to the suspicion of others (particularly if it develops that he is less ill than you had imagined!). In looking for further information, you might broach the subject casually by asking, "I am worried about Silas—he doesn't seem himself lately. Have you noticed anything different about him?"

Finally, please bear in mind that the purpose of this book is to educate you, to help you help and understand the patient. It was *not* intended as a manual for self-help, or to make you into a psychiatrist. The symptoms and diagnoses described here have varying nuances and degrees of severity, so their final interpretations must be left to a competent professional; no book can substitute for his opinion. And of course the same holds for treatment; even the physician who treats himself has, as they say, a fool for a doctor and a fool for a patient. But the well-informed layman *can* intelligently influence for the better the course of his relative's illness, from selecting the doctor right through to helping with after-care. And in the next chapter we will take up the first problem: selecting the physician.

5.
Going for Help

So you have made your decision: Uncle John, or Brother Bill, or someone else you know really needs professional help. Now what do you do? If you are like most people, you may still feel tempted to "let the problem take care of itself." You may fear what the doctor will say—that the patient's severe mental illness is incurable, or that it was inherited and threatens the rest of the family. The wife of a paranoid patient fears she will make him even more suspicious if she talks about him, not realizing that his illness is so severe that people *really* talking about him can add little to what he already believes. Shame at being related to someone "tainted" by a nervous disorder can also delay your seeking evaluation as can, ironically, guilt feelings at not having sought help earlier. The only remedy for this dilemma is to cast your worries to the winds and plunge in.

Once matters come to this point, one of two situations usually obtains. You may find a bewildering array of mental health professionals and paraprofessionals to choose from, but perhaps more frequently you have no idea where to turn. In the following pages, we will discuss the relative merits and points of view of these possible sources of help.

You may be well-advised to make an appointment first with your family physician, because the psychiatric complaints which worry you can be symptomatic of organic (medical or surgical) conditions which he may be able to identify by examination or laboratory tests. Mary's "depression" may be due to iron deficiency anemia; her husband's hyperactivity and rapid speech could be caused by an overly active thyroid. A second reason for starting with the family doctor or internist is economy of time; many psychiatrists will refer a patient to him at the outset for a complete medical evaluation. Third, your doctor has referred patients to a number of psychiatrists in the community, and by experience knows which of them give the best service.

Unfortunately, not all physicians are equipped to evaluate psychiatric problems. Some doctors, just like some relatives, feel uncomfortable when confronted with mentally disturbed people —their own feelings get in the way of proper evaluation. Others have not had training current or thorough enough to spot severe emotional difficulties, to understand the special interview methods which must be used to elicit information from psychiatric patients, or to appreciate the value of obtaining history from outside informants.

> Until the age of forty-five Joseph Strong had been a calm, pleasant, easy-going husband and father, who had worked steadily as a machinist for over twenty years. None of his several past episodes of mild depression had been severe enough to warrant visiting a physician.
>
> About two months before, he had suddenly become severely hyperactive, rushing about from one project to the next, completing none, but planning ever more grandiose schemes. His energy boundless, he seemed to need only a few hours of sleep a night before he would awaken refreshed, ready for another very active day.
>
> When his wife finally insisted upon treatment, his internist evaluated him first for a thyroid and then for a gallbladder disorder. Finding neither, the physician, whom he regaled with some extremely funny stories and several fine cigars, pronounced him in the best of health, noting only that he talked a lot.
>
> The condition progressed. His wife observed that his mood became ecstatic, that his speech was extremely rapid, and she found it "nearly impossible to get a word in edgewise." He withdrew four thousand dollars of their life savings to buy a boat, and his sexual demands upon her skyrocketed. But when in desperation she finally called the doctor again, he became

irate, accusing her of sneaking around behind her husband's back to give unsolicited information.

A few days later, Mr. Strong was brought stark naked to a psychiatric hospital, having been found streaking down the median strip of an interstate highway, scattering flower blossoms which he had plucked from the bushes.

This case, although true, is among a small minority—generally the family physician is an excellent place to begin, and he may be able to provide all the care needed, particularly for a relatively uncomplicated case. But if you have seen no improvement within a short time (two or three weeks, say), or if symptoms actually worsen, you should take further steps to insure proper consultation. For openers, you might do worse than to "let your fingers do the walking" through the yellow pages of the telephone book, where in any medium-sized city you will find a motley of mental health professionals.

PSYCHIATRIST

Your telephone book may list him separately from other physicians, but he may be right there with all the rest, identified by notations such as "practice limited to general psychiatry" or "child psychiatry only." After receiving his medical degree (four years of post-college training), he goes on for a three-year specialized residency program during which he intensively studies the symptoms and treatment of mental disorders. In addition to office patients, he may have a hospital practice where he cares for those who require the seclusion and more intensive treatment best afforded there. Like any "real" doctor, he can prescribe medicine, and he may administer electroconvulsive therapy (ECT). In common with all other professionals, he also uses psychotherapy (the "talking treatment," further discussed in chapter 17), to help people with their emotional problems. Some psychiatrists also employ behavior modification therapy, in which they train a patient to alter the manner in which he responds to certain circumstances or feelings.

Some psychiatrists have special interests, such as treating families together, marital or couples therapy, sexual disorders, or problems of alcohol or drug abuse. Others specialize in the treatment of a particular age group, such as children and adolescents. (Cynics accuse some of specializing in diseases of the rich, but that is not nice.) Most, however, regard themselves as general psychiatrists, the type you will most likely see.

Many people worry about the cost of psychiatric treatment, and with good cause; the initial evaluation by a private psychiatrist runs close to eighty dollars with subsequent charges at over a dollar a minute. These fees seem high (outlandish, you say!) compared to a general practitioner's, but remember that the nature of the psychiatrist's work demands that he usually see only one patient at a time, whereas the general practitioner may run back and forth, keeping four examining rooms going at a time. Insurance defrays a varying proportion of these fees, and Medicare, Medicaid, and CHAMPUS (the civilian medical coverage for dependents of military personnel) supply all or most of the cost for many. Perhaps more to the point is the question of the total cost per episode of illness. For a depression not requiring hospitalization, the cost may be two hundred dollars over a several week period—not inconsiderable, but minor compared to the disability which might otherwise result.

Psychiatrists have been trained to detect and treat many forms of emotional or mental disorders. Being medical doctors, they can also recognize when mental symptoms result from an organic (medical or surgical) problem. If one is found and treated, the emotional symptoms are often relieved. Because psychiatrists have broader training than any of the other mental health professionals, and because they offer a variety of treatment modalities, your search for specialty treatment is best begun here.

PSYCHOANALYST

Some psychiatrists have a special interest in the field of psychoanalysis. These physicians have had the initial training of the general psychiatrist, but in addition to medical school and residency, their interests lead them to a specialized study of the mental processes by the technique of in-depth interview. Psychoanalysts probe deeply into early (often childhood) experiences which, they believe, can cause psychiatric illness to develop. Psychoanalytic theory holds that symptom removal occurs through psychotherapeutic resolution of conflicts which have arisen during these early stages of development.

The problems usually treated by psychoanalysts include the less severe forms of mental illness, neurosis and character pathology foremost among them. They also try to help basically healthy people to understand factors in their personalities which contribute to problems of living. Psychoanalysis has been advocated as a treatment for the more severe conditions which we cover in this book, but many psychoanalysts will refer such patients to a general psychiatrist when hospitalization or intensive drug treatment appears indicated.

PSYCHOLOGIST

The clinical psychologist's training includes, after college, several years of specialized graduate school during which he studies theories of the development of human behavior, psychological testing techniques and other disciplines pertaining to the workings of the mind. Because he receives his degree in psychology, not medicine, by law he cannot use drugs or hospitalize his own patients. He uses IQ and other tests to evaluate possible organic (brain lesion) causes for nervous and mental disorders. He helps to unravel patients' conscious and unconscious ideas, attitudes and motivations through other psychological tests which include storytelling, interpretation of ink blots, card-sorting techniques, and various pencil and paper tests. By putting the data from several tests together with his own observations of behavior, the psychologist arrives at a diagnosis and (often) suggestions for treatment.

The psychologist sometimes treats patients by psychotherapy, and his sophistication in certain of these techniques may be greater than that of the psychiatrist with whom he often works. But because he has not had training in general medicine, more severe mental conditions requiring medication and hospital treatment, as well as mental disorders which may be caused by physical illness, should be first evaluated by the psychiatrist.

SOCIAL WORKERS

The social worker's particular interest in environmental factors has led him to specialize in dealing with social and family problems which can affect patients. Those who help psychiatric patients with their problems often work closely under the supervision of a psychiatrist. Usually the holder of either a bachelor's or a master's (rarely a doctor's) degree, depending upon level of training and experience, social workers can solve such problems as making living arrangements for someone who can no longer live at home, obtaining financial assistance, or finding temporary foster home placement for children whose mother has been hospitalized. They may help the family locate and utilize such special facilities as child care centers, day hospitals, sheltered workshops, or arrange for job retraining and placement.

Many social workers have had additional training and experience qualifying them to do psychotherapy. Some specialize in family and marital counseling or in group therapy with adolescents or adults. If you take your relative to see a social worker, it should be upon the referral of a psychiatrist. Then, with medical aspects of the problem already cared for, this specialist can help you resolve the marital, job, or other social problems which either result from the patient's illness or which may be incidental to it.

Marriage Counselor

A marriage counselor may be any individual with a special interest in the problems married people have with each other. He approaches these conflicts psychotherapeutically or behaviorally; in education, he may be a fully-trained psychiatrist, or merely a layman who has attended a seminar in marriage counseling. Whereas some states require licensing of marriage counselors, in many you have no assurance that he has had any special training whatsoever. Although mental and emotional illness, particularly when severe or of long standing, can certainly produce marital problems, the marriage counseling approach is better saved until the underlying illness has been diagnosed and treated.

Agencies and Institutions

For a number of reasons, including finances and lack of availability, it may be necessary to seek treatment outside the private medical sphere. Fortunately, a number of alternatives exist, particularly in larger cities and towns. In the major metropolitan areas, a considerable number of services may be available, usually at nominal (often sliding-scale) fees, or in some cases at no charge whatever. But the very diversity and scope of these resources can confuse you as to just what services each may provide; a telephone inquiry in advance should help decide which agency can help you with your problem.

Mental Health Center

Many areas have federally-funded mental health centers. Staffed by psychiatrists, social workers, psychologists and other mental health workers, they often provide a full range of services, including even hospitalization in some areas. Some smaller clinics exist as "store-front" operations which offer only counseling, crisis intervention, and group therapy. A psychiatrist (often employed on a part-time basis) supervises all treatment, and he will also prescribe medication when indicated. Workers at a mental health center (or at any other institution) who have been properly trained to spot symptoms of psychiatric illness can refer a patient to the doctor for appropriate medical treatment. Because of the volume of patients seen here and the shortage of physician time, many people spend little (or no) time with the doctor, and receive their care more or less exclusively from social workers and psychologists.

Medical Schools

All, or nearly all, of the 115 four-year medical schools in this country have training programs in psychiatry, and most of these offer psychiatric treatment on a reduced fee basis. Typically, a patient who does not need hospitalization will be evaluated and cared for by a second- or third-year resident in psychiatry—a doctor who has completed medical school and is now taking his specialty training. These young physicians, working under the supervision of the medical school faculty, can prescribe medication, do psychotherapy, and, should it prove necessary, refer the patient to the university's hospital for inpatient care. There, treatment is usually provided by a first-year psychiatric resident, working even more closely under the supervision of a fully-trained faculty psychiatrist.

Because the resident physicians are young, energetic, and have a thirst for knowledge, and because the faculty supervisors are usually interested in new developments in the field, treatment at such university hospitals and outpatient clinics can be quite good. Of course, as with any other setting, the treatment your relative receives will be as good as the individual physician(s) who care for him; just because you have come to the "ivory tower" seeking help does not relieve you of the responsibility for constantly checking up on the quality of that care. Another advantage to university and other major hospital training centers is that they usually maintain a resident physician on duty twenty-four hours a day, affording you care in a crisis right now, without having to wait for a regularly scheduled appointment.

General Hospital

Some general hospitals, particularly those in large cities, have psychiatrists on their staffs and psychiatric beds available. Even at those with no psychiatric house physician (resident or intern) immediately available, the doctor on duty in the emergency room can refer you to a psychiatrist on the staff. Emergency room personnel also often know a lot about the agencies in the community which can help you with emotional problems. If your relative has become agitated and needs help immediately, a trip to this emergency room may stabilize him and help you set your course for the future.

Other Community Resources

In metropolitan areas additional resources include free clinics and community crisis clinics, which usually provide emergency-oriented counseling on a no-fee basis. These facilities often offer evening appointments, but do not always provide medical services. Although community resources are more limited in smaller cities, you may actually find it easier to find help for your problem because of better communication between agencies in these locations. Welfare departments located through city and county listings in the white pages of the telephone book employ social workers who know about other community resources and who can refer their clients to psychiatric treatment facilities as necessary. In small communities social service agencies may be quickly discovered by contacting traditional centers for care such as general hospitals, health departments, and civic organizations.

Many larger communities maintain hot lines such as suicide prevention center telephone services. The professionals and lay people who man hot line phones can refer patients as necessary to other social service organizations, psychiatrists or hospitals. The disadvantage of hot lines is the lack of personal contact with the patient, which may limit the amount of information the worker obtains from the individual or his family.

State Psychiatric Hospitals

These venerable institutions, much maligned of late, served for years as virtually the only resource available to the severely mentally ill. Prior to the 1950s, the populations of state hospitals increased steadily as individuals became less willing and able to care at home for their deranged or demented relatives. Overcrowding resulted, contributing to the image they evoke of countless blank faces pressed against barred windows, a picture which often falls not far short of the truth. And those who enter echo the stygian admonition to "abandon all hope."

In the past few years, state hospitals have come increasingly under fire as the public has become aware of the deficiencies in care provided by these psychiatric behemoths. Successful lawsuits requiring the state either to treat or to release patients have made headlines recently, but less heralded has been the real progress made in the past decade in many places. As hospital populations contract, more attention can be given to those patients remaining, and more emphasis given to those recently admitted.

If one of your relatives' options is to go to a state hospital, you can help by checking it out, firsthand if at all possible. During a brief visit with the admissions officer you can learn what sort of therapy they provide, how many patients each doctor cares for, and how much time each patient spends with his psychiatrist. The scope and vigor of the activities can provide a useful index of the excellence of the hospital in question. Are new arrivals segregated from chronic patients? Do patients spend much time in structured activity, or do they mostly sit around the ward? Is the occupational therapy department well staffed and equipped? Do the physicians offer a spectrum of treatments including electro-convulsive therapy, drug and psychotherapy? Is the decor pleasant?

Is the lighting adequate? Does the hospital have a university affiliation? Does it have resident physicians? A "yes" to all these questions suggests a progressive program which can be truly therapeutic for your relative, regardless of the age of the building, or who operates it.

Veterans Administration Hospital

Although most VA Hospitals provide some psychiatric care, the quality of their service varies as widely as their locations. Some, particularly those affiliated with a university medical school, offer diagnosis and treatment as thorough and sophisticated as any medical center in the country. But many suffer from the same problems as any other government medical service: understaffing and overutilization. Consequently, the individual patient may get lost in the shuffle and receive treatment less than optimal for his condition. The comments about state hospitals apply equally well to the VA.

Pastoral Counseling

Counseling offered by clergymen of various faiths and denominations has become available over the past few years. Most seminaries now require considerable training in counseling and human psychology, often including clinical experience obtained through medical training facilities. Some psychiatrists will even occasionally refer patients to clergymen for spiritual counseling. Pastoral counseling sometimes is offered for a fee, although it is often provided as a non-fee service to parishioners. The quality of such services varies greatly; although some are excellent, many pastoral counselors lack the expertise to know which mental disorders are serious enough to require psychiatric attention.

This criticism can be applied equally well to many of the agencies (and individuals) discussed here. Although most can probably adequately treat the more commonplace, simpler problems, many workers (and not a few physicians) have difficulty in identifying serious mental illness. It is much like delivering babies: 90 percent of the time the process is so easy anyone can do it— but the other 10 percent of the cases require years of training! The last few resources may serve you best, at least at first, as avenues of referral for more definitive care. Your relative's illness may be complicated, confusing, hard to diagnose, and perhaps harder to treat; you will probably be most satisfied with care obtained from a psychiatrist, whether he be located in the public sector of medicine or in private practice. But wherever you obtain treatment, be satisfied with nothing less than individual, personal attention from your doctor, who must care about your relative, you, and what he is doing.

6.
What Is Good Care?

With the wide variety of resources offering therapeutic services of varying types and (as we will learn) degrees of effectiveness, small wonder that you feel at a loss to evaluate the care you have paid for. Your confusion is particularly understandable in the light of the disagreement among professionals as to what constitutes good care. Some truly memorable brouhahas have been touched off simply by inviting two psychiatrists of differing persuasions to the same cocktail party. With the profession sorely at odds, most patients would not recognize good care if served it on a skewer— after all, a lot of doctors do not know how to prepare it. The following discussion will consider the characteristics to look for in any treating physician or institution.

CASE HISTORY

Good care requires first a complete history of the illness, obtained not only from the patient but from his family, his friends, and as many other informants as seem needed. School records, evaluations from teachers, employment and military records may each bear on the initial evaluation. The history includes not only an account of the current episode (present illness), but also any similar problems in the past. Inquiries related to the patient's health in general should also be made to determine what possible medical or surgical disorders have contributed to his present mental condition.

The field of psychiatry allows (in fact, demands) its practitioners to be almost incredibly nosey. With care they examine the social history of the patient, detailing his entire life from birth on. Relationships with parents and siblings, schooling, sexual and marital history, military service if any, religious preferences, habits, hobbies, and attitudes all will be covered in this portion of the examination. From the informants the physician pieces together a picture of the patient's character as it was before he fell ill, called the premorbid personality. We will see later that this personality type can influence the kinds of psychiatric symptoms which may appear when illness strikes.

Because mental illness often runs in families, the careful interviewer obtains a history of psychiatric conditions in all blood relatives, particularly parents, siblings, and children. He will be especially interested in illnesses similar to the patient's, but any history of alcoholism, "nervous breakdown," suicide, drug abuse, mental hospitalization, "neurosis," or criminal behavior may be pertinent.

PHYSICAL EXAMINATION

If your relative enters the hospital (sometimes even if he does not), he should have a thorough physical examination. Most psychiatrists do this personally, but some prefer to refer their patients to an internist or general practitioner so that he can "do the dirty work."

The physical exam is indicated:

1. whenever the patient is hospitalized;
2. when he has a history of physical illness which may be related to his mental condition; and/or
3. when a neurologic disorder may account for the mental symptoms.

The specialized part of the neurological examination which psychiatrists always evaluate in depth (and which *all* doctors should evaluate) is called the *mental status*. This formal assessment of mental functioning, which includes the symptoms discussed in earlier chapters, is one of the basic tools used by the psychiatrist to judge the type of illness and the degree of incapacity resulting from it. It also provides a useful yardstick by which to measure improvement as treatment progresses. Most of the time you will not realize when the doctor is evaluating the mental status, because much of it involves observing behavior and listening to the patterns and content of speech. But do not be surprised if at some point he begins to ask your relative to subtract seven from one hundred, or to name the past five presidents—that is part of the mental status.

Diagnosis

The careful physician makes the best diagnosis possible based on the information he obtains from the history and examination. But often he will not be able to make a definite diagnosis after the initial evaluation, and will instead draw up a list of possibilities called "differential diagnosis." Then he will use further tests, observation, or simply the passage of time to help him select the final (and, one hopes, correct) diagnosis. The psychiatrist may request consultation from other physicians, particularly neurologists and internists, to rule in or out medical illnesses and from other psychiatrists when special problems in diagnosis arise. He may also use laboratory tests (blood, x-rays, special neurologic exams) to help with diagnosis, but in most cases he can make an adequate evaluation without these specialized techniques.

It has been common practice, even fashionable in some areas, to make no diagnosis at all. As Dr. Fuller Torrey has recently stated, most psychiatrists do not "use formal diagnostic labels in their day-to-day practice." This, as we shall see, goes a long way to explain some of the sorry practices perpetrated upon patients in the name of therapy. Some doctors will say that a diagnosis is only a meaningless label and does not aid in the care of the patient. While it is true that diagnosis as made by some physicians has little to recommend it, denying the importance of all diagnosis can be a tragic mistake.

> At the end of one long corridor at Golden Days Convalescent Home was the bedroom of Emanuel Trimmer. By virtue of his long-term residence at Golden Days, he had moved up from the ward to a four-bed room; because he was well behaved and no trouble to anyone, he had not advanced to a bedroom of his own. And on this morning, having tired of the morning talk

shows which poured from the TV in the tattered day room, he had retired to this niche, which he called his "sanctum dormitorium." There he sat on the edge of his high, hospital-type bed, one foot touching the floor for balance, the other leg dangling off the edge of the mattress.

At sixty-three, Emanuel's hair was grizzled about his slightly furrowed face; but he was clean-shaven, and his dark trousers and frayed white shirt bore the look of a man who still cared about his appearance. Although he had had few visitors of late—vanishingly few in the past year—he appeared at ease as he motioned his caller to the room's single straight-back chair, next to his bed.

"It isn't much, Doctor, but it's yours." His voice, resonant and friendly, bore the smile which his face could not. For his features had long since been frozen into a fixed expression which gave him the appearance of wearing a mask.

"I'd offer you a cigarette, but I gave them up several years ago when the trembling started." One noticed the shaking immediately—a rhythmic back-and-forth of thumb upon fingers, the motion a child might use to roll a spitball.

"It started just after I got depressed and they gave me the tranquilizers. I was so bad I went to the state hospital, and there they thought that I was hallucinating."

"Why did they think that?" the doctor asked.

Mr. Trimmer shifted his position uncomfortably on the bed and leaned forward confidentially. "Well, Doctor," he responded, "I'm kind of ashamed to tell you, but I think I really must be a little crazy. Ever since I was a young man, these thoughts have run through my mind. I know they're silly, and I've tried to get rid of them, but I can't—they just keep coming back."

He sighed deeply, and after a moment went on. "You see, I get this idea that I won't be able to get to sleep. But if I get out of bed and say to myself 'go to sleep, go to sleep, your worries will keep,' then I relax, and I can go to sleep. At least, that's the way it started out. After a while that wasn't good enough, and I had to repeat it three times—like magic, it was. And later it took three times three, and I crossed myself in between threes. Then I could go to sleep."

With upturned palms, he shrugged, "what's the use," then dropped his hands back into his lap. In a moment, his fingers had restarted their rhythmic oscillations.

"So, when I went to the state hospital four years ago, they saw me repeating my little nonsense and thought I was crazy. And I guess maybe I am. But I don't feel depressed anymore, and I think I could work in my shoe repair shop again"—his eyes dropped uncertainly to his hands—"except for the shaking."

In his chart, the attendants' notes covering the past few months took up but a page or two. "Chronic schizophrenic stands at foot of bed at night, apparently hallucinating. Doctor called. Thorazine increased."

"I don't think I'll ever get back to my shop now. But could you talk to my doctor—could you get him to cut down my medicine? I'm so frozen up I can't move. I'm not depressed— I don't wish I were dead, though I might as well be. Sometimes I wish I really were crazy, so I could just sit quietly and listen to voices and not think about the past."

Mr. Trimmer's shakiness and frozen facial expression are due to the neurological disorder called Parkinson's disease, caused in his case by tranquilizing drugs. When an illness like this one which keeps a patient in a nursing home, unable to work, with no prospects for the future, has been caused by a doctor, it is called *iatrogenic.* The whole sorry story represents a cruel contradiction to the first rule medical students learn when beginning clinical training: *Primum non nocere*—first do no harm. Iatrogenic complications, bad enough when they occur (as they may) in the course of the correct therapy, are intolerable when they result from unnecessary treatment given for a mistaken diagnosis.

What was actually wrong with Emanuel Trimmer? His recurrent fear that he would not be able to sleep we call an *obsession,* which he counteracted with a *compulsion,* the magical rhyme he repeated over and over. The illness in which they occur together *(obsessive-compulsive disease),* while relatively rare, can thoroughly incapacitate the patient as he spends most of his waking hours ruminating about and trying to combat his "crazy" thoughts. But these people are by no stretch of the imagination psychotic; they realize that their obsessive thoughts are silly, and they vigorously try to resist them, but to no avail. Many a normal person has obsessional thinking, but usually it is mild and responds to the simple reassurance that he is not seriously ill. Indeed, society profits from that degree of obsessiveness that prods the accountant to recheck his entries, the scientist his results, or the carpenter his plumb. Mr. Trimmer had tolerated his condition for years and might yet be a productive citizen had not his home, his business, and his friends been wrested from him by a careless diagnosis. *Primum non nocere!*

Without a doubt, the history of Emanuel Trimmer ranks with medicine's all-time tales of horror. Experiences like these have contributed to the drive among some psychiatrists against making any diagnosis at all. After all, the reasoning goes, if it can do this much damage, who needs it?

A second, perhaps more telling hindrance to the use of diagnosis has been the popular notion that all mental illness exists on a continuum—that as a person becomes ill he progresses from normalcy through neurosis and personality disorder to psychosis. In other branches of medicine, this sort of argument was discarded as scientists discovered that, for example, the ancient chest complaint *phthisis* actually comprised a variety of discrete disease entities. But imagine a physician today suggesting that all lung ailments are but different stages of the same disease process, that the chronic cough commences as a cold, continues through consumption to conclude as cancer—he would be laughed right out of his stethoscope! So why must we abide this nonsense in psychiatry?

Probably because, like most popular misconceptions, this one contains a germ of truth. As Karl Menninger put it, "The labeled patient is not so different from you and me," a sentiment with which we can only agree, remembering that psychotic or sane, neurotic or not, we all have appendices and adrenal glands—and all the additional structures which make us resemble one another. And it is certainly true that, as we have previously discussed, normal people do have symptoms. The error lies in leaping to the assertion that, *ipso facto,* each of us is slightly deranged. Psychiatrists have for years been biting hard on that particular chestnut, but we learned in chapter 4 that merely having symptoms is not enough—you need the right symptoms, in the right combination. And that, we shall see, is what makes manic-depressives different from schizophrenics, and separates both of them from the rest of us.

Let us consider what diagnoses correctly made can gain us. A sound diagnosis has only one real value: it allows the physician to make predictions about the outcome of the illness, to select the treatment which is likely to be most effective, and to decide how best he can advise you. The practice of proceeding without a diagnosis, though not uncommon, is, in a word, foolish. It encourages desultory thinking—or no thinking at all—about the patient and leads to therapeutic efforts which are not specifically directed to his problems.

Physicians are sometimes quite secretive about making diagoses. Dissembling may be appropriate at times, as when the patient, his family, or friends temporarily must be guarded from the knowledge of a condition which they fear. In such a case, the physician can use the time gained to explain the situation to them carefully, in as nontraumatic a manner as possible. But generally you and your relative have the right to be fully informed about his illness, and your doctor should be as clear as possible in discussing with you the diagnosis and what he intends to do about it.

When no diagnosis can be made with certainty, the doctor should say so. Unfortunately, physicians often hesitate to admit that anything is less than crystal clear to them, even in a case so complex that no one could give an immediate answer. The practice of saddling such a patient with a definite diagnosis under these conditions can only be condemned, as it leads to inappropriate pigeonholing. The danger is this: any label that sounds official tends to stick, whether correct or not. And once he makes a diagnosis, any physician tends to become comfortable with it and to stop thinking of alternatives. If he is right, well and good; but if he has erred, his faulty labeling can lead to therapeutic stagnation instead of the frequent reevaluations a complicated patient requires and deserves.

We can boil all this down rather easily to a paraphrase of an old maxim: if you cannot say something *right* about a patient, say nothing at all. The "good" diagnosis helps us select treatment; the "bad" one may defeat treatment. The lack of independent methods for validating diagnoses handicaps the psychiatrist, who alone of all physicians lacks laboratory tests for the diseases he treats. But, fortunately, over the past twenty years we have developed clinical criteria which allow us to do better than fly by the seat of our collective pants; now we label 80 percent or more of psychiatric patients, confident that years from now their subsequent course will not prove us wrong. To more definitively state the principle: if the features of an illness meet the criteria for a diagnosis which allows accurate predictions about the patient's outcome and treatment, that diagnosis should be made. If these criteria cannot be satisfied, the patient should be regarded as "undiagnosed but psychiatrically ill," enabling the physician to keep an open mind and a weather eye out for new developments.

How long should it take to evaluate a new patient? As frequently happens in psychiatry, we will indulge ourselves with a bit of a cop-out: a great deal depends on the complexity of the problem. In a typical mild-to-moderate depression, an hour-long interview in the office should be perfectly adequate. More complex problems may take several interview sessions to obtain information from other sources such as previous physicians and hospitals. But most initial evaluations should require no more than an hour or two before the doctor has a working diagnosis (or list of differential diagnoses) and a plan for further evaluation and treatment.

TREATMENT

Flexibility is the key to successful treatment. The careful physician does not put all his therapeutic eggs into one basket—even patients with the same illness may require different forms of treatment. Effective treatments include drugs, electroconvulsive therapy (ECT), and various forms of psychotherapy, and the therapist equipped with only one of these, though he may be perfectly adequate in caring for some emotional disorders, cannot offer the full range of treatment needed by the more serious psychiatric illnesses. We will fully discuss types of treatment in chapters 14 through 17.

APPROACH TO THE PATIENT'S FAMILY

The physician should not only inform both you and the patient of his diagnosis and plan for treatment, but should explain the alternatives and possible dangers involved both in treatment and in lack of treatment. He should involve you in his plans for treatment so you can reinforce his methods and plan on the same goals. He also relies heavily upon you for information as to how therapy is progressing; after all, you observe the patient more hours in a week than he could in a year. And as we will discuss later (chapter 18), you may also be of help in administering treatment at home.

Because patients are sick twenty-four hours a day, the doctor should be available either by telephone or in person at all times; when he plans to be away, he should leave his practice in charge of a colleague who has similar training and background and who can be reached at any time if needed in an emergency.

SEEKING A SECOND OPINION

Occasionally, despite the best of care, things just do not seem to go right, and you want a second opinion as to whether the course you are pursuing is the right one. Unless the doctor has suggested it himself, you may be reluctant to ask that another physician be consulted, but this reluctance is ill-founded. Good doctors do not take offense at requests for consultation; they know that the family has the patient's best interest at heart, and, being of like mind, comply without rancor.

Several circumstances might suggest the need for consultation.

1. When there is a question about diagnosis, you may believe that the physician has not given proper weight to certain historical information or other aspects of a patient's behavior. Through reading or discussion with acquaintances with similar difficulties, you may have arrived at your own impressions as to the source of the problem. A confirmation of the diagnosis can set your mind at ease, enabling you to cooperate more fully with the treatment plan. On the other hand, a differing opinion may point your physician in another direction which he has previously not considered and which may prove more beneficial to the patient.

2. When you are dissatisfied with the progress of treatment, a reevaluation of diagnosis may again lead to differing therapeutic efforts with improved results. The consulting physician may, at the request of the family, the patient, or the referring physician, assume care for the patient at that point, particularly if he advises another type of treatment in which the referring physician lacks expertise.

3. The therapist himself may request consultation with a colleague, particularly if the case is not going well or if he believes

it warrants another form of treatment which may be new or controversial.

4. Some physicians and patients simply do not hit it off well together. This usually is not the exclusive fault of either. Personalities can clash for a variety of reasons—perhaps as a residue of an unfavorable first impression (doctors and their patients often meet under trying circumstances), or because one reminds the other of, say, his mother-in-law. If your relative should find himself irrevocably at odds with his doctor, everyone including the psychiatrist will probably be better off if you face the problem squarely and make a change.

Part II

Knowing: Major Mental Disorders and Their Causes

7.
Depression

To one degree or another, the experience of depression is almost universal. Nearly everyone who has felt sad when things were going badly has expressed his emotion by saying, "I feel depressed." Although statements like this may only reflect a passing mood, they create an unfortunate confusion between the commonplace symptom of depression and the actual illness we call, among other names, depressive disease. This confusion affects not only patient and relatives, but many doctors as well—even including some psychiatrists.

SYMPTOMS

The problem lies in defining just what illness is and what it is not. As we discussed earlier (chapter 4), symptoms alone do not mean disease. Only when certain constellations of symptoms occur over a specified period of time should we call someone sick. The same symptom pattern appearing in a number of patients constitutes a *syndrome*. The scientist studies such groups of patients in the hopes of discovering a common cause, course, or treatment for the condition (which may then be named after him).

But because we use the same word to mean both the symptom and the syndrome of depression, people often take one for the other. Back in the early days of psychiatry, when its practitioners, then called alienists, commanded no specific treatment anyway, the terminology used made little difference—the doctor could do little more for his patient than lock him up or hold his hand. But from decades of research, we have now inherited such a variety of treatments, more or less specific for certain well-defined psychiatric disorders, that we can no longer afford the luxury of mistaking syndrome for symptom, or vice versa. To do so risks treatment which is improper, excessive, or inadequate, any of which can be a mortal sin. Psychiatric diagnosis must be "right on."

One of the commonest syndromes is that of *reactive depression,* sadness which occurs in reaction to a traumatic life event (Great Aunt Tillie dies and leaves her millions to the Red Cross). This gloomy mood will persist until the stress has been withdrawn or the memory of it fades. Our aspiring sales manager, Gary Grindstone, provides one example of such a stress-related mood state; later in the chapter we will meet another.

The term "reactive" implies, of course, that *non*-reactive depressions also exist, which indeed they do. These conditions (we will give them a less cumbersome name in a moment) constitute what has been the most misunderstood, misdiagnosed and mistreated problem in psychiatry, if not in all of medicine. Their very existence still evokes amazement (and often, at first, disbelief) in patients and doctors alike. For it seems contrary to logic that many depressions occur not as a reaction to stress at all, but strike unprovoked and unheralded, apparently from "out of the blue." Because they are not stress-related, springing from within, so to speak, we refer to them as *endogenous.* Lois Downing gave a history quite typical of a severe, progressively worsening, endogenous depression for which no clearly precipitating factor could be pinpointed. Experience with countless patients suggests that at least half of all depressed patients are similarly at a loss to name the cause.

This is the condition responsible for the majority of the seriously ill patients seen by psychiatrists either as office patients or in the hospital. But because it comes in many guises, even doctors may fail to classify it as endogenous or sometimes to recognize it as depression at all. No laboratory tests exist for depression; we have only the symptoms to guide us in detection and diagnosis. So for the balance of the chapter, let us carefully examine the symptoms and syndromes of this illness, considering along the way some of the names it has been given.

Foremost among symptoms is disturbance of *mood*. All of our depressed patients so far have shown a clearly lowered affective (mood) state, which Lois, had she been asked, would have readily identified as "sad." But sometimes anxiety, irritability, or "nervousness" are the only abnormal emotions a patient recognizes in himself, and occasionally he may deny that anything at all is amiss. "Nonsense," he says, "I'm just tired (or worried, or nervous)." Then it falls upon you to point out to his doctor the definite change in the way he relates to friends and to relatives. Children and adolescents particularly have trouble identifying their moods, probably because they lack sufficient experience with normal mood to realize that they feel different.

You may wonder, Where do I draw the line between a normal reaction to stress and depression which has clinical significance? Of course, we cannot say with certainty that the two-day blue spell will not develop into a long-lasting endogenous depression, but length of illness usually serves as a pretty good index to type. Research psychiatrists demand that a patient have symptoms for a month or more before they diagnose depressive disease, and in clinical psychiatry this rule serves as a practical guide; most patients have been ill for at least a month before they or their relatives realize that they need help and seek it. Even in the case of the grief reaction which follows death of a loved one, if the symptoms persist past the first month or two, the clinician suspects that an endogenous depression has supervened.

Lois's physiology had got the best of her. Her biological clock, which in each of us regulates sleep and other body functions, was running out of step with the rest of the world. When she first became ill she had difficulty falling asleep, but later she awakened in the early hours of the morning. This early morning awakening (terminal insomnia) often is a hallmark of severe depression. But if she greeted the dawn tired and miserable, she also noted an improvement in her mood as the day wore on, a form of *diurnal variation* often encountered in endogenous depressions. Other patients experience just the opposite pattern, feeling nearly well in the morning, but gradually worsening as the day progresses. *Appetite and weight loss* also typify the endogenous depression; even today the psychiatrist occasionally sees a patient who looks like a refugee from a concentration camp.

But some depressed people experience exactly the opposite of the physiological changes we have mentioned. They sleep too much, as if to escape their depressive feelings; the amount of food they consume rockets skywards, and their weight gain may be as impressive as it is distressing. These symptoms typically occur in the teen- or college-age patient, and, as a result, his parents, thinking him merely lazy, inattentive, or greedy, may nag or otherwise harass the luckless fellow for his supposed moral turpitude.

Depression leads to *crying spells,* which sometimes seem to occur "over nothing at all." Saddened by gloomy thoughts, the patient may suddenly dissolve into tears with little apparent provocation. Others wish they could cry but cannot; they are "all cried out" and say they would feel better if they could only shed some tears.

To his friends and relatives, the patient appears *listless* and *disinterested,* as he shows little enthusiasm for his work. One man, an amateur (and capable) mechanic who had always kept his cars in good running order, developed the notion that he could no longer change spark plugs, so he and his car wound down together. Such apparent lack of motivation, particularly when combined with the *irritability* so frequently seen in depression, provokes angry feelings on the part of those close to the patient. Their remonstrations increase both his *guilt* feelings and his depression, widening the rift within the family. *Loss of sex interest* with, in males, inability to achieve or maintain an erection, creates further suspicions and ill-feelings between spouses. Either men or women may enter into extramarital affairs as they attempt to reawaken decreasing sexual interest, often resulting in severe marital difficulties, including separation and divorce.

Other physical complaints develop. The anxiety which frequently accompanies depression causes shortness of breath; in his panic the patient breathes too rapidly *(hyperventilates),* becoming weak and dizzy from the effort. His *heart beats* too rapidly or skips beats, and although physically in perfect health, he may imagine that death beckons. Some patients, increasingly strained by financial worries and family obligations, complain of tension-type *headaches:* a dull, aching pain localized at the front or the back of the head, often radiating down the neck. During moments of stress it worsens, but can usually be relieved by aspirin, rest, or heat.

The depressed patient can be a veritable walking textbook of *physical symptoms.* He is nauseated and may try to vomit; he complains of bloating or heartburn; his bowels become·irritable as diarrhea confines him to the bathroom. He may first seek treatment from his family physician, who may diagnose "masked depression" and refer him to a psychiatrist when all test reports come back "negative."

Phobias (unreasonable fears) sometimes develop during the course of depression. These include fear of germs, of going out-of-doors, of animals, of being alone (or of being with people), or of almost any other conceivable thing or situation. The phobic patient suffers from intense *anxiety*—he feels that something is terribly wrong or has the sense of impending doom. In a typical anxiety attack, his heart beats too quickly or skips beats; he breathes in short gasps, causing dizziness and fatigue. The pains in his chest and the tingling sensation about his mouth or in his hands or feet convince him that his body is failing and that he will die. For some, these anxiety attacks are the only readily apparent emotion; the doctor must search diligently for signs of depression.

On the edge of her chair sits Eula Mac Trimble. This forty-five-year-old black lady has worked since her early twenties as a registered nurse, and she is a good one, holding together the often-stressed fabric of a large city hospital's outpatient clinic. Her job, which involves coordinating the activities of the twenty doctors and nurses who serve nearly three hundred patients seeking care each day, she has handled with ease for years, yet over the past month she has suffered from anxiety attacks of increasing severity.

Sitting rigidly, handkerchief clutched tightly in both hands, she describes the fear of being away from home which gripped her suddenly six weeks before. Unable to identify its source, she knows only that she frequently becomes preoccupied with the idea that something terrible will happen to her. Then she feels the intense compulsion to rush home, undress, and get into bed, which in fact she has done on several occasions. Increasingly she has felt fearful upon leaving the house in the morning, and for the past few days she has not been able to go outdoors unaccompanied at all.

"When I go away from home," she explains, "I can feel something tighten up inside my chest. It's like someone puts his giant arm around me and keeps me from breathing. My heart beats so fast I think it will jump right out of my chest, and I just know that if I don't turn around and rush home, I'll fall down dead." For two weeks her internist has prescribed tranquilizers in increasing amounts, but without improvement. Today he has learned that she quit her job, so he refers her to a psychiatrist for an emergency consultation.

Not satisfied that he has obtained all relevant information, the psychiatrist questions her husband, who has brought her to the office. Mr. Trimble notes that despite their continuing closeness, several times during the past month his wife has said she has felt lonely; more than once he has seen her wiping her eyes with a handkerchief. He recalls that a decade earlier she had a similar illness when she felt anxious and fearful, much as she does now, and which also resulted in quitting her job. Then he had done the marketing himself for the nearly six months she remained afraid to go outside, but with time she had gradually improved and within a year was well and back at work.

Suspecting depression, the psychiatrist prescribes a mood elevating drug, and within three weeks Mrs. Trimble returns to her nursing duties.

The history illustrates the importance of looking beneath the presenting symptom (anxiety) for the underlying depression, something that many physicians regularly forget to do. *Anxiety depression,* as this syndrome has been called, may progress to such extreme agitation that the patient cannot sit still longer than a moment. He wrings his hands, paces the floor, hammers his head with his fists, and groans aloud in anguished frenzy. He clings to you or to the doctor, begging that you not desert him, and no amount of reassurance seems to calm him. Severe anxiety depression produces a terrific strain upon patient and family alike and is usually best treated in the hospital.

With more severe illness, the symptoms of endogenous depression become more obvious (and more frightening). The patient complains that his *thinking* has *slowed down.* His *memory fails,* his thoughts elude him as his *concentration wanes.* Objectively, his speech is retarded as he hesitates between words or phrases. Sentences seem to stick in his throat, and an eternity may pass before he answers a question. Talking to people with *psychomotor retardation* like this can be an excruciatingly drawn-out process, exhausting patient and interviewer alike.

Physical processes other than speech slow down, too. The retarded patient may appear virtually immobile as he drags himself from bed to chair and back. He suffers from paralysis of his will, agonizing over every small decision. Once he does make a choice, he obsessively wonders if he has considered every factor bearing upon it and once again begins his ruminations.

Because of advances in treatment over the past four decades, today's patient does not usually lose touch with reality. But the fact remains that, untreated, melancholy can lead to feelings of *guilt* and guilt to the conviction of evil-doing or sin.

The large, stolid-looking woman who sat in the corner of the day room had become nearly a fixture there. Over the past decade, Olive Bard had been admitted to that psychiatric hospital yearly, usually in the fall just before school took up. Her dedication to her students caused the school where Miss Bard taught English and literature to make allowances for the repeated episodes of her illness, which had begun several years into her fourth decade. Thereafter, she continued living much as before, save that she gave up the small house she had rented upon first returning to her hometown, moving once again into her parents' large one.

"Since then she's always made her home with mother and me," her father had said the day they brought her back to her hospital. Her parents, fixtures themselves by now, were thin, elderly, somewhat ascetic and appeared not a little melancholy themselves, needing only farm clothes and pitchfork to complete the picture.

"Well, it's happened again," continued her father. "She was all right for quite awhile after the last time. Took up her reading again and started making lesson plans for the next year. We really hoped she wouldn't get depressed again this fall, her mother and me, and we decided to take her on a trip to Chicago and east. Had a good time, too, for about a week, but then she decided that she wanted to ride in the back seat instead of up front with the two of us, and we could see the change coming over her face again—the corners of her mouth turned down, and her brow wrinkled together. When she does that, she always looks like she's trying to figure something out. "Then she allowed as how she'd been unpleasant to the manager of the hotel where we'd stayed the night before," the old man continued, "and she couldn't figure out why she came in the first place, so she commenced to feel guilty. Thought maybe she'd done something wrong. But when she stopped eating— said she couldn't figure out what was right to eat when we stopped in Chillicothe—we knew that it was coming down on her again, and we brought her straight here. Drove fourteen hours yesterday just to get her back."

He stood to leave, dejectedly turning the rim of his derby hat through his fingers. "I guess you've got everything else in the old chart. Thank you for your time, Doctor."

Seated in hospital pajamas across the table, the schoolteacher looked distinctly nonprofessional. Her round face was contorted by the worried, unhappy expression she wore, and she repeatedly screwed her brow into an anguished grimace. Sitting quietly in her chair, she laced and unlaced her fingers, rubbing her palms back and forth together in a continuous gesture of anxiety.

"I ... just ... can't figure out ... why ... I took that ... trip, Doctor. How ... could I .... have been ... that ... cruel and thoughtless?" Her speech was agonizingly slow, as she struggled to summon new reserves of strength every few words.

"I ... know ... that ... I've hurt them ... terribly. Did you see ... my father ... turned his hat ... in his hands? It means ... he ... should turn ... away ... from me." At the thought her face reddened, and tears streamed down her cheeks, "Oh God ... I deserve it. I deserve to ... die."

Olive Bard's belief that she had sinned was typical of the delusions which, before the advent of modern therapy, were often encountered in severely depressed people. Like many patients, she accepted her depression as a punishment she richly deserved for the guilt she felt. Another patient[1] became so ill at age sixty-three that she believed everyone on earth had died due to the enormity of her sins. Before shock treatments cured her, she spent several days lying in bed and moaning about her wicked folly. Her husband

---

[1]Another name sometimes given to those who first become ill in middle life is *involutional melancholia,* so called because its onset coincides approximately with the "change of life" (menopause). There is little evidence to support this relationship (especially hard to explain in men, who do not have change of life), but old habits die slowly, and the term lingers.

could not understand. "This is crazy, Doctor, that she believes these things—the only place she's ever been in her life is to church!"

Other patients may believe that demons, the police, or the CIA hound them; they hear the voices of dead relatives beseeching them to repent; total strangers call them degrading names or taunt them to commit suicide. The patient may believe he is infested with cancer or that his heart is beating so slowly that his blood pressure will fall to zero. Olive Bard's belief that her father had "turned away" from her was a delusional misinterpretation of his actual gesture. And occasionally a patient becomes so ill that he thinks he has already died. One young man hospitalized after several months of growing depression startled the laboratory technician by telling her: "There's no point in drawing my blood—it's all gone. And you can forget about the electrocardiogram because my heart stopped beating days ago."

The wealthiest of patients may express delusions of poverty. Because he fancies that the bank is about to foreclose the mortgage, he must sell his farm or business. His fright becomes so great, his suffering so real, that he quite convinces his relatives. In a misguided attempt to placate him, they may actually agree to sell the house, business, farm, or yacht to cope with the imaginary fiscal crisis. One of the jobs the physician faces is to set apart real fears from those which are delusional; you can imagine how important an interview with a relative is in helping to discriminate fact from fiction. For example, one middle-aged man, temporarily unable to work because of depression, became convinced that he would have to sell his property to avoid the poorhouse. His wife laughed nervously as she pointed out to him (for the fourth time that afternoon) that his job was secure until he recovered and that his disability insurance and sick pay produced a greater income than he had when working!

As her feelings of worthlessness and hopelessness about the future grew, Lois Downing's morbid thoughts about death became more and more prominent. Death became an increasingly attractive alternative to her hopeless, tortured existence, and she began to plan her nearly successful suicide. When it comes, a suicide attempt usually has been foreshadowed by days or weeks of gloomy predictions about the future. As the desperation increases, these subtle hints broaden to frank statements of suicidal intent which even *then* may be ignored by acquaintances. Hints and threats alike represent a clarion call to immediate action on the part of both relative and physician and should *always* be taken seriously (see chapter 13).

Occurrence

Depressive illness occurs far more frequently than is recognized. Three to five percent of all people at some time in their lives will have an episode of depression similar to those which we have described and severe enough to need treatment. This means that as many as ten million Americans have been or will be affected by depressive disease, a number which ranks this disease among the most common that humans experience. Yet so few receive treatment that if all visits to physicians for depression were evenly divided among all medical doctors in this country, each physician would see a depressed patient only once every two months. This important disease may well be the most underdiagnosed, under-treated and misunderstood in the history of medicine.

If most of the patients we have met so far have been female, it is with good reason: depressed women outnumber men about two to one. Although there are no racial preponderances, the disorder tends to be diagnosed less frequently in blacks, either because they, being poorer, less often consult psychiatrists, or because white, middle-class psychiatrists less readily understand the problems of black people. Encountered at all social and economic levels, depressions have been recorded in widely varying cultures in all countries of the world. Although some of the individual symptoms vary depending upon the culture, the basic syndromes are quite constant from place to place.

The typical patient is a woman in her middle forties, but you may encounter depression in people of all ages from youth to senescence. Depression of one degree or another frequently appears in the elderly, particularly in those who must live in nursing homes or hospitals. Although many such people may "only" be sad and lonely, others do suffer from treatable depressive disease. If psychiatrists would take more careful clinical histories and treat accordingly, a number of older people might be salvaged from too-early consignment to the slag-heaps of society. But with geriatric psychiatry still in its infancy, so to speak, physicians are often poorly informed about the mental illnesses of this age group. Once again, responsibility for recognizing this common disease must rest with the concerned family.

Of all the types of depression encountered, those which occur in childhood seem to be the hardest for people to accept. Despite our advancing sophistication of the last several decades, we still recoil at the thought of children suffering the failings of adults, whether these be sexual, criminal—or merely mental. When a child becomes depressed, as happens more often than we realize, the adults in his family are likely to overlook it until it is far advanced.

Until he turned seven they called him "Tiger," which pretty well summed him up: cheerful, positive, and irrepressibly bumptious. But for a year or more he had withdrawn from his family, become generally sad and often irritable. And now they called him "Tony."

"And that in itself should have told me something," said his mother, nervously crushing a handful of hankies as she related his history.

When, in the second grade, he had begun to stand at the edge of the playground or stay indoors during recess to read a book, his mother tried to force masculine socialization upon her son by having him participate in the Little League; he cried throughout his first game. Believing that he was "only going through a phase," his parents redoubled their efforts. In Cub Scouts he again hung back from the others, spending most meetings off in a corner playing with the cat. At school his grades dropped from superior to unsatisfactory, and he preferred the company of girls; the boys, he said, were mean to him. Although his weight held steady his appetite seemed poor, and his mother commented that he lacked his usual pep and energy. "Spooky" dreams frequently disturbed his restless sleep, and some nights he would sleepwalk. In the morning, he felt tired and wished he did not have to go to school. He took no interest in family activities but spent afternoons and evenings in his room, where he was often seen with tears quietly streaming down his cheeks.

At length, his parents realized this was something more than just a childhood phase. Their family practitioner, who had not seen Tony for some months, noted that he appeared listless and sad, and, after the physical examination, sat down with his small patient to talk. What he learned alarmed him. Tony admitted to such profound depression as is usually seen only in adults.

"I'm not a very nice kid—I hate myself," he admitted with a little prodding. When asked what he would like if he could have any wish granted, he replied, "I wish we had a big tree in our yard. I could climb up and jump off a high branch and break my neck."

The same afternoon, they took him to a psychiatrist. Tony responded quickly to medicine, just as an adult would, and soon returned to his normal, outgoing way of doing business. In adults, permanent alterations in personality do not follow depression. But depression during a child's formative years may leave him unsure of himself, lacking social graces, and chronically "one down." He may lose time from school through psychosomatic complaints or school refusal (sometimes called "school phobia"), or if he does go, his inattention may cause him to fall behind in his work. Early detection and rapid treatment of depression are even more important in childhood and adolescence than in adults. And the very young patient depends completely upon his family to see that he receives the help he needs.

Mild and Masked Depressions

The clinical examples we have examined so far are, in a sense, misleading, for they suggest that all depressive symptoms are severe and seriously incapacitating. Nothing could be further from the truth. Depressions are like auto accidents: mostly minor, inconvenient at the time, but not very newsworthy. Only a few are big and bad enough to make the headlines.

The average depressed patient has symptoms so mild that he often escapes medical attention completely. His mood is one of mild sadness which he may not even recognize as abnormal; and if he has any of the bodily symptoms previously described, they, too, will be mild: sleep delayed by an hour or so of tossing and turning, appetite slightly diminished—perhaps at last he can rid himself of the "spare tire" he has packed around for years. If the depression affects his social life, it annoys him but does not put him out of commission. Although his efficiency at work may fall, at least he is able to *get* to work. It is at home in the bosom of his family, where loss of functioning will less likely threaten either income or social stability (relatives can absorb a lot of punishment!) that the effects of mild depression most frequently appear. Identifying the one or two key symptoms which disrupt family relationships can solve the puzzle of mild endogenous depression.

"Boy, you should've seen this couple I talked with a month ago!" George Goodfellow, the family practitioner from Rancho Bravo exulted to the physicians gathered around the table in the hospital dining room. "One of the most unusual and gratifying cases I've seen in months.

"This gal—she was about forty years old—and her husband came in complaining of marital difficulties. Seems that ever since she had her right breast removed for cancer a year ago she hadn't wanted sex. Of course, she blamed her husband, saying that he was being too demanding of her, and there they'd go again with another argument. Her menstrual periods were still regular, and she hadn't complained of hot flashes or any other symptoms of menopause, so I didn't think putting her on hormones would do the job. And she really wasn't worried about a recurrence of the tumor—both she and the surgeon seemed pretty well convinced that they had got it all. I was afraid to send her to a psychiatrist. From my experience with some of those fellows, he'd get tangled up in the symbolic loss of her femininity and all that b.s., and she'd *never* get well." He chuckled to himself and finished his soup, slowly, savoring both it and the interest of his colleagues.

"What I finally decided," he continued, toying with a package of crackers, "was that she must be suffering from a masked depression. She didn't *say* that she was depressed, and she frankly didn't even *look* depressed—hair nicely done, eyebrows in place and all that. But she was so irritable, and she'd always enjoyed sex before, and now wanted no part of it—they hadn't had relations for the past three months. That's a pretty definite change! So I told them I wasn't exactly sure what was wrong, but that depression was a good possibility, and we ought to try an antidepressant for a couple of weeks.

"You know, when I saw them later, she was sleeping well, eating better, and she said that now she felt so cheerful she *must* have been depressed before. As for the sex part, I knew that was better, too, when I saw the huge grin her husband wore. I could have charged him a thousand dollars for that visit and he'd've asked me, 'How do you want it, in twenties or fifties?' "

Patients like Dr. Goodfellow's drag along for months or years at a time, feeling moderately tired, cranky, and unable to experience joy in everyday life. Their symptoms include trouble making minor decisions, intermittent anxiety, vague uneasiness—in fact, nearly every nonpsychotic symptom previously described, but to a lesser degree. If these people do see a physician, it will seldom be a psychiatrist. Usually the doctor will diagnose "neurotic depression" and treat with tranquilizers, which reduce anxiety but leave the basic mood disturbance untouched. Left unattended, as they often are, mild depressions can become severe, and this "great oaks from little acorns" phenomenon sets the scene for one of the more important examples of preventive medicine in psychiatry. For if friends and relatives can learn to recognize the mild endogenous depression, the psychiatrist's job and the patient's life will both become considerably easier. And once more, the key to recognizing depression is change in personality, in habits, and in attitudes in a previously stable man or woman (or child).

By now you may be wondering what the various syndromes of endogenous depression have to do with one another. Are psychotic and anxiety depression really distinct diseases with different causes and courses? Or have doctors simply renamed the same basic illness over and over again with terms describing this or that prominent feature, failing to recognize the important similarities of the conditions they treat?

The names themselves set up an unfortunate dichotomy; if we call delusional depressives "psychotic," then by the same token are all others neurotic? This artificial distinction, subscribed to by a great number of mental health workers, ranks among the lesser contributions psychiatry has made to medicine. Inasmuch as depressed people can be psychotic during one episode and non-psychotic during the next, and because most of the so-called neurotics function normally when not depressed, the term is about as useful as track shoes for turtles. It should be summarily discarded.

When we look into the problem of symptoms more closely, we find that not even the "obvious" distinction between reactive and endogenous depressions can be clearly supported on the basis of symptoms alone. Let us meet another person with reactive depression—but unlike Gary Grindstone, a real patient.

Until the previous two years, Rhoda Crews' health had been excellent, and she had worked hard keeping an immaculate house. But at age twenty-seven, the roof fell in.

When her two grandfathers died, she grieved but seemed to adjust. In the next year, her stepfather, her biological father, and her closest friend all died, and her depressed mood became more sustained, and she cried a lot. Nonetheless, she bore up well even when her husband lost his job and remained unemployed for six months. It was not until his new job with the highway maintenance department required him to live away from home for several weeks at a time that she really "broke down."

Missing the support of her husband, she began to have difficulty falling asleep at night; in the morning, it was equally hard to get up. Once awake, she felt reasonably energetic but was "completely washed out" again by nightfall. Her appetite diminished, and she lost six or seven pounds. Because she felt happier and more secure when distracted from her problems, she spent a good deal of time at her neighbors, but wondered aloud how they could stand her because she was "so bitchy." When she began to have thoughts about dying, she reported them to her family physician, who referred her for psychiatric hospitalization.

The morning following admission, she seemed considerably brighter, the result of a good night's sleep. The hand-wringing and crying had diminished, and she could relate her story coherently. Her husband obtained a leave of absence from work and eventually found another job closer to home. Six days following admission, she returned home to her husband and her houseful of children; her mood now returned to normal. The low dose of antidepressant medicine initially prescribed was quickly tapered and discontinued.

Without medicine, she has been well since.

In onset and course, Rhoda's depression was certainly classically reactive. The onset appeared to have been precipitated by a number of traumatic events, culminating in separation from her husband. Again typically, the depression subsided without medicine or other specific treatment as soon as the stress abated. But look at the symptoms: sleep disturbance, diurnal variation, appetite and weight loss, death wishes, but to a less intense degree.

Rhoda's sleep pattern—initial insomnia or trouble getting to sleep—seems just the opposite of Lois', and has been claimed to typify reactive depression. But either type of sleep disturbance can be seen in either type of depression; there are no simple answers in the diagnosis of this illness. She could be distracted from her misery by the society of her coffee klatsch friends, whereas Lois could not have cared less about companions—another feature often said to differentiate the two types of depression. But again, "it ain't necessarily so." In either type, appetite and weight may decrease, though the magnitude of loss is usually more severe in the severe endogenous depression. In the final analysis, you simply cannot base this differentiation on symptoms alone. So the careful clinician often goes ahead and treats for endogenous depression, because it is relatively easy, cheap, safe—and it just might work (see chapter 14). Too often doctors take at face value a "clear" precipitating circumstance and diagnose reactive depression, failing thereby to treat as vigorously and thoroughly as they should.

What knowledgeable psychiatrists are finally coming to appreciate is that *none* of the labels we have encountered so far predict much about the patient's future. But fortunately, a path has been hacked out of this nettlesome and somewhat depressing thicket. In the next chapter, we will discuss some other terms which can help the doctor with treatment, but for now let us admit frankly that by and large only two groups of depressed patients can be clearly differentiated: primary and secondary. By *primary depression* (or *primary affective disorder*), we mean simply that prior to the current episode the patient has not been ill with another diagnosable psychiatric condition; it implies nothing else about cause or severity.

When someone has had another psychiatric problem like alcoholism, neurosis, or personality disorder prior to the onset of depression, "secondary affective disorder" describes the chronological relationship between the two illnesses.[2] Why bother with this distinction? For two reasons.

First, the clinician can usually decide whether the depression came first or second in, say, a patient who drinks excessively— a decidedly easier job than interpreting which depression is "en-

---

[2]Those depressions caused by physical conditions such as brain tumors, thyroid disease, birth control pills, steroids, and some blood pressure medicines could also be classified as "secondary." Their treatment, obviously, is to remove the causative factor, which must first be identified.

dogenous" and which "reactive." But more important, the primary-secondary concept allows him to make those vital predictions about treatment and outcome which other diagnoses do not permit. For example, secondary depressions respond poorly to the standard drug and physical treatments which have proven so effective for the primary affective disorders (chapters 14–17); on the other hand, secondary depressions are likely to be of briefer duration, and may be less likely to result in suicide.   ·

All the depressions we have described in this chapter (with the exception of Rhoda Crews') are primary, and all can be treated in about the same way. And all carry the same prognosis: excellent. Cumbersome and confusing names like involutional melancholia can at last be retired in favor of a simple, logical classification which anyone can easily learn to use. But the various clinical pictures should be kept in mind, to help identify primary affective disorder when it crops up.

DIAGNOSIS

As we have learned, depression can take as many forms as it has names, and to make a firm, valid diagnosis requires the training and experience of a professional. But before your doctor can diagnose depression, he must see the patient, which he will never do unless someone suspects that a problem exists. To help you help your doctor, the most important of the depressive symptoms which we have discussed are listed in Table 1. If your relative has had a *mood change* which *persists,* so that he seems *different from his usual self,* and if he has several of the other symptoms tabulated, he may well suffer from a primary depression and should be carefully evaluated by a doctor.

OUTCOME

Severe depression can be a most debilitating illness, uncomfortable for patient and family alike. In a sense, though, it is a "good" illness to have; psychiatrists will sometimes tell a depressed patient, "If you had to have a mental illness of some type, you picked the right one." The reasons for this are several.

First, even before the advent of modern psychiatric treatment, it was well known that people with depressive disease almost in-

---

Table 1
Common Symptoms Suggesting Depression

Mood Change:
    Sad, blue, depressed, "down in the dumps"
    Irritable
    Anxious
Mental Symptoms:
    Loss of interest
    Indecision
    Poor concentration
    Slowed thinking
    Feels worthless
    Future hopeless
    Guilt feelings
    Death wishes
    Suicidal ideas
Social Symptoms:
    Unable to work
    Decreased sex interest
    Withdrawal from friends
    Drinking, drug use
Physical Symptoms:
    Sighing
    Tiredness
    Headaches
    Dry mouth
    Constipation
    Restlessness
    Poor appetite
    Weight loss
    Crying spells
    Insomnia

---

variably recovered. As one doctor put it in describing the course of his patient's mood, "What goes down must come up." Depressions may end quickly, within a few weeks, but more often they persist for six to twelve months. A few may last for years. But no matter how long they last, nearly everyone recovers fully, meaning that once well, each patient returns completely to his former personality with no evidence of residual mental disorder. This means that friends, relatives, physicians, and the patient himself will be able to agree that he seems no different from his usual self. He will be able to enjoy life, to work, to love and to be loved by his family. This excellent prognosis holds for all primary affective disorders, whether they have been called endogenous or reactive, psychotic, neurotic or anxiety depression, or involutional melancholia. And regardless of how severely ill the patient has become, the outcome can still be summarized in one word: recovery.

There is a second reason for this optimistic outlook on depression: during the past forty years, extremely effective treatments have been developed for even the most severely ill patients. Essentially all depressions will eventually resolve by themselves, but no one need endure months or years of misery while awaiting his spontaneous remission. Through one means or another, as we will discuss in chapters 14–17, this is one illness in which you should have every expectation of rapid, substantial relief.

The case of Olive Bard illustrates the point of recovery nicely, for despite her severe incapacitation when ill, she was able to continue her teaching duties between episodes. Her story also shows one disquieting feature of the illness—the tendency for some depressions to recur. First, the good news. About 50 percent of patients have no recurrence; their depressions will be a one-time illness. And then the bad news: the other half will have one or more subsequent episodes of depression. This is not so terribly dreary, because the average patient need expect only two or three episodes during his entire lifetime. This means that if Aunt Sally becomes depressed after childbirth when she is thirty, she may never have another sick day until she is sixty-five. And a thirty-five-year interval between illnesses is not such a terrifying prospect, especially when each episode is as easy to treat as is true today.

Patients like Olive Bard are the obvious exception to this rule of infrequent recurrences, yet even here there is cause for optimism. We met her as she appeared over a decade ago, at a time before some of the newer modes of therapy had been developed. Today, more definitive prophylactic treatment might well prevent further difficulty with her disease.

One other point should be reemphasized: the ever-present danger of suicide. Some patients attempt it, some merely talk about it, while others actually die by their own hands. But in one of these ways suicide plays a role in many patients with primary affective disorders. It is the one complication to depressive illness which can seriously (fatally) affect patients' lives. This is such an important subject that an entire chapter (chapter 13) will be devoted to it later on. Suffice it to say for now that suicide or suicide attempts, often encountered in depressions of the sort we have discussed in this chapter, are even more likely to complicate the picture of manic-depressive disease, the subject of the next chapter.

8.
Mania

For many patients, depression is only half the story. About a quarter of all those with affective disorder will at some time have an episode of mania. In chapter 2 we met Gilbert Grand, whose mood was the exact opposite of depressed. As with Gilbert, the manic's excessive good spirits often cause quite a bit of trouble for himself and his friends. His mood and optimism rise to overpower his judgment, and what he says and does he later comes to regret.

During his lifetime a patient may have a number of episodes of mania, interspersed with periods of depression identical to those described in chapter 7. The inconvenience caused these *manic-depressive* patients can be considerable, as you can see in the following letter from a woman.

Dear Doctor:
   You don't know me yet, but you soon will as I have an appointment with you next week. I am writing this letter to apprise you of some of the early details of my case history, and I am sending it to you as either a challenge or a threat, depending upon how you choose to regard it, and me.
   I'll skip lightly over my childhood and early adult life. Not much to growing up the apple of your parents' eye in East Jesus, Oklahoma, or being the brightest scholastic light in a high school graduating class of seventeen. I had always been rather bubbly and outgoing, and it stood me in good stead in obtaining a position with an advertising firm after college. By the time I was thirty-five, my drive and energy carried me to

an important executive position. Then the difficulties began. Over a period of several weeks, I seemed to lose my interest (and talent) for my work, and I started each morning a little gloomier than the last. I felt increasingly blue and down. I was irritable and didn't care to be with people, and my decreasing concentration caused my work to suffer. In desperation I finally sought the help of a psychiatrist (my first!), who advised me that my trouble was due to my sexual hang-ups and advised me to go to bed with the two men I had dated from time to time until my illness. And so, my dear Doctor, I lost my cherry on a medical prescription and felt none the better for it until six or eight months later, when I gradually began to feel more like my old self.

Unfortunately, it didn't stop there. As my mood improved, it seemed to me that everything was going just right. I felt that I loved everyone, to the point where sometimes I could hardly stand it. When I got back into my work again, I found that I could think more clearly about it than ever before. It was good times in the office in those days, and we laughed a lot. My colleagues said that I talked incessantly at the brainstorming sessions, and I guess I did, but I frankly didn't give a damn! Ideas—good ideas—would flash into my head faster than I could note them down. Fortunately, I had plenty of time to work them up, because now I felt terrifically energetic on only three or four hours of sleep a night. Not that I didn't spend plenty of time in bed, mind you—I became sexually quite active, and even learned to climax!

After six or eight weeks I settled down to normal once again, where I remained for a short time before once again becoming depressed. Thus began the pattern of mood swings which was to continue with me for the next eighteen years: four months down, a month and a half up, with precious little space in between. The up periods were a lot of fun and I did get things done, but I knew each time that I would have to pay for it later with depression.

Are you still with me, Doctor? Because you ain't seen nothing yet! I was thirty-nine, well off financially, and just swinging into my semi-annual "high," when I met Harvey. Six days later I married him and moved halfway across the country. In the next two weeks, I learned he was a feckless liar, the marriage was a bust, and I was out of a job.

As my mood swings became worse, I began to drink to get to sleep. Over several years this led to sneaking drinks at parties, then seeking out parties for drinks, and finally, when I was forty-nine, to my first psychiatric hospitalization—for alcoholism. By the time I finished chasing the snakes and mice off my bedclothes, I swore I would never take another drink, and up to the present time I have not done so, for which I thank God for Her infinite mercy.

Although at times I think I might as well have. While in Paris one summer, I raced into a beauty shop to request (I thought) a Joan of Arc haircut, which was the style that year in France. Three weeks later, I awakened in a sanitarium where I had had sleep treatments for a psychosis, in which (they told me later) I kept insisting they follow me to Orleans. Back in the States the next year, I bought football uniforms for the girls' soccer team of Terre Haute, to "guarantee them equal opportunity," as I phrased it in the twenty-five-page accompanying letter I wrote. During a business trip to the Soviet Union, I had oral sex with two women from the Urals, which I found distasteful. Back home, I became very aggressive with members of my own family. (Probably the worst thing I ever did was giving my sister-in-law, a lifelong staunch Republican, a recording of speeches by Hubert Humphrey and making her listen to them.) All the while, more psychiatrists and psychoanalysts, none of whom told me what was wrong.

Then, about two years ago, I saw an article in *Time* magazine about manic-depressive disease, and the description fit me like a pair of stretch panty hose. The article suggested lithium could control this condition, so I trundled off to my GP and made him prescribe me some. The poor man knew less about the drug than I did (he hadn't read the article), but I bullied him into it and started taking two to four tablets a day, depending on how I felt. From time to time we had a test done to find out how much lithium was in my blood, which Dr. *Time* said we were supposed to do, but because neither of us knew what it meant I didn't pay it much attention.

It was great! I still had highs and lows, but it was as if someone had come along and chopped off the peaks and filled in the valleys so that most of the time I was pretty stable. No drinking, no violence, no sex (well, almost!), no medicines (except lithium) and, perhaps best of all, no psychiatrists.

I am moving to your town in three weeks, and I've been told that in the "big city" it is darn near impossible to get lithium without seeing a shrink. So I'll be in to get a load of you, and as I said at the beginning, you may take this as a warning or as a challenge: I've spent fifteen years in Hell and seen eleven psychiatrists who have collectively destroyed my life. But I have found lithium, need lithium, and I will have it. And if you try to offer me any nonsense other than lithium, you will find yourself having to deal with a menopausal hypomanic who is madder than a boiled owl.

Sincerely yours,
Donna Updyke

Needless to say, Ms. Updyke received her medicine, along with a gratuitous discussion of her illness, which went something like this:

Like depression, mania is primarily a disorder of the mood, or affect. But the manic's affect is quite on the opposite end of the scale from that of the depressed patient—indeed, he feels too well, happier than usual, euphoric, or exalted. "I feel like a two-year-old kid," is the way one ninety-year-old man put it, tossing down his cane and dancing a jig in the hospital corridor. Some manics like Gilbert Grand become uproariously elated and bumptious, a rollicking circus of unfaltering good humor. Donna Updyke's mood was elevated, but at first only to a glowing sense of contented well-being, a feeling of happiness and love for all people. Later in her course of cyclic mood swings, her euphoria was overtaken by the pronounced irritability which can also be quite typical of mania, as her luckless sister-in-law discovered. Either mood can exist alone, or they may occur together in a single manic patient, but one of these two must be present for the diagnosis of mania to be made.

The manic laughs often, long and loud. His infectious laughter elicits the "funny-bone sign" of mania, the irresistible urge of his listeners to laugh with (at) him. With a twinkle in his eye, he may recount a dozen droll stories, sing the refrain from a ballad he has just composed, or regale you with a lengthy account of his latest (prodigious) sexual exploits. One manic patient scampered about the ward pinching several of the nurses on their breasts. When called to account, he indignantly replied, "What's the matter—haven't you ever seen a nervous titter run through a room?"

Unfortunately, one of the most typical features of mania cannot be reproduced in print. That is the rapid manner of talking which psychiatrists call *push of speech*. Whereas in normal conversation each speaker pauses from time to time to allow the other to respond, manic patients typically talk on and on in a sort of verbal diarrhea. Manic speech is really a monologue, and whoever tries to "get a word in edgewise" does so at the peril of being run over with a filibuster.

Almost always push of speech is accompanied by a rapid shift of the manic's thought from one subject to the next, known as *flight of ideas.* Although he may wander far afield of his subject during his soliloquy, when you analyze his speech you can usually understand the connection between one subject and the next. A middle-aged lady who had become manic on a transcontinental airplane flight responded, when asked how she felt, by saying, "I feel wonderful, just plain wonderful!—When the plane took off, I took off.—What do you want me to take off, my dress?—Aren't you going to do a physical?—You look so quizzical!—I'm in great shape, always run on the beach every night." You can see that the links in her train of thought were controlled not by logic, but by punning, rhyming, and other similarities of sound and idea. The manic patient may be distracted by noises in the hallway or irrelevant details he notices about the room, and the original point of his discourse may be forever buried in the verbal avalanche which results.

A manic may say almost anything, proper or not. The informal censoring device which keeps most of us within the bounds of social propriety short-circuits in manic speech. A manic person may call the doctor by his first name (doctors hate that—it destroys their sense of majesty). A manic woman who rattled on about her varied sexual interests cackled as she explained, "I'm as pure as the driven slush." Gilbert Grand's thought was preoccupied with his plans for a monorail; others spend their time writing poems (or books), constructing financial empires of greater or lesser worth (or reality), or simply interfering with the lives of relatives and neighbors.

For all his activity, the manic's energy supply seems inexhaustible as his activity increases to a frenetic pitch. He endlessly cleans and recleans his house; over the weekend he spades the entire lawn for a garden which he never sows. As his excitement mounts, he becomes unable to sit still longer than a few moments, so he spends his time in ceaseless activity, running, pacing, or jogging in place. (One young man devoted the first interview with his psychiatrist to turning front- and back-somersaults about his room; later, he foiled his attempts at physical examination by repeatedly biting the stethoscope.) In the days before modern treatment, some of these extremely ill patients actually died, burning themselves out in what was called "manic exhaustion."

Miraculously, all this activity is fueled on very little sleep. The manic arises early, refreshed and "raring to go" for another marvelous day of hyperactivity—to sleep more than a few hours would be a criminal waste of precious, creative time! Attention to hygiene may suffer: his hair goes uncombed, his beard becomes tangled, his clothes become bedraggled as he joins the ranks of the great unwashed. Appetite may be ignored, and a severely manic patient loses weight, although his energy level remains high.

His euphoric mood and faltering judgment lead to grandiose thinking in which increasing overestimation of his own ability produces greater and greater excesses of behavior. He begins to believe he has exceptional powers denied the rest of us: he can work faster or better than anyone else in the factory, and indeed, with his increased energy level and quickness of thought, he may actually do so for a time. Those who have not yet reached the height of their mania may actually become quite creative for a time, sometimes making a good deal of money before the boom goes bust. The manic's exalted feelings may reach the proportion of delusions, and like Ms. Updyke, he may believe that he is Joan of Arc, Jesus Christ, or any other V.I.P.

Thus the manic sometimes becomes quite psychotic. Completely out of touch with reality, he briefly enters a world of his own in which he believes that he can control people's actions or thoughts, that the pictures on television move by his command, or that he can read minds. He hallucinates the voice of God commanding him to go out and save mankind, or he envisions family and friends standing near. One severely manic sixteen-year-old girl, believing she could hear the heart of her dead father beating from the grave, would pause in her manic frenzy to weep, only to return within seconds to her agitated euphoria. These so-called *micro-depressions,* occurring in the midst of a full-blown mania, are a typical if sometimes confusing feature of the illness.

The combination of energy with grandiosity often delivers a one-two punch to the patient's life. Gilbert Grand's plans were so outrageous that he was not taken seriously, but many are less fortunate. The business man engaging in numerous money-making schemes overextends himself into bankruptcy; the housewife who had purchased food enough for a month lets it rot in the sack for lack of storage space. Manic patients have been known to drive their families deeply into debt by buying several new automobiles at once, engaging in ill-conceived business deals, or giving away large sums of cash on street corners. One manic woman, admitted for treatment in April, sneaked down to the hospital's tiny gift shop and spent four hundred dollars on Christmas presents, much to her psychiatrist's chagrin.

Other social problems may be merely embarrassing at the time, but they can cause repercussions for years to come. Increased sexual drive occurs in women as well as in men, and can lead to promiscuity and pregnancy. Bizarre combinations of clothing (or no clothing at all) set tongues wagging in the community. Family members exhaust themselves trying to keep up with their energetic relative, following him from store to store cancelling debts and hauling him through one scrape with the law to the next. Because manics usually lack the insight that they are ill, they sometimes resist treatment so vigorously that involuntary hospital commitment becomes necessary to avoid even more serious social consequences.

In the throes of a manic state, some patients abuse alcohol. Although they appear to be jolly, many later recall their "euphoria" as more of an uncomfortable agitation which led them to try to dampen their activity with the only "medicine" available: alcohol. So it occasionally happens that a patient admitted to jail or to a detoxification center for "drying out" will, once the acute effects of the liquor have worn off, show the typical symptoms of mania. In fact, heavy abuse of alcohol occurs in about half of all manic patients. Although many do stop drinking once the euphoria has subsided, in some cases heavy alcohol abuse continues, an enduring social consequence of the original illness. Abuse of other drugs such as marijuana, barbiturates, narcotics, and the hallucinogens may also mask the more classical symptoms of mania.

Although neither Gilbert nor Donna actually lost a job because of mania (Donna quit, but that does not count), both had trouble in functioning at their usual occupations. Whether it be the house-wife's ability to care for her home and family, a student's preparation for examinations, or a physician's attention to his patients, problems on the job are a frequent early symptom of manic illness. Happily, once the attack of mania subsides, most patients return to their usual occupations. Unlike some other victims of psychiatric illnesses, they do not suffer a deterioration of job performance level subsequent to an attack of this illness.

HYPOMANIA

So far, we have discussed only the extreme (and bizarre) form of this illness. But many people with manic-depressive disease never become so obviously ill. They may have periods when they feel much better than at other times, show overactivity and a mild push of speech, but the other symptoms which we have already discussed, if present at all, are neither noticeable nor troublesome. These conditions are called *hypomanic,* meaning "somewhat less than fully manic."

Holly Dahl had never sat in a psychiatrist's office before her forty-second birthday. But today she was celebrating that anniversary by telling the doctor of her ten-year history of mild mood swings, occurring on the average of once or twice a year. During her "down" phases, she felt blue and lethargic, had little use for people, and stayed pretty much to herself. But after several months of life as a semi-recluse, her spirits would pick up again, and she would spend the next few months in a moderately euphoric state, having a great deal of energy and bubbling over with enthusiasm.

"I really don't mind this part of it, Doctor," she said, lighting a cigarette. "I manage to accomplish a lot—you can when you get up at three or four in the morning, you know. Then we go to a lot of parties, and I get drunk sometimes and feel embarrassed later. But all in all, everyone should feel this way!" She wiggled her eyebrows suggestively at the psychiatrist and crossed her legs.

"I write poetry, too," she continued. "It's mostly doggerel—Ogden Nash type stuff—but I think I do rather well with it. Last week I bundled up thirty-six poems I had dashed off and sent them to a publisher. I realize now they weren't really polished, and, if I had spent some more time with them, I'd probably get more than a big fat rejection slip in the mail. But that would have to be some time when I'm feeling a little less energetic than I am now—I can't sit still long enough to polish my nails, let alone poems.

"But it's the down periods that neither my husband nor I can stand. I don't cry much, but I do get bitchy and pretty thoroughly irritate everyone. During the last one several months ago, my family doctor put me on an antidepressant and said that I should see a psychiatrist next time I went up. He said you might have something to keep me in better balance. So here I am."

Because people like Mrs. Dahl do not appear frankly ill, they often go unrecognized through manias and depressions alike. During high periods they are ebullient and carefree, really delightful to be around. The ex-wife of a hypomanic physician reported that their life together was like living on a carousel. "We would fly back and forth to South America whenever the mood struck, with never a worry about tomorrow. He was a great lover, worked long hours, and brought home fantastic money. But then the down phases became longer lasting, and took over, and the merry-go-round stopped, and I got off." Feeling depressed, these people may be simply "bitchy," or they may withdraw and not communicate with their families much for weeks or even months on end. As time goes on, the pattern of mild ups and downs can change to emphasize one or the other phase, or either affective state becomes increasingly severe, until family and social difficulties eventually lead to recognition and treatment. Although lithium (chapter 16) can effectively prevent further episodes of hypomania and depression in these patients, the vast majority of such people never come to psychiatric attention.

On the positive side, a certain amount of hypomania may have real benefits for some people, and by extension, for society in general. The business man whose hypomania is sufficient to increase his capacity for work, but not to diminish his judgment, may become a real empire-builder, if his euphoria lasts long enough. Some writers become quite prolific and creative during their hypomanic phases, and may actually resist treatment on the basis that it hampers creativity. When toting up the debits and credits of hypomania, we should not forget the "lift" in the spirits of each one of us which can come from associating with a hypomanic individual. If only each office, schoolroom, or production line could be issued one controlled manic as standard equipment, the world might turn a little more cheerfully (and quickly).

Bipolars and Unipolars

Because highs and lows of mood do seem to occupy the opposite ends of a spectrum of mood states, the condition in which both are present at different times has recently been called bipolar affective disorder. More than just a fancy new name for manic-depressive disease, this term helps us to distinguish two types of patients with primary affective disorder—those who have both depressions and manias (bipolar disease), and those who have depressions alone (unipolar). This distinction allows us to make some observations which were hidden by previous classifications of depression.

People fall ill with bipolar disease at an earlier age than with unipolar illness: the average age of onset at first attack is around thirty years for bipolars, forty-five years for unipolars. Therefore, someone who becomes depressed when young has a greater chance of having attacks of mania in the future.

Although depression occurs fairly commonly in children and adolescents, curiously enough the bipolar form of the illness almost never develops before puberty.[1] In fact, only one well-documented case of bipolar disease in a child has been reported in all the world psychiatric literature. We do not know the reason for this discrepancy, but the hormones released during the onset of puberty probably play an important role in the development of the bipolar disorder.

The sequence of manias and depressions in any individual patient is only modestly predictable. One patient regularly cycles between ups and downs—you can almost "set your calendar" by his

---

[1]Of course, some children (and especially boys) show behavior which may appear quite manic; restlessness and hyperactivity, short attention span, low frustration tolerance, impulsiveness, destructiveness, and rapid speech are the hallmarks of the hyperactive child syndrome which affects about 5 percent of grade school youngsters. Although these children can be helped psychiatrically, the medicines and psychological approach which are indicated are all quite different from those used in mania. The two conditions have no more than a superficial resemblance to one another.

mood swings. Another has several widely spaced depressions before coming down (or better, coming up!) with his first attack of mania. One man suffered seven attacks of depression over a twenty-five-year period, recovering completely from each one, before he experienced his first episode of mania in middle age. Although some investigators have discussed the possibility that "unipolar mania" may be a different disease, most authorities agree that patients who have had only manias will eventually develop a depression if they live long enough.

The form of individual attacks of bipolar disease can vary considerably. Although some attacks occur as straightforward mania or depression, returning after a period of illness to a normal mood state (Figure 8.1A), the typical attack is more commonly biphasic or even triphasic. The biphasic attack (Figure 8.1-B) begins with either mania or depression of variable length and progresses directly to the opposite affective pole, before returning to normal. In the triphasic variety (Figure 8.1-C), three distinct mood swings of variable length will be encountered, beginning and ending with either mania or depression. The importance of recognizing that bipolar disease can be bi- or triphasic is, of course, that it alerts us for sudden shifts from one mood to another. Whereas it can be disconcerting to see a patient catapulted from despondency into a hyperactive frenzy, the real danger lies in failing to recognize the transition from mania to severe depression, a plunge which can sometimes occur with appalling swiftness. One twenty-year-old man who had been treated in the hospital for a severe, psychotic mania shifted overnight from euphoria to deep depression characterized by constant weeping and the conviction that he should die. He was swiftly started on antidepressant medicine and has been well since.

But the important feature shared by unipolar and bipolar patients is recovery. Careful follow-up studies and extensive clinical experience indicate that 95 percent or more of patients with primary affective disorder will recover even without treatment (the outcome of any untreated illness is called its *natural history*). And by the time the full spectrum of modern psychiatric treatment has been employed, virtually 100 percent of all patients can expect a complete recovery.

COURSE OF BIPOLAR ILLNESS

A. Monophasic

B. Biphasic

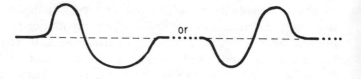

C. Triphasic

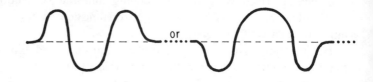

TIME ⟶

Figure 8.1.   Course of Bipolar Illness

But how "complete" is that? As with unipolar illness, any bipolar patient should expect to return to his former personality, with no defect discernible to his family, his friends, his physician, or to himself. This means he will be able to work at his usual job, to take care of his family, to form new friendships and to enjoy old ones. His friends and relatives will be able to say, "He has returned to his usual self." But two problems cause some concern.

For one thing, residual social problems may be more severe than in unipolar patients. Alcoholism and drug abuse are more likely to develop, and the manic patient may run his family into debt or alienate friends with his outrageous behavior. He may spend more time hospitalized, or under a physician's care, and he may have more trouble holding a job or advancing in his chosen area of work.

What about the chance of recurrence? Although about half of all unipolar patients will never have another episode of depression, bipolar patients are quite likely to have recurrence. On the average, they can expect an episode of either mania or depression every two or three years. But even this forecast seems less gloomy now than it did a few years ago, before the development of newer treatment methods. New drugs now allow even those with severe illness to function with little or no disability for years at a time and to receive a minimum of psychiatric attention.

Because bipolar patients often act bizarrely, have difficulty in communicating, or have delusions or hallucinations, psychiatrists frequently diagnose them as "schizophrenic." In fact, until recently, when the advent of lithium heightened psychiatrists' awareness of manic-depressive disease, most bipolar patients received the diagnosis of schizophrenia at some time or other during the course of their illness. This mistake is a serious one, leading to incorrect or incomplete treatment, longer hospitalization than necessary, and difficulty later obtaining jobs, security clearances, or insurance. A doctor will blithely advise against marriage or childbearing for people who spend 99 percent of their lives as healthy as he. Because the social consequences of misdiagnosis of bipolar (and to a much smaller degree, unipolar) affective disorder can be so incapacitating, these problems of diagnosis will be more thoroughly elaborated in the next two chapters.

The symptoms of primary affective disorder can be frightening, puzzling, irritating, and sometimes incapacitating, but both forms —bipolar and unipolar—are truly compatible with a productive and happy life. Abraham Lincoln and Winston Churchill both suffered from severe periodic depressions (Churchill called it "the black dog"). Pulitzer Prize winning author Bernard De Voto probably suffered from bipolar affective disorder, and prominent theater producer Joshua Logan recently described his experiences with mania and depression to a gathering of the American Medical Association. When properly recognized, these conditions become among the most manageable in all medicine, to the point that patients with primary affective disorder can be told in truth, "If you had to have a nervous disorder, you picked the right one."

9.
Schizophrenia

"Oh dear, there's that fellow from my philosophy class." Mary Chase glanced over her shoulder at the figure rapidly advancing toward them. "I'm afraid he's coming our way. He always looks at me so *queerly*."

In a moment the two girls were joined by a thin, callow man of about twenty-five who fell into stride beside them. "Hello, Mary," he ventured, then walked with them in silence. Suddenly he asked, "How are we this evening?" He gazed steadily at Mary, gray eyes unblinking, without expression. "How are *we*?" he repeated, meaningfully.

"Oh fine, Lyonel," replied the girl. "Jackie, this is Lyonel, uh . . ."

"Child."

"Lyonel Child," she repeated.

"Hello," Jackie said.

As they strolled along the quiet path, he occasionally glanced at the girls. He moistened his lips several times to speak, but appeared to think better of it. Then, as they reached the walkway, "This is where I turn off . . . I'll see you in class tomorrow, Mary." He finished uncertainly.

For reply, she half waved her hand, then spying ahead of them a youthful figure wearing a letterman's sweater, the two girls quickened their pace. As he retreated across the lawn toward the street, Lyonel looked back to see the three of them talking animatedly together.

A vignette of his life, he thought, as he scuffed his way home along the quiet Midwestern street. That's the way it had ever been.

The oldest of four children, Lyonel had always felt somewhat set apart. His sisters and he had been well cared for, their

99

clothes neither ragged nor too rich for the public school they attended. Yet from kindergarten on, in his classes as in his family, his had been an isolated, somewhat melancholy existence. There had been friends in the earlier years, but he had never really understood them. Although he joined them at play and laughed when they did, he lacked any real grasp of how they thought or felt; as a result, he occasionally found himself the butt of their jests.

Through the first few grades, he hung back and by the age of ten was regarded as "nervous" by adults and peculiar by other children. That year his parents took him to a psychiatrist, complaining of his nightmares and persistent fear of the dark. He cried some and talked little; when he left therapy after a few sessions, neither he nor his doctor was much enlightened— or sorry.

During his early teens he became interested in religion, and his decision to become a minister led him to spend long hours in his room learning Bible passages by heart at the time his classmates were beginning to date. At the university he sporadically flirted with other subjects, but invariably returned to his "first loves," religion and philosophy. Looking back now, he could ruefully concede that he wished he had spent less time with the Good Book and more with a "bad broad." But now he would try to make up for lost time. A minister needed a wife, after all, so the search for a girlfriend could still be considered a Christian endeavor.

Back in his room, Lyonel examined his eyes in the mirror. Deeply set beneath heavily furrowed brows, they stared back at him more piercingly than ever before. Eyes filled with meaning, he thought, eyes which in their steady gaze held secrets, held truth. His face, broad and bulging at the forehead, narrowed towards the chin where it tapered further into a nascent goatee. He drew his fingers several times across the umbilicated scars which dotted his cheeks, a remembrance of the teenage struggle with his complexion. He sighed heavily and plopped down upon the bed. Head cradled in the palm of one hand, he stared absently at the dingy yellow ceiling and thought about the girl.

When he had first encountered her in class, his heart had skipped a beat, and he had wondered if that was a sign. Particularly arresting were her pale blue eyes, which seemed able to penetrate the murky fathoms of his soul. During the first two or three weeks of the new school year he had often seen her in the dining room. He had wanted to date her but held himself in check, trying not to betray too great an interest. For several weeks he had contented himself with saying "Hi" after class, but then one evening before supper he had asked her out. Politely, but firmly, she refused.

This was the queer part about it, he reflected. She was friendly and open with him during the day, but perceptibly more reserved at night. "Matutinally cheerful enough, but aloof, cool, almost disdainful at vespertide," he had confided to his journal. The reasoning or force behind the discrepancy he could not define, but there was no mistaking it; it had happened several times now. Was she a butterfly perched daintily upon the branch of some bush, whom he could admire from a distance but could not approach lest she fly away? He knew that here, somewhere, there was a message, and its elusiveness made him feel indecisive, shy, less forceful in his affairs. His thoughts had speeded up, at times tumbling over one another so rapidly he could not keep up or sort them out. He sensed a waning of his usual mental energy. He must endeavor to build himself up.

During spring break he consulted his family physician. "I seem to have gas forming on my intestines and it presses on my prostate, giving me erections. I've tried controlling my diet to get more protein-substance into my muscles—they seem all flabby to me." Though his brow furrowed occasionally as he spoke, his voice was quiet and his recital oddly detached. "Could I be having wet dreams?"

Doctor Goodfellow was suspicious. "How has your mood been, Lyonel?"

"Why do you want to know? What's that got to do with my problem?"

"Well, when people feel sick, they often get irritable or in low moods, and we'd like to be able to help that, too. And then, sometimes a state of mental depression can make our bodies act up. Have you had trouble sleeping?"

"I have had some trouble sleeping—you see, I keep getting these erections, which are very disturbing to me, and I wake up. But there's nothing at all wrong with my mood."

The physician leaned back in his swivel chair and smiled, reassuringly he hoped. "Well, I wonder if it wouldn't be a good idea to get another doctor's opinion on that?" As he reached for notepad and pen, Lyonel abruptly stood up.

"No siree, by God, you're not going to get me near one of those nut docs! Just give me something to help me sleep better, that's all I want from you!" They compromised on a prescription for a tranquilizer, which Lyonel crumpled and threw into the wastebasket as he slammed through the outer office.

With summer vacation, thoughts of Mary continued to weigh on his mind. Through the long, boring days of midsummer (he had neglected to look for a job this year), he spent many hours in his room considering their relationship. And at first he thought, then knew, that she was thinking of him. So he wondered why she had not contacted him, and he began to suspect that something was keeping them apart. This, then, would be his Christian endeavor: to plumb the depths of the mystery, to reunite the couple as one.

Whenever he thought about the problem, his physical symptoms became more intense. A ringing in his right ear caused him to wonder if he was going deaf. His fear seemed confirmed when he noted as if for the first time the label on the rear window defroster control in his car: REAR DEF. A clear sign of deafness, right ear, he thought.

He visited the doctor again, and this time he mentioned some of his fears. "I've noticed that my eyes will sometimes become unusually brilliant and lustful. And people seem to be putting gas pressure on my prostate. It gives me erections at three or four in the morning, and I have to rub my muscles, or burp, or pass gas until it goes away. Sometimes I masturbate."

The doctor doodled as he listened: a stick figure criss-crossed by lines, a reflection in a shattered mirror. Lyonel's bizarre symptoms and lack of insight into the false nature of his ideas suggested the possibility of schizophrenia. This time he did make the referral to a psychiatrist, even calling him on the telephone to confirm the appointment before Lyonel left the office. But instead of seeing the psychiatrist, the following afternoon Lyonel Child visited a sporting goods shop and purchased a rifle—a 30.06 with a 6-power hunting scope.

Back in his room he pressed the cool smoothness of the stock against his cheek and sighted down the barrel. The single extracurricular activity of his adolescence had been the three years he belonged to the school rifle club. He had become a marksman of considerable ability, capable of squeezing off five shots in as many seconds, clustering them into a bull's-eye. Although he had not touched a weapon in the intervening ten years, its heft, familiar to his hands, seemed an extension of his self.

For some time he had known that she was near, and on several occasions he sensed that he had just missed her. Then his thoughts would boil over the edges of his skull, becoming so nearly audible that other people appeared to know the content of his troubled mind. From the watchful, darting looks in their eyes he divined that in their hearts they knew he was right and wanted to help him recover his loss. The situation was becoming intolerable, and he knew that he must end it. He made and rejected a number of plans, at length settling upon a letter.

Dear Miss Chase:

I am writing to you to request your help in an Endeavor in which I am at present engaged. It has become most difficult for me to reconcile the feeling which I know you bear for me with that behavior of yours which has been observed by me. I have noted and appreciated the helping hands proffered me in this Endeavor by others, but of late they seem to have grown disgusted with me for my failure.

... my situation in the university has become intolerable, and I have withdrawn my matriculation for the coming semester. It is impossible to study, knowing that at every turn I miss you by minutes.

My solution is this epistle, in which I ask that you achieve correspondence with me and acquiesce to my request that you become my betrothed. ...

He waited through the early football weeks of autumn, but when a month had passed without an answer he admitted that which he already feared: there would be no answering letter.

Lyonel moved back into his parents' house, where he kept to his own room. Isolated and brooding, he wrote voluminously, but destroyed most of his output. Although he occasionally ventured out to the campus to look for Mary, his main activity, besides writing, was to read the Bible critically, marking certain passages.

As winter gripped the town, Lyonel's suspicions held him tighter still. The signs were obvious. Now his relatives were involved in it as well, trying to apprise him of her whereabouts by the wink of an eye or the enciphered tapping of fingers on a table top. But it was no good: she continued to elude him, sometimes by scant minutes.

Then one day in deep December he found himself in his Volkswagen van driving the hundred miles or so to the farming community where she lived. The bloated feeling had returned, causing him to stop every few miles to press on his abdomen and painfully pass gas. He assuaged the fluttering, electrical anxiety which mounted through his chest by patting the long, narrow box propped against the seat beside him. A chance remark from an acquaintance had set him off on his quest—the observation that Mary had returned to her home for the holidays. As he hurried through the shops that morning preparing for both the unexpected and the inevitable, the people he passed on the street nodded and winked at him in the old way, signaling their comprehension and approval of his plan.

And now he stood beneath the naked branches of a small stand of oak trees fifty yards from her front door, bundled in parka and boots against the biting wind which swept out of the northern plains. His loaded rifle leaning within easy reach against a tree trunk, he peered through the gathering dusk toward her front porch. It had been nearly a year since his relationship with her had begun, and now the signs had become clear. He felt relaxed, free of doubts, happier and lighter than he had in months. The soothing voice within his brain spoke with unusual clarity, reassuring him: "You know the way to a girl's heart. . . ."

It was a Christian endeavor.

The tormented Lyonel Child was driven to the point of murder by a condition which has been around a long time, though physicians did not recognize it as a separate illness until fairly late in the last century. Its early name, *dementia praecox,* expressed the belief that the adolescents or young adults it typically victimized were reduced to a state of dementia, or inability to think. With newer forms of treatment, this illness, which we now call schizophrenia, only infrequently leads to severe intellectual deterioration. As we will learn later, the outcome of this condition is not nearly so grim as it used to be.

SYMPTOMS

The case of Lyonel Child provides an excellent example of a life course typical of schizophrenia. From the beginning, his shyness and lack of sociability set him apart from other children. When quite young, he was different enough that his parents sought psychiatric help; but, despite their efforts, he remained withdrawn, shy, and sensitive, corresponding to the so-called *schizoid* personality type which often precedes the development of actual psychosis. Typically, the shy child gradually develops the clinical illness— a change which often occurs so slowly and quietly that even the most painstaking interview cannot pinpoint its beginning. This explains why many schizophrenics come to medical attention only after months, even years of clinical illness. Their condition progresses so slowly that the family does not notice the change.

Disorders of thought form the cornerstone of schizophrenia. As we learned in chapter 3, psychiatrists recognize two types of thought disturbance: either the content of thought (delusions and hallucinations) or the flow of thought may be affected. Lyonel's illness dramatically affected his content of thought, leaving undisturbed his flow of thought (you could understand what he said and meant). Less fortunate was the young man who wrote this note during one of many hospitalizations:

> I found out that the English tea which the British drink. And that clam chowder isn't different, like Indian corn is American food. But England has a king, queen and a prince. Princess Ann is married to an Englishman. Now medication is for help of accidents, sickness, burned people and blackouts and dizzy spells like me. The truth of Europe, in fact Japan has tea, too! And America. Thanks.

This remarkable document (unfortunately also typical of the way the patient spoke) demonstrates the pattern of expression called *tangentiality* encountered in a few seriously ill schizophrenics: one thought bears no sensible relation to the next. We will encounter a less garbled example later.

Tangential speech may occur alone or in combination with disordered thought content, which can take the form of delusions or hallucinations or both. Lyonel was troubled by delusions of persecution, particularly relating to the luckless Mary Chase who, he fancied, persistently avoided him. False beliefs that one is spied upon or plotted against are called paranoid, and patients in whom this symptom predominates are called paranoid schizophrenics.

Other paranoid patients may believe that they are hounded by the police, the FBI, the CIA, or a Senate investigating committee. A veteran of World War II believed for years that Nazi soldiers followed him around, foully cursing him in German (of which he understood not one word). His doctors could easily judge the severity of any current attack. When his illness was well controlled, the soldiers kept a respectful distance—skulking about a block behind him—but when he worsened, they came right up behind to shout their Teutonic taunts directly into his ear. Another patient, homosexually inclined, believed that the city government for which he had once worked had sent out spies to observe him in public rest rooms. This poor man became so fearful of being watched that he abstained from sexual relations with anyone, male or female, for seven years.

Paranoid ideas are very real to the patient, who cannot be shaken from them no matter how much logic you bring to bear on the subject. If you suggest that he is mentally ill, he may become angry at your impertinence or simply incredulous, demonstrating the complete *lack of insight* characteristic of schizophrenia. Sometimes paranoid patients become quite grandiose, fully believing in their own divinity or that they have special powers which can save the world. J. C. Schmidt believed that his initials signified he was really Jesus Christ; for hours at a time he would stand at the hospital window making the sign of the cross over the multitudes he fancied had gathered below.

> Delusions of marital infidelity afflicted one seventy-year-old lady, who angrily accused her husband of nightly flashing coded messages with the venetian blind to a widow who lived across the street. The husband, even more elderly than she, reported that he would awaken at night to find her standing over his bed, glaring fiercely and daring him to make a move for the front door. Once she had sprinkled the hallway outside his room with carpet tacks so she would hear him scream if he tried to keep his nocturnal tryst. As he concluded his story, he shook his head sadly. "You know, Doctor," he said, "I haven't had sex with anybody for fifteen years—the ability just hasn't been there."

Lyonel's interpretation of the "rear defroster" label in the van represented a *delusion of reference,* a term used to mean that ordinary objects or events have a special meaning for the patient. A Protestant woman believed that her Catholic neighbors had bugged the telephone so they could spy upon her children. She moved several times to try to elude the ecclesiastical eavesdroppers, but to no avail, as they followed her relentlessly. For years another woman, the wife of an electronics engineer, believed she was involved in a scientific experiment in which researchers controlled her actions and thoughts through electrodes implanted in her brain. What upset her most was that, rather than pay her for her trouble, the hospital kept charging her for her room!

Lyonel's delusions far exceeded his hallucinations—he did experience a voice in his brain which occasionally commented on his thoughts or actions, but, as we shall see, other patients suffer hallucinations of much greater intensity. To become familiar with other typical symptoms of schizophrenia, let us walk through the wards of a mental hospital and meet some of the more severely ill patients there. Most people are not allowed to visit psychiatric facilities, so we will join a group of medical students who are being conducted on a tour by a professor of psychiatry.

As the entry bell rings, you crane your neck to peer through the small wire-reinforced window cut into the heavy steel door. Abruptly, a face appears at the window and glares out menacingly—surely a hostile, paranoid patient, possibly violent. Then a key turns the lock, and the door opens to reveal that the face belongs to a young attendant, and a smiling one at that. He politely conducts you inside.

The hospital ward itself fails utterly to meet your expectations. Far from a dingy, drafty, high-ceilinged institution (where are the chains on the wall?) with barred doors and padded cells, the hallway is wide and well lighted. As you walk down the corridor toward the nursing station, you glance into some of the rooms. Most contain only two beds and are well appointed with comfortable furniture, a sink, and private bath.

In the sunny, uncrowded dayroom patients talk with each other or watch the color television. Some play pool or ping-pong in the recreation areas, and through the open doorway leading to an enclosed patio you see several engaged in a vigorous game of volleyball. Mingling with the patients are the nurses and their assistants who, because they wear street clothes, can be identified only by a small name tag. They sit talking with individual patients or participate in the athletic events and other activities. In all, an atmosphere rather more social club than hospital.

The students cluster around the professor, who is saying, "This is our acute receiving ward. All newly admitted patients come here to be evaluated for at least twenty-four hours before they are transferred to an unlocked ward. I thought I'd bring you here first to meet some people with more severe psychopathology."

You crowd into a room where sits Anthony Yelle, a slightly built, heavy-lidded black man. The following dialogue takes place.

Professor: Good morning, Mr. Yelle, how are you today?

Anthony: Oh, not so good, not good at all, Doctor. It's these voices—these voices are giving me the misery in my head. They won't let me alone!

Professor: What are they like?

Anthony: They're miserable, Doctor, miserable! They come at me from all around, from up on the ceiling and from behind the radiator. And they a–a–aggravate me and they won't let me alone!

Professor: What do they say?

Anthony: Oh, they tell me all sorts of bad things! They say I did a lot of bad things to–to–to my mother. They call me a bastard, and a fool, and a—lots worse things, Doctor. They tell me that I should go kill myself. And when they talk louder and louder like this I have to scream and curse to drive them out of my mind.

He stands up, takes his jacket from the bed beside him, and violently slams it down on the writing desk. All jump back as the professor motions everyone out of the room. Two attendants speak quietly with the patient for a few minutes until he becomes calm once again. When you last see him he is swallowing some medication from a small paper cup.

In the hallway, the professor is speaking. "Mr. Yelle has heard these voices for five years now, ever since he was thirty-two. As he told us, they come from outside his head, and they are just as real to him as my voice is to you. They call him filthy names and comment on his sexual proclivities; often they suggest that he commit suicide. They are less troublesome during the day when other people are around to distract him, but at night they scream right into his ear so that he cannot sleep. They improve greatly, even dissolve entirely, when he takes his medicine. But he suspects the medicine has been poisoned. The voices tell him to "spit it out," which he often does, so he keeps coming back to the hospital.

"Mr. Yelle suffers from *paranoid schizophrenia.* It is the one form of schizophrenia which really does not fit well into the old concept of dementia praecox—it neither begins early in youth, as do the other forms, nor does it lead to dementia. These patients may retain their delusions and hallucinations for many years and still be able to converse rationally on other subjects. If you were to ask him the date, or where he is, or to name recent presidents, he would do as well as any of you—perhaps better, for he reads the newspaper cover to cover every day. It is only when we come to the content of his thought—his hallucinations—that he appears in any way abnormal. And while we are on the subject of hallucinations, does anybody know what type of hallucinations you encounter most frequently in schizophrenia?"

No one answers, so he continues. "Auditory hallucinations are most common, followed by visual. But in any patient with visual hallucinations, you should think first of illnesses other than schizophrenia; alcohol withdrawal syndromes like delirium tremens for one and drug abuse for another. Hallucinations of smell, touch, or taste also occur, but then you worry about brain diseases like epilepsy. A special type of hallucination of touch is the sensation of bugs crawling on or beneath the skin, called *formication*—but be careful how you pronounce it!"

The professor chuckles to himself, then goes on. "One of the features you should particularly note in Mr. Yelle is the range of his affect. Did you notice how angry and upset he became when describing his hallucinations? His affective response—that is, the emotion he showed—seemed to be perfectly appropriate to what he was thinking. This preservation of affect is typical in paranoid schizophrenia, but many other schizophrenics show little or no affect at all. Let's move on and meet some of these other patients."

The tail of his white laboratory coat flapping, the professor strides down the hallway, trailing a fleet of students in his wake. You stop at the pool table where Miles Brodeur deftly banks the 6 and 7 balls into the side pocket. In his late teens or early twenties, Miles is tall and slim, dressed casually in a sports shirt and slacks. The smile he has worn while making his shots widens into a grin as he recognizes the Professor.

Miles: Oh, hello Doctor. How are you today?

Professor: Fine, thank you, Miles. Could we interrupt you for a few minutes?

Miles: Sure thing, Doctor. I love to play pool, you know.

Professor: Could you tell these young doctors why you came to the hospital?

Miles: Sure thing, Doctor. Oh, there were certain reasons and other reasons.

Professor: What were they?

Miles: They thought I should come in for a checkup—the people where I was working.

Professor: Where was that?

Miles: Well, it was certain Space Academy groups. I was with them in a remote capacity, I guess because of military reasons.

Professor: What did you do?

Miles: Well, I worked around the power plant. If people became vaporized, it could run with only twelve people working it. Mostly I swept up around the pool, but I wasn't paid by the space industry—I got my money from home.

Professor: You mean your family supported you?

Miles: Yes, I was a guinea pig.

Professor: Guinea pig?

Miles (smiling broadly): Yes, you have to consider the possibilities of deep space. It was the physical implantation of a person on the moon. I was going to be sent there to stay.

Professor: That must have upset you, Miles.

Miles: Yes, it knocked me on my butt. (Laughing.) It's a healthy project, but then there are people who need healthy minds. Why, I can recall—

He pauses in mid-sentence, then smiles, winks broadly, and returns to his pool game.

Out of earshot, a student asks, "What was he talking about? Most of his sentences made sense by themselves, but I couldn't follow the point of his thought."

"What you have just heard is one of the most characteristic features of schizophrenia," says the professor. "This type of speech, where you cannot understand how the patient gets from one subject to the next, is called tangentiality. It differs from flight of ideas, the type of loose associations encountered in manic patients, in that you can generally understand how manics get from one idea to the next: there is an understandable connection between thoughts which you don't find in tangential speech. Another characteristic of schizophrenic speech is the stilted, complicated expressions which Miles used, such as "physical implantation of a person on the moon." And did you notice how he suddenly stopped in mid-sentence, then did not go on? This is *blocking,* and it has also been described as typical of schizophrenic speech. Likewise the concrete, or very literal interpretation which he gave to my use of the term *upset*—he took it literally to mean "knock you down." This is sometimes tested by asking the patient to interpret proverbs. A typical response to the question "What does 'don't cry over spilt milk' mean?" would be "If you spill some milk on the floor, just mop it up." But there was something else peculiar about Miles which is typical of schizophrenia. Can any of you tell me what that is?"

"He smiled a lot," someone ventures.

"Exactly," says the professor. "His silly, rather inane grin is typical of the disturbed affect seen in some schizophrenic patients. He laughed and appeared to enjoy himself, but unlike the manic patient there was no infectious quality to his mood. It seemed oddly out of place, and it made you feel uncomfortable. Other schizophrenic patients may show no affect whatsoever. They will converse on almost any topic without expressing either sadness or joy, regardless of their subject. This is called flattening or *blunting of affect.*

"Miles has *hebephrenic schizophrenia*—and a pretty typical case at that. The main features are the disturbances of affect and flow of thought, as we have just discussed. Although disordered thought content—namely hallucinations and delusions —may occur in hebephrenia, it is not nearly as prominent as in paranoid schizophrenia.

"Patients with hebephrenia fall ill much younger than paranoid schizophrenics, usually in their teens or early twenties. And unfortunately, the outcome of hebephrenia is often less favorable than that of paranoid schizophrenia. These patients may have difficulty in working and in caring for themselves, and their faulty affective responses and trouble talking in a straight line often forces them into a pretty solitary existence—they really lose contact with the rest of the world. But with modern treatment even these people can be helped greatly. Drugs can correct their thought disorders and quiet their hallucinations and delusions, just as they do for the paranoid patient."

"What about Miles' affect?" asks a medical student. "Will medication correct it also?"

"To some extent. His affect will become warmer and more appropriate, but sadly enough, even with continuous medication, it may never become entirely normal." The professor shakes his head and is silent for a moment, than starts down the hallway. "But let's go see another patient, a new arrival this morning who shows an extremely interesting condition. And what's more, her situation is much more hopeful."

In the room nearest the nursing station, where the most severely ill patients are kept initially for close observation, you gather about the bedside of a young woman. She lies on her back, head resting on a pillow. Her eyes are open, pupils widely dilated; she quivers slightly with the tension of her tightly clenched fists.

"This is Wilma Freese," says the professor, standing at the bedside. "Although she appears not to notice us, she is nonetheless quite alert, and later on, when she's better, she may remember a considerable amount of what we say now. Wilma is an old friend of mine, as we have met here on several previous occasions, and she won't mind if we spend a few minutes with her.

"Wilma is in a state of catatonia. See how every muscle trembles with tension so great it seems she must explode." The professor reaches down and gently removes the pillow; miraculously, the patient's head remains suspended an inch or two above the mattress.

"The most characteristic feature of catatonic schizophrenia is disordered motion," continues the professor. "The phenomenon you see here, called 'psychological pillow,' is only one example of the way a catatonic patient will maintain an uncomfortable position. At another time she might strike a pose spontaneously and remain in it for many minutes, sometimes for hours. Another typical disorder of motion is her *waxy flexibility*.

"If you," he says, pointing to the medical student standing at the other side of the bed, "will try to bend her arm you will see that you can do it. But notice the resistence to motion which you encounter, like bending a wax rod—hence the name. And notice further what Miss Freese does with the limb once you have moved it."

The student standing next to you, gingerly at first, then firmly, grasps the patient's arm above and below the elbow and lifts. Slowly but smoothly the arm bends. With continued force he at last raises it high above the bed in a kind of salute. As the medical student releases his grip the arm remains in midair, as if suspended by an invisible thread.

"You may drop your arm and your head now," says the professor, but Wilma Freese maintains her bizarre position, apparently without discomfort. The professor once again leans over the bed, placing himself fully in view of her still widely staring eyes. "Miss Freese, you can relax now," he says, firmly but kindly. Slowly the patient turns her head away from the professor to gaze steadily at the opposite wall.

Back in the nursing station the professor once again comments. "Turning away like this is called *negativism,* and it also typifies the catatonic state. We don't know why catatonic patients behave this way. Although they may be confused or disoriented, when they at last awaken many patients will tell you they were actually alert and vigilant. Perhaps too vigilant: some will say that for ill-defined reasons they felt afraid to move. Others have expressed the fear that if they spoke they would somehow be punished.

"Although some catatonic patients appear retarded or stuporous like this, others become extremely excited, leaping and screaming around the room, tearing off their clothes or smearing themselves with their own feces. In fact, back in the bad old days before shock treatments, excited catatonics sometimes became so active and slept so little that they died of exhaustion. Nowadays, of course, this never happens. With modern treatment these people can usually be returned to work and to their families fairly quickly. Miss Freese, for instance, has suffered through several attacks, and with a few electric treatments can usually be discharged within two or three weeks. She then gets along pretty well for months or years at a time, maintained on medicine.

"Besides these three classical types of schizophrenia, other diagnoses have sprung up in recent years," the professor concludes. "With early drug treatment we sometimes have trouble in telling one form of the illness from another, so a lot of psychiatrists now take the lazy way out and use the term "undifferentiated schizophrenia" for most patients. But the careful physician can still usually decide whether his patient has paranoid schizophrenia or something else—a useful distinction in that paranoid patients usually do somewhat better at follow-up. Other terms such as simple, pseudoneurotic, and borderline schizophrenia are also thrown about a good deal, but they probably refer to patients who do not really have schizophrenia at all. Whenever you encounter one of those terms you should pay close attention to the symptoms and try to form your own conclusion as to what really is wrong with the patient."

Leaving the ward you pass by the pool table; Miles Brodeur grins broadly at you and winks.

OCCURRENCE

From the clinical cases encountered in this chapter we can draw a few generalizations about the syndromes called schizophrenia. In the first place, the symptoms can be extremely variable; perhaps the only constant finding from one patient to the next is that all are thoroughly psychotic, at least during the acute phase. Second, schizophrenia characteristically begins during adolescent or young adult life. As the professor noted, paranoid schizophrenia has the latest onset of the three classical subtypes; a paranoid patient rarely falls ill in middle or old age. Third, females are as likely to develop schizophrenia as males—right down to the last percentage point. And this illness knows no racial or religious preferences, affecting people in all stations of life and in every country in the world. Although, for reasons we will discuss later, people from lower socioeconomic backgrounds stand at slightly greater risk for schizophrenia, the children of bankers and brickmasons, actors and arsonists may develop the illness.

Epidemiologists—scientists who study illness in large populations to learn its cause—have found that schizophrenia develops in about eight out of every thousand people, making it nearly as common in the general population as bipolar affective disorder, but much less common than unipolar depression. More than half a million people have schizophrenia in this country, and the total number of those alive today who will probably develop the condition approaches two million. Although a greater proportion of schizophrenics are now treated as outpatients, in a recent year this illness accounted for nearly two-thirds of mental hospital beds and nearly a quarter of all hospital beds in this country. The annual cost has been estimated as high as nineteen billion dollars nationwide, two-thirds of which is due to lost production. At least the problem is not getting any worse. A study of psychiatric hospitalizations in the state of Massachusetts found no increase of psychosis in young people from 1840 to 1940, suggesting that there are proportionately no more schizophrenics now than there were one hundred years ago.

If we see so much less schizophrenia than affective disorder, why has so much more effort been directed toward the care and treatment of schizophrenia than toward that of manic-depressive disease? Partly because of its potential for chronicity, schizophrenia has had a far greater impact upon the economics (and emotions) of our society than have the affective disorders. Once a person contracts the illness he may need care for a long time—the rest of his life, in 10 to 15 percent of all cases. From the dual standpoints of manpower lost and treatment cost, schizophrenia takes a heavy economic toll indeed.

It has been only in the last twenty years that effective outpatient care for schizophrenics could even be contemplated. Prior to 1954, most of these people faced chronic hospitalization, leading over the past one hundred and fifty years to the establishment of vast state hospital systems for the warehousing of human beings. But today most patients do not need long-term hospitalization; drug treatment has even enabled many chronically incapacitated patients to seek a new life on the outside. At the same time it is clear that for the foreseeable future we can expect no reduction in the number of patients falling ill; schizophrenia will continue to be a public health problem of the first magnitude.

History

But so far, we have talked about a collection of syndromes as if they represent a single illness. How did this come about, and is it reasonable to continue to regard it (them?) as a single entity?

Until a little over a hundred years ago, one psychosis was regarded as pretty much the same as another. However, during the latter part of the nineteenth century, French and German psychiatrists began to differentiate the conditions of paranoia, hebephrenia, and catatonia; for several decades these *were* regarded as separate illnesses. It took the genius of Emil Kraepelin to recognize late in that century what these conditions had in common—psychosis with a (relatively) early age of onset, and frequently (inevitably, he thought) a deteriorating course, thus clearly differentiating them from manic-depressive disease. He therefore hypothesized that they were simply different forms of a single illness, for which he borrowed the term *dementia praecox*—a name which lasted barely fifteen years. For in 1911 the Swiss psychiatrist Eugen Bleuler noted full recovery in patients whose symptoms appeared identical to those Kraepelin had described. He retreated to the idea of several, perhaps many, similar diseases for which he coined the term *the schizophrenias,* using the new name in the plural to emphasize his belief that they were not a single disease. He believed that the basic underlying defect was "splitting of the mind," meaning that with the illness all aspects of the personality became fragmented. The divorce of Miles Brodeur's affective response from his content of thought, resulting in inappropriate giggling, is one example of splitting.[1]

Since Bleuler's time many other theorists have proposed what they consider to be the "core" or central pathology of schizophrenia. Various psychological tests have demonstrated that schizophrenics have defects in one area or another of the mind, but as yet no one has found a specific defect. Equally in vain have pathologists sought evidence of coarse brain disease; no one has ever found clear evidence of any structural abnormality in the substance of the brain. Tumors, deterioration of brain tissue, abnormal deposits of fat or other substances—none of these factors can account for the symptoms of the patients we have met here. So

---

[1]The popular (and unscientific) term "split personality" is often erroneously associated with the syndrome of multiple personalities (*Sybil; The Three Faces of Eve*), but the women portrayed in these books suffered from personality disorder, not schizophrenia. If you did not know this, you have a lot of company.

frustrating has the search become that a few voluble psychiatrists have responded by relegating to the status of myth this and every other mental illness, a bit of dialectic sophistry the irony of which can be fully appreciated only by a relative who has faced the bitter reality of mental illness.

Outcome

Uncertainty as to cause undoubtedly contributes to the sense of helplessness felt by families when they learn that a relative has schizophrenia. "My God," you say, "we have a chronic illness on our hands, and there is no cure." Natural reactions to this intelligence run the gamut from despair to desertion, from hopeless acceptance of the inevitable to frenzied visits to every quack and mysticist in the country who holds out a shred of hope for cure. But just how serious a threat does this diagnosis pose?

The answer, as we have emphasized over and over, depends on diagnosis, without which no worthwhile predictions can be made. The thorny problem of accurate diagnosis attains briar-patch proportions in the field of schizophrenia, through which we will attempt to hack a trail in the following chapter. When a competent clinician takes a careful history and makes a thoughtful diagnosis of schizophrenia, we can expect that most patients will continue to show some symptoms far into the future. But we have progressed a long way from the time when a deteriorating personality leading to chronic hospitalization was the inevitable outcome of this disease. Indeed, the slow decline into imbecility so often noted by Kraepelin and other early writers may have been caused by the stultifying atmosphere of the hospitals of that era, rather than by processes inherent in the disease itself. And even when the diagnosis has been made by the most conscientious of psychiatrists, some patients still recover completely. Recovery is more likely in catatonic schizophrenia than in any other subtype, but it can occur in others as well.

More commonly, the patient will improve enough that he can return to his life in the community and often resume his job or schooling. But even after the acute attack many patients complain that they continue to feel "nervous," and relatives may notice that they remain mildly apathetic, vague in their thinking, or that their range of affect has become restricted—they do not express either joy or sorrow to quite the extent of which they were formerly capable. Therefore, some complain of difficulty communicating with other people; others, whether single or married before the onset of their illness, become less interested in intercourse, either social or sexual. These relatively mild residual changes in personality may also contribute to the difficulty some people have in regaining their former level of job competence. A medical ·student, stricken with paranoid schizophrenia in his third year of school, never completed his degree; a secretary sought new employment doing housework; a young man trained as an accountant felt unable to withstand the pressure and worked as a school custodian. Others may be temporarily unable to work at all and must rely on state aid or the support of their families. But this is by no means inevitably the case; 40 percent or more of patients can be fully employed after hospitalization.

Today the concept of the "hopeless schizophrenic" has become as outmoded as the outhouse, though this expression is still used by some psychiatrists in discussing prognosis. Contemporary treatment can provide hope of marked improvement and useful life to even the most severely ill of these patients.

10.
More Schizophrenia: Variations on a Theme

Lyonel Child and the others we met in the previous chapter presented with histories typical of chronic schizophrenia: most psychiatrists would have no trouble agreeing on their diagnoses. But not all patients psychiatrists call schizophrenics have such classical cases. In fact, a lot of people whose illnesses at first look like Lyonel's actually differ in important ways, including the all-important factors of prognosis and treatment of choice. Many, perhaps most, patients who receive the diagnosis of schizophrenia actually do very well at follow-up. Just because Cousin Jake develops a psychosis does not mean he has bought a one-way ticket to the "funny farm." Unfortunately, most doctors, even including some psychiatrists, don't have the training to tell the difference between those psychotic patients who can recover completely and those, like Lyonel, who will always require medicine to keep them functioning.

Several years ago a study frightening enough to be picked up by newspapers across the country appeared in *Science* magazine. Its findings carry a valuable object lesson for all of us and for psychiatrists in particular. It reported an experiment conducted by psychologist D. L. Rosenhan, whose volunteers presented themselves at various psychiatric emergency rooms with stories just a *little* contrived, to test the acumen of the psychiatrists they encountered. Actually, these normal people falsified nothing but name and occupation—and the assertion that they heard muffled voices which said "empty," "hollow," or "thud." To a man, the doctors admitted these psychiatrically well people to the hospital for observation; within hours each "patient" experienced a miraculous recovery. But whereas each proclaimed that he no longer heard voices, treatment continued apace. The doctors prescribed powerful drugs (which the "patients" did not swallow), and hospitalization dragged on for periods ranging from a week to nearly two months. Each patient was finally discharged with a diagnosis of "schizophrenia in remission," and no doctor suspected that any patient was a completely normal—if devious—human being.

The appalling feature of this caper is not that psychiatrists are so easily fooled (they are, after all, physicians and not fortune-tellers) but that these psychiatrists so readily volunteered to look ridiculous. For the admitting symptoms of these pseudo-patients no more indicate schizophrenia than a cough means lung cancer; after all, coughs *can* occur in less serious illnesses: colds, for example. "Real" hallucinations of course occur in schizophrenia, but they can also indicate a variety of less serious psychiatric conditions. And as hallucinations go, these fabricated voices were pretty unexciting, barely worthy of the term. Labeling anyone, pseudo-patient or real, sane or insane, on the basis of a single symptom is a knee-jerk reaction clearly pointing to an incompetent diagnostician. Any conscientious third-year medical student (or reader of this chapter) would easily avoid the error. But Rosenhan's embarrassing little study indicates that a considerable number of American psychiatrists fail utterly to tell the difference between, metaphorically, colds and cancers.

If this approach to diagnosis is distressing, the resulting treatment is often deplorable. Over the past twenty years or more, medicines have been developed which can control hallucinations in almost anyone, regardless of what caused them. Therefore many doctors find it easier to cover over a hallucination than to unearth its cause, contributing to the diagnostic torpor into which psychiatry has slipped over the last few years. Of course, not all American psychiatrists are as quick on the diagnostic draw as those encountered by Rosenhan, but the unfortunate tendency to shoot from the hip does seem to run in the national family. Another recent experiment neatly documented this tendency to diagnose schizophrenia, no matter what.

British and American psychiatrists viewed videotapes of various patients, then made independent diagnoses from the same recorded material. The British, a more conservative race, preferred not to call anyone schizophrenic unless his history and symptoms strongly indicated it; uncertain cases might be called "depressed." But for the Americans, schizophrenia stood out head and shoulders in popularity for any patient who had hallucinations or delusions, regardless of the other diagnostic possibilities. The difference between these two countries supports the Rosenhan finding that American psychiatrists tend to be somewhat knee-jerk in their diagnostic styles, basing their decision on—what? Certainly not on criteria which rigorously define schizophrenia as a discrete entity —otherwise, the Rosenhan travesty never would have happened. On what, then?

In this country, the traditional basis for diagnosis has been the work of Eugen Bleuler, the Swiss psychiatrist who coined the term *schizophrenia* in the first place. Early in this century, he opined that certain symptoms are so characteristic that they virtually demand the diagnosis. Among these symptoms Bleuler included loss of continuity of *associations* (we would say tangentiality), peculiarities of *affect* (flattening, inappropriateness), *ambivalence* (feeling both positively and negatively about something), and *autistic thinking* (in which the patient becomes detached from reality, including not only delusions and hallucinations but daydreams and fantasies as well). These symptoms, traditionally referred to for convenience as the "four A's," provide a convenient way to remember some of the important features of schizophrenia, but they fall far short of constituting the essence of the disease, or even of creating a valid basis for its diagnosis. For example, we have already noted that flattening of affect can occur in severe depressions, as can autistic thinking (depressives can be thoroughly deluded— remember Olive Bard, who wrongly believed that she had said something terribly unkind to people she had met on her trip). Ambivalence, too, can be a perfectly normal state of mind. For example, consider the mixed emotions of a man whose wife loses thirty pounds at the Golden Door health spa and looks great, but it costs him a thousand dollars!

Even loose associations can be normal in certain circumstances, as demonstrated recently when a group of psychiatrists tried to select which of a sample of writings had been produced by schizophrenic patients, which by manic-depressive patients, and which by authors like James Joyce. The doctors failed miserably to define the line between inspiration and insanity: they couldn't even tell the psychotic patients from the (presumably) healthy authors, identifying a "thought disorder" more often in the writers and manics than in the schizophrenics. The psychiatrist who·tries to distinguish mental illness on the basis of thought disorder alone does so at his (and his patients') peril. So Bleuler's criteria provide a slender reed against which to lean the diagnosis of schizophrenia, yet to generations of psychiatrists they have served as the basis for understanding the disease. And as a result, thousands—perhaps over the years, millions—of patients have stumbled through life erroneously labeled (or libeled) as schizophrenic.

Egregious errors likewise emerge from relying too heavily upon the results of psychological tests. Now, psychiatrists like these tests for obvious reasons. They are easy to do (a psychologist gives them), they require no thinking (on the part of the psychiatrist), and because their conclusions come buttressed by statistics, they wear the mantle of authority. For example, the Minnesota Multiphasic Personality Inventory (MMPI) derives a numerical score for schizophrenia based upon responses of the patient to a few of some five hundred questions, which are then compared with the responses given years before by supposedly "typical" schizophrenics. Unfortunately, the patients used to standardize the test were chosen by criteria suspiciously similar to the "four A's." So all the test does is dignify with numbers the same errors doctors have been making for generations.

But still worse is the tendency of some physicians to use no criteria at all, instead basing their impressions on something called "the schizophrenia feel." This means that as the years go by and the doctor supposedly becomes expert, he develops a sort of sixth sense about schizophrenia and discards even the four A's in favor of his instincts. Following hunches is fine when he visits the track —it's his money, after all. But when he tries to apply the same method to taking care of your relative, the stakes are higher, and the potential for disaster is enormous. Other luckless patients do not even need to emit a "schizophrenia feel" to receive the label—having any old hallucination or delusion will do nicely, as Rosenhan demonstrated.

Well, so what? What does all the bother with names really matter? Had we considered this question twenty years ago, the answer would have been "not much." Psychiatrists then had little to offer their patients other than shock treatment. But beginning in 1954, medicines of various sorts began to pop up like mushrooms, and many of them have specific indications for use. Obviously, drug (or any other) treatment will only be used to its full value if these indications are fully appreciated and followed. But if a doctor regards all his patients as having essentially the same illness, regardless of important but sometimes subtle differences in history and symptoms, chances are that he will treat each the same, too, and never mind how poorly the formula happens to fit an individual patient.

So how should psychiatrists (or relatives) separate "real" schizophrenics from others who only seem to have the disease? Actually, they can't, because as yet no one knows what schizophrenia really is. But an approach nearly as useful began to appear almost before Kraepelin finished describing the chronic, unremitting course he believed characterized all patients with *dementia praecox*. Early in this century, other psychiatrists (Bleuler foremost among them) pointed out that many psychotics *did* in fact recover. If only a way could be found to tell in advance which patients would recover and which would not, a useful diagnosis could be made—one which could predict something about the future.

Through the years psychiatrists have tried many times to identify symptoms which *always* mean poor outcome; these attempts have uniformly failed. Even such "obviously" schizophrenic symptoms as audible thoughts (the patient believes his unspoken thoughts can be heard by others) and complete auditory hallucinations (two voices comment on his actions) can occur in patients who recover completely. In short, the *cross-sectional* approach—evaluating symptoms present at one point in time—cannot predict outcome. But beginning in the 1950s researchers both in this country and abroad found that certain features of their patients' histories (the *longitudinal* approach) could usefully predict outcome. These criteria are so clear and easy to understand that even a layman can quickly learn to use them. We will examine them in detail in the next few pages.

PREVIOUS ILLNESS

Anyone with a history of previous psychiatric illness from which he has recovered completely already has a leg up on a good prognosis for any later episode. The rule that "the best predictor of future behavior is past behavior" applies to psychiatric patients as well as to race horses. Had the psychiatrist who admitted Emanuel Trimmer to the hospital bothered to obtain the history of a previous episode of depression from which he had recovered, years of misery might have been avoided. At least he could have forecast that poor Mr. Trimmer would recover again, if only left alone.

Shirley High at age fifty-six had had an eight-year history of recurring psychosis. Every two years she became psychotic, irrationally throwing away perfectly good clothes from her closet, speaking unintelligibly, winking and smiling suggestively at whomever she met. Her first psychiatrist called her a "hebephrenic schizophrenic" and hospitalized her four times in six years. When her husband swore that each time she had returned to her normal personality, the psychiatrist who took over her care during her fifth episode became suspicious and dug deeper into her history. He found evidence of ups and downs of mood during her "normal" periods, eventually leading to the rediagnosis of manic-depressive disease. On lithium therapy (chapter 16), she has since had fewer mood swings and no psychosis.

The simplest explanation of this case is that many manic-depressive patients become so psychotic during their more severe episodes that they automatically receive the label of schizophrenia. So of course these people recover—all manic-depressives do, provided their physicians let them. Any patient who has had a previous episode of illness with complete recovery should *never* be called schizophrenic until the possibility of affective disorder has been carefully considered.

RAPIDITY OF ONSET

In typical schizophrenia, the patient develops symptoms gradually, often so slowly that, like Lyonel Child, change from one stage to the next is hardly noticeable. Most people who become ill suddenly do not have schizophrenia, but do have a better prognosis.

Curtis Cummings had been well until one Sunday morning when he awakened in his college dormitory room talking a blue streak about Jesus and health foods. During the next week he developed auditory and visual hallucinations and became convinced that everyone he met was plotting to kill him. His first doctor diagnosed schizophrenia and prescribed Thorazine, an antipsychotic drug, at which time Curt ran away to Los Angeles. There the police picked him up two days later for wandering about, half-clothed; and he was admitted to a private psychiatric hospital. The following morning he told his psychiatrist, "This seems like a girls' hospital because I'm here."

His psychotic thinking notwithstanding, the sudden onset and hyperactivity (he spent several hours that first day jumping up and down in his room as if riding a pogo stick) prompted a diagnosis of mania. This impression was confirmed by a brief episode of severe depression which occurred shortly before his discharge five weeks later. Treated with lithium carbonate, he recovered completely and has remained well since.

Even when the psychiatrist cannot diagnose manic-depressive disease, a sudden onset still predicts recovery. Your rule of thumb: if the patient has not been continuously ill for six months or more, do not diagnose schizophrenia.

These two factors, previous episode with recovery and rapid onset, are so important in determining prognosis that if either is present, schizophrenia *must* not be diagnosed until further exhaustive investigation turns up no reasonable alternative. In the following pages we will discuss seven additional factors, no one of which by itself actually excludes the diagnosis of schizophrenia, but which together suggest that another illness may be responsible for the psychotic symptoms.

AGE OF ONSET

Schizophrenia typically begins early. Someone who first becomes ill later in life—after the age of forty—most likely has a different psychosis.

When the Ward Chief encountered Brian Zell, this fifty-year-old man had already been deteriorated for several years, but his history of good mental health until age forty-two piqued the chief psychiatrist's curiosity. Mr. Zell had been as well adjusted as any Marine could be during the early days of the Viet Nam build-up, but for no apparent reason he became disoriented and began to hallucinate and to scream at his family. With the diagnosis of schizophrenia, he was boarded out of the service and packed off to a Veterans Administration Hospital where he had lived since. Now, a decade later, he could neither walk nor speak, and he smelled of the urine he constantly dribbled into his pajamas.

In the Ward Chief's mind something clicked. Dementia, trouble walking, and loss of bladder control formed the classic symptoms of normal pressure hydrocephalus, a neurological disease caused by the accumulation of fluid inside the brain. This accumulation produces symptoms by compressing nerve tissue, but when caught early can be treated by inserting a valve to drain away the excess fluid. A special laboratory test confirmed the diagnosis—nine years too late to save Brian Zell.

Several diagnoses are more likely than schizophrenia when psychotic symptoms develop at a relatively advanced age. These include psychotic depression, mania and various alcohol withdrawal states, all of which carry a good prognosis. Therefore, anyone whose illness begins when he has passed considerably beyond the first flush of youth stands a much better than average chance of recovery (a point also illustrated by the case of Shirley High).

Wouldn't you know, one significant exception to this rule does exist. A few old people develop paranoid delusions in a pattern which appears identical to paranoid schizophrenia. Often associated with isolation from family or friends or with loss of vision or hearing, this condition has been called "late paraphrenia," which is a fancy phrase meaning "paranoid schizophrenia developing in old age." With treatment, which is the same as for younger patients with similar symptoms (chapter 15), the outlook for these old people is satisfactory: medication can return them to normal activity. But they represent rare exceptions to the general rule that psychosis starting after age forty is usually *not* schizophrenia.

While we are on the subject of age, we should briefly consider the problem of "childhood schizophrenia," a term often applied to small children afflicted by symptoms of the condition more properly known as *infantile autism*. Described by Dr. Leo Kanner in 1943, these children behave bizarrely, playing with stereotyped, repetitive motions as they twirl tops, sticks, or themselves almost without end. Many have marked trouble communicating, and some never develop useful speech at all. Autistic children cannot relate affectively to others; even as babies they do not cuddle or respond normally to affection. But with these symptoms the similarity to adult schizophrenia stops, and the two conditions are entirely unrelated. This very rare childhood disorder probably results from brain damage sustained during or before birth, and there is no genetic predisposition as there is for schizophrenia (see chapter 12). The treatment and course of the illness likewise set this unhappy condition well apart from schizophrenia. The term childhood schizophrenia should be expunged from the dictionary; its use can be confusing to the physician, injurious to the patient, who may be inappropriately treated, and pejorative to the parent, who often finds himself unjustly scapegoated for the tragedy.

PRECIPITATING FACTORS

Any psychotic illness which develops following some psychologically or physically stressful event also stands a better than average chance of falling into the "good outcome" category. Childbirth, major surgery, or experiencing an emotionally traumatic event like combat may precede such an acute psychosis.

After his hernia repair, Michael Popper's surgeon remarked about how quickly his patient had bounced back. That was the trouble: he kept bouncing, higher and higher. Two days later, dragging his intravenous bottle on a stand behind him, he tried to waltz a nurse down the hall. Later, any nurse not fleet of foot found her backside the target of the "mad pincher," who could also quite suddenly turn nasty and become the "bad pincher." All but his wife were relieved when he finally returned home, whistling, jigging, and shadow-boxing as he departed.

A week later he had exploded "right through the roof," as his wife put it, "just like last time." She told the admitting psychiatrist that Michael had had a similar episode twenty years before, just after gallbladder surgery. Then he had required several weeks in a psychiatric hospital, but ultimately recovered completely. This time when he returned home, he had become gradually more excited, striding about the house with his arms outstretched in a benedictory pose, or forming the sign of the Cross over all who ventured near his path. Occasionally he would stop to declare, "I am not God" before resuming his gesturing. When he became combative and his speech lost all coherence, the police brought him to the state hospital, where he entered with the statement, "I am God!"

"Schizophrenia" wrote the admitting physician.

The following day, his wife had him transferred to a private psychiatrist who successfully treated him for mania.

Alcohol and Drugs

Abuse of these substances represents a special type of precipitating event which also helps to predict recovery from psychosis. This factor may seem paradoxical at first; we don't usually think of the abusers of either as doing well at anything. But compared to chronic schizophrenia, the course of toxic drug or alcohol psychosis is placidity personified. Withdrawal from amphetamines produces a paranoid psychosis which exactly mimics the symptoms of schizophrenia. The sufferer who fancies a whole gang of *mafiosi* in hot pursuit may even leap through a window to make good his escape. In *delirium tremens* (DTs), one of the psychoses which sometimes accompanies alcohol withdrawal, patients see animals, bugs, or Lilliputian people—symptoms which have often been mistaken for schizophrenia, although the restlessness and confusion should make the correct diagnosis obvious to any competent physician. In yet another alcohol withdrawal state, *alcoholic auditory hallucinosis,* the patient begins to hear threatening voices when he stops drinking.

All of these psychoses clear rapidly within a few days, and none is closely related to true schizophrenia. Yet time and again each has been mistaken for schizophrenia by physicians who either don't know or don't care about accurate history-taking.

Premorbid Personality, Marital State

These factors are related, so we will discuss them together. Many people who go on to become chronic schizophrenics have always appeared set apart from the rest of the human race. Lyonel seemed "programmed" for schizophrenia all his life: throughout childhood and adolescence he had had no close friends and had participated in few of the extracurricular activities offered by his school (the rifle club was a notable exception). He never felt comfortable with other children—his hypersensitivity to the slightest insult earned him a lot of teasing, but more frequently his schoolmates simply ignored him. Psychiatrists call this personality type "schizoid," meaning that these people resemble schizophrenics in their social isolation without actually being psychotic. Schizoids sometimes progress to frank schizophrenia, though this is by no means inevitable. It is as if the two conditions existed on a continuum, the one sometimes imperceptibly developing into the other.

You can easily understand how someone as peculiar and withdrawn as Lyonel would be unlikely to attract a mate. But even in someone with a normal premorbid personality, the frank psychosis often attacks before he has had the opportunity to marry. Hence another of the prognostic criteria: single people are likely to do worse than those who have married by the time illness strikes. Several of the patients we have already met in this chapter illustrate these two criteria for recovery.

FAMILY HISTORY

In a later chapter (chapter 12), we will examine the proven axiom that when psychiatric illnesses run in families, they run true to type. This means that a manic-depressive is likely to have relatives with affective disorders, just as the relatives of schizophrenics will probably have schizophrenia, too, if they are ill at all. Sometimes the type of illness in a patient's family can help the psychiatrist with diagnosis in a difficult case.

By the age of eighteen, Gregory Mendel already had had two long psychiatric hospitalizations for "schizophrenia" during which voices had told him to kill himself. Now he had been readmitted with complaints of depression, fear of crowds, and "problems with my vision, like seeing the lawn move." Because he had abused LSD, barbiturates, marijuana, and cocaine in the past, the history he told the consulting physician was "a tangled mess."

But his family history proved enlightening. Years ago, his mother had recovered from depression with electro-convulsive therapy, and his brother had once attempted suicide. His sister, five years his senior, had been hospitalized earlier with a diagnosis of schizophrenia. When the consulting psychiatrist reviewed her records, he found that her "schizophrenic" symptoms had included overactivity, feeling "too happy," and talking too much—a misdiagnosed manic psychosis from which she had subsequently recovered completely. Greg's diagnosis was changed to depression, and he received antidepressants for the first time in his life. He recovered within two weeks.

From this case we learn that the psychiatrist not only must pay attention to the fact of illness in a relative but also can't take someone else's word for diagnosis—it may well be wrong. Generally, if a relative has recovered completely from a major psychiatric illness, the patient is likely to recover also.

PROMINENT AFFECTIVE SYMPTOMS

Finally, significant depressive or manic symptoms point away from chronicity, toward recovery, a fact already demonstrated in several of the cases we have summarized in this chapter. The explanation is, of course, that many manic-depressives have psychotic symptoms which lead the unwary psychiatrist to diagnose schizophrenia, often using the term "schizophrenia, schizo-affective type" to indicate the affective features of the illness. But the emphasis is all wrong. Most clinicians classify them with schizophrenia, but the few research psychiatrists who have studied these patients know that many of them fall into the good prognosis group. Perhaps the term "affecto-schizive" would be more appropriate; at least it would clearly indicate which of the two components was the more important for prognosis.

> Beatrice Moody was thirty years old when her mother first brought her to the attention of a psychiatric consultant. Two years before, Beatrice had developed euphoria, overactivity, and the notion that she had a divine mission in life. Her doctor had called her a "schizo-affective" and had treated her with tranquilizers. Six months later she lost all her pep and energy and took to her bed, looking and feeling depressed. "Schizophrenic withdrawal," said the doctor, who had been treating her at a community mental health clinic. "She'll have to pull herself out of it."
> "Manic-depressive," suggested the consultant. "We should try antidepressant medicine."

Before jumping the gun with *any* predictions, we should remind ourselves that none of these factors predicts outcome by itself. A patient may suddenly fall ill, yet pursue a chronic course; another with a schizoid personality like Lyonel Child's recovers anyway. But it has been proven repeatedly that several of these factors can gang up together to predict course of illness in most patients. Table 2 summarizes the criteria we have discussed, grouping them ac-

Table 2
Summary of Factors Differentiating Schizophrenia from "Good Prognosis Schizophrenia"

Factor	"Poor Prognosis" Schizophrenia	"Good Prognosis" (Schizophreniform)
A. Previous illness* Onset*	Never recovered Insidious (more than 6 months)	Complete recovery Acute (less than 6 months)
B. Age at onset	Under 40	40 or over
Precipitant	Absent	Physical or psychological stress
Alcohol or drug abuse	None within past year	Heavy use prior to onset of psychosis
Premorbid personality	"Schizoid": shy, secluded, sensitive, loner	"Normal": outgoing, personable, has friends
Marital state	Married at least once	Single
Family history	Schizophrenia; no recovery	Affective disorder; recovery
Affective symptoms	Not prominent	Marked manic or depressive features

*These two factors are critically important to the diagnosis of schizophrenia: if a patient's history for either falls into the "good prognosis" category, schizophrenia *must* not be diagnosed except by exclusion and (preferably) by watching him over a period of several months. The remaining criteria are less absolute, indicating but not dictating diagnosis.

cording to importance. If a patient has four or more of the "good prognosis" criteria from Group B, he stands a good chance for a favorable outcome. Conversely, four or more Group B "poor prognosis" criteria suggest a more chronic course with a smaller chance for complete recovery. But even if your relative has only one of the "good criteria," we still cannot be *certain* that he will do poorly. These predictions only indicate outcome, they do not determine it. And if your relative has several of the "good outcome" features in his history, but has been diagnosed as having schizophrenia, you should arrange a competent psychiatric consultation at once. It could literally save his life.

The power of these criteria to distinguish between the two outcomes was recently demonstrated by some researchers from the University of Iowa who studied five hundred patients hospitalized with psychosis back in the 1930s. Each patient had been called schizophrenic by highly competent attending physicians who made the diagnosis only if they were *sure*. But though these psychiatrists were as good as any in the country at the time, they had no guiding criteria better than the "four A's" and their own instincts. So, thirty years later, the research psychiatrists found that, by the strict crieria we have discussed, only two-fifths of these patients fell into the "poor prognosis" category. And at the follow-up significantly fewer of this group of "real" schizophrenics had recovered. The study demonstrated that even the best of psychiatrists cannot see into the future—unless they are willing to rely on factors so simple that any layman can learn them.

Although these criteria can help us "read" the future for an individual patient, they do not themselves constitute the essence of schizophrenia. They were derived from numerous studies of actual patients and have been proven over and again to predict outcome validly, but still they tell us nothing of the cause, theory, or nature of the illness itself. In effect, they are something of an optical illusion, a bit of psychiatric prestidigitation by which we appear better acquainted with the illness than we really are. For to tell the absolute, embarrassing truth, we know little more about this disease than Bleuler did nearly three generations ago. Over the years, psychiatrists have proposed a gaggle of theories invoking nearly everything from high anxiety levels to disorders of perception to abnormalities of thought itself to explain the basis of schizophrenia. But we simply do not know for sure.

This uncertainty as to what we have defined by "schizophrenia" leaves us somewhat in the dark about the "good prognosis" patients as well; do they simply have a form of bipolar psychosis, or is their condition more closely related to schizophrenia? Or is there a third major endogenous psychosis lurking darkly in the woodpile? Like the examples we have examined in this chapter, many "good prognosis" schizophrenics suffer from affective disorder; some have other illnesses entirely (Mr. Trimmer with his obsessions, for example) and a few may actually have no psychiatric illnesses at all, à la Rosenhan. But some do turn out to have a chronic illness of greater or lesser proportions which, as time goes by, cannot be distinguished from schizophrenia. In recent years, some careful psychiatrists have begun to call this group of patients "schizophreniform," meaning that they look like schizophrenics and may turn out to be schizophrenics but that right now the criteria do not allow this diagnosis to be made with certainty.

And "certainty" most certainly must be the name of the game in schizophrenia, where we are playing for high stakes indeed: people's lives. The greatest single pitfall in the diagnosis of schizophrenia, confusion with affective disorder, sets a trap which yearly enmeshes thousands of patients (and their psychiatrists) in its coils. As desirable as the step would seem, in the next few years we cannot hope to reeducate all our physicians as to the importance of careful differential diagnosis. Eventually this reeducation will take place, and psychiatric patients will be able to look forward to competent treatment as a matter of course. But until that millennium arrives, the care your relative receives may well depend, reader, upon you.

11.
What Causes Psychosis: Psychological Theories

If all the social scientists, psychologists, and psychiatrists who have tried to explain what causes psychiatric disease were laid end to end, they would probably get up and start fighting. Although nobody has any solid data about etiology (cause), everybody thinks he knows the reason. And the combat that results when a few of these good people get together is enough to make a Gurkha blanch.

Nothing so trivial as the absence of fact has halted the veritable avalanche of proposed etiologies which theoreticians have tumbled forth to fill the yawning gaps in our knowledge. And as often as not the cause claimed by these theories is you, the patient's relative.

For years many psychiatrists have placed the blame for mental illness squarely upon the very family which has struggled in vain to cope with life with a psychotic. These undoubtedly sincere yet misguided savants have portrayed you as a jailer who prevents the patient from regaining his mental health, rather than as someone who can help him through his illness. Now, if somehow you have caused your relative's illness, you should be informed so you can correct the problem. But it is equally important to know when you are *not* at fault. Then you, your doctors and relatives can stop blaming each other and get on with the important job of treatment.

The most effective treatment for any illness attacks its cause. This truism is the second important reason for trying to clarify your family's role in the development of mental illness. Many treatments, some of which psychiatrists still advocate, are based upon theories of etiology which are just plain wrong. If we debunk these ideas, we can eliminate a lot of useless and expensive treatment and get on to provide some real help. And finally, hope springs eternal that finding the cause of an illness will someday allow us to prevent it.

A list of the theories of mental disturbance proposed over the past few decades would reach from here to next week. Most of these blame factors in the patient's environment. They include psychological, social, and moral models; a model blaming harmful interactions within the family; and a conspiratorial model which supposes that various elements of society "gang up" on the patient to make him sick. In contrast, a medical model which regards mental illness as essentially no different from bodily ailments has limped along in near obscurity for years, at best ignored, often vilified. In the next two chapters we will examine these factors implicated in the etiology of psychiatric illness.

FAMILY DYNAMICS AND PATHOLOGY

From the time we are old enough to toilet train, we learn that, from depression to drug abuse, from psychopathy to schizophrenia, whatever ill befalls us must have its roots in early childhood. Many a distraught parent has been told that had his child only been reared with more love (or less), had he been given more freedom (or more discipline), had he not been the favorite, eldest child (or pampered youngest), he would have stayed well. For years parents and other close family have been the targets of a psychiatric inquisition—particularly in the case of schizophrenia, for which many more environmental causes have been proposed than for affective disorder. But faulty child rearing has also been implicated in manias and depressions; we will briefly consider them later in this discussion.

In the several forms of family pathology thought to cause mental illness, everybody's all-time favorite "heavy" is Mother. Because she is the most constant object in the small child's environment, she has been a sitting duck for criticism, which through the years she has received by the apronful. Psychiatrists have called mothers of schizophrenics monsters and pictured them as malevolent creatures possessed of a perverse sense of motherhood, devoid of human feelings. Whether she is aggressive and domineering or rejecting and insecure, cold and unfeeling or fussy and overprotective, whether she wills it or not, by her behavior Mom supposedly creates a schizophrenic of her child. So sure have psychiatrists been of this ground that the term "schizophrenogenic mother," meaning a woman who in one way or another relentlessly drives her son or daughter up the wall, has gained a stranglehold on their vocabularies. It makes little difference that in most families only one child is affected, while the rest remain normal. The difference does not lie in the children themselves but in the varying degrees of affection Mother gives to each. When the child falls ill, it is her fault. But what if he improves—did Mom pull him through? No, his therapist bailed him out.

The story of how mothers produce schizophrenia in their children varies according to the theoretician. Some believe that the children learn their crazy behavior by imitating crazy Mom, despite the fact that only five percent of these women have schizophrenia themselves. Others say that Mother sets herself up as a martyr, drawing the child closely to her and restricting his freedom to investigate, to grow, to develop normally. The unnaturally strong bond forged between mother and child leads to a "symbiotic psychosis" where neither child nor parent can survive without the other. Another particularly complicated theory points the accusing finger not just at Mother, but at *her* mother as well. Because Grandma rules the roost, her daughter (the patient's mother) cannot mature normally herself; instead, she adopts Grandma's domineering manner and represses *her* child right into a breakdown. A tangled web, to say the least.

To give the family pathologists their due, they are not completely sexist in their orientation—fathers gather in a small share of the blame. In counterpoint to the fussy overprotectiveness of his wife, Dad is described as a passive, inadequate gentleman who contributes to Junior's illness by failing to serve as a suitable model for his development. So the little fellow's ego never learns to withstand life's vicissitudes and he sinks into the morass of psychosis. An alternative explanation accuses Father of brutally assaulting his child, verbally or physically threatening him into a nervous breakdown.

Parents of either sex have been accused of confusing the patient during his formative years with "mixed messages." They encourage him to seek greater independence ("Of course you should take a date to the dance") at the same time they remind him of his filial obligations (". . . if you don't care that I'll be here alone at night.") The parent effectively, if not willfully, puts his child into a psychological double-bind where he feels equally damned whether he does or he doesn't. So the preschizophrenic child grows up in a ferment of contradictory permission and denial from which he finally escapes into psychosis.

Other fathers and mothers have been told that their children's psychoses developed out of their own irreconcilable differences. These parents supposedly stay together for one reason only: their mutual love of fighting. Casting about for an ally to support his side of the conflict, each seizes upon the child as a weapon to use against the other. Drawn willy-nilly into the fray, the child internalizes (adopts as his own point of view) the pathological family relationship which he can neither understand nor control. Because he cannot identify with either parent without fighting the other, he adopts their distorted perceptions of reality and eventually develops psychotic symptoms.

Yet another theory blames the parent for being so egocentric that he does not recognize his child as a thinking, feeling person who needs to express himself. Because his self-centered, restricting parents did not foster his individuality, the child is forced to adapt to their needs and he becomes egocentric and *parent*-centered. He then begins to think of himself as centrally important to everyone, including his family, friends, the FBI, and ultimately to God himself. This grandiose self-view develops into frank delusions, and another schizophrenic thought disorder is born.

To a degree, the affective disorders have also been beset with dynamic interpretations. For example: the forceful, overbearing parent demands obedience and excellence from the future manic-depressive patient, particularly during his first two years when he is learning about cause and effect. The parent capriciously alternates these demands with periods of unearned permissiveness. As the child learns that his parent's alternating punishment and praise are unpredictable, his mood, too, becomes unpredictable. In the shadow of great inconsistency the child enters adolescence burdened by parent-induced mood swings which eventually blossom into full-blown manic-depressive disease. Or: at age three, the child is toilet trained too strictly, inhibiting free emotional expression. Because he never learns to express anger, he later turns it inward where it festers into a depression.

We can evaluate these theories succinctly. After years of looking, there is still no evidence that family pathology, particularly maternal "schizophrenogenesis," has anything at all to do with the development of schizophrenia or affective disorder. Families of schizophrenics do often communicate differently from families of normal people. But even this consistently reported finding has never been proven to cause the illness. Some writers claim that relatives of schizophrenics show abnormalities of affect by which patients "learn" to appear blunt or unresponsive themselves. But other studies have reported schizophrenics' relatives as rather livelier than the average. It is hard to be especially impressed with the importance of any cause supported by evidence no more consistent than this.

In a 1975 essay in the *American Journal of Psychiatry,* Dr. Silvano Arieti wrote that only about 25 percent of the mothers of schizophrenics fit the classical mold we have described. And he said something else, which someone should have pointed out years before: no one has any idea what percentage of *all* mothers fit the so-called schizophrenogenic prototype. Perhaps a lot of moms are sometimes cold or rejecting, or make contradictory statements to their children. If so, the apparent relationship between maternal behavior and psychopathology is due purely to chance and has no bearing at all on the cause of schizophrenia.[1]

Especially and increasingly troublesome to the careful thinker is the habit of blaming the same cause for several illnesses. If psychiatrists claim (as they do) that Dad's passivity and inade-

---

[1]Doctor Arieti's statement appears the more remarkable for its disavowal of his former position in the vanguard of those who support family dynamics theories. At last, psychiatrists are coming to grips with a number of illogicities too quickly accepted as truth by the profession's leaders of yesteryear.

quacy causes not only schizophrenia but homosexuality as well, poor Father's failings seem less convincing as the cause of either condition. The family dynamics theories are further weakened by their very number. So many different "causes" are put forth for the same disease that one suspects their advocates of casting blame on whatever is there, rather than more scientifically looking for factors which differentiate histories of schizophrenics from those of other psychiatric patients. Every family, no matter how intact or normal, has a few peculiarities which appear increasingly deviant and pathological the more you scrutinize them. Close observation rattles skeletons in the cleanest of closets.

But for the sake of argument, let us say that mothers of schizophrenics *do* appear unusually cold, distant, anxious, or unsympathetic to their children. Can this be explained, other than as a deliberate attempt by Mom to destroy her offspring? The distant attitude of a son or daughter like Lyonel Child just might "turn Mom off" from expressing normal maternal concern or love. If it really happens this way, those who blame Mother have confused cause with effect: Junior's illness affects Mother's personality, rather than the other way around. It is the old fallacy of *post hoc, ergo propter hoc.* Demonstrating that B follows A does not mean that A causes B. The apparent relationship may be purely coincidental, or B may really have caused A. Or both may have been caused by C, a hidden third factor. (A pertinent if hoary example of cause confused with effect was the medieval belief that loss of love caused the spermatozoa or menses to be dammed up, producing madness. Psychotics do sometimes lose interest in sex or stop menstruating, but the sexual symptoms result from the illness, not the other way around.)

Much of the information which provoked the theories of family pathology was gathered from patients during psychotherapeutic sessions, and that, psychologist Paul Meehl wrote, is methodologically next to worthless. Psychotherapists usually allow the patient's evaluation of his own childhood to stand unchallenged—no one interviews family or friends for their version of the story; old records gather cobwebs, unread. Lacking substantiation from outside sources, the psychiatrist uncritically accepts the story which may have been unconsciously doctored to fit the patient's (or the doctor's) biased concepts of etiology. You cannot blame the patient if he has an axe to grind; everyone colors what he says to favor his own point of view, and a patient may be psychotic to boot. But the psychiatrist, who is presumably seeking truth (and who is, we hope, sane), should manage better than this. He *must* set aside theoretical models and listen critically to the patient, evaluating his story by the yardstick of outside information.

Until it hits your family, you cannot believe the anguish caused by revisionist history-taking. After days, weeks, sometimes months of trying to cope with a situation which you cannot understand and which worsens day by day, at last you screw up the courage to consult a "shrink." After listening a few moments to the patient's story, and perhaps paying no attention at all to yours, he delivers himself of the opinion that it was all *your* fault. The effect can be devastating.

> A physician and his wife took their teen-age son to a psychiatrist, telling him that for weeks the boy had been depressed, alienated, and irritable. The father came from a long line of manic-depressives and had been severely depressed and preoccupied himself. Imagine his consternation when the psychiatrist told him first that his son had schizophrenia (wrong!) and concluded by saying, "*You're* making him sick—you've got to get out of his life."

Why? Why have mental health workers for decades dished up these indigestible points of view? In answering, we should be careful not to adopt the same condemnatory attitudes which some professionals fling at relatives. Most mental health workers are honest, dedicated people earnestly trying to create order out of the chaos of psychosis. Their only fault lies in the way they do it, by forcing facts into some dynamic model of etiology. Gripped by the urge to explicate the unexplainable, they earnestly dig at what they suppose to be the roots of the pathology. They don't realize that in so doing they risk killing the plant.

Because coping with severe emotional illness frustrates relative and therapist alike, each tends to seek relief by scapegoating the other. With relatives quick to blame the doctor if treatment goes poorly, at some unconscious level he must feel that turnabout is fair play. Or perhaps the guilt he feels when he cannot cure his patient sets the therapist's defenses in motion, causing him to blame the hapless relative, who will more than likely accept the blame with open arms. Anyone, but particularly a parent, would be intimidated by those accusations from a source as authoritative as a psychiatrist. When you bring your relative for treatment, you are already fearful of the possible diagnosis, guilty that you have delayed so long, and apprehensive about the outcome. You have the need to believe in the doctor's infallibility; after all, if he is wrong about the cause of the illness, is he likely to know how to treat it? So you'll swallow almost any interpretation, no matter how ill-founded or insulting, as long as it holds promise of help. In effect, your anxiety crowds out your ability to judge what is likely and what is not.

Doctors as a class hate to admit ignorance. By training a pillar of knowledge and strength, by predilection omniscient and omnipotent, the practicing physician seldom has to prove the statements he makes. So he accepts less and less critically the wisdom of his own *ex cathedra* pronouncements, until he believes them as religiously as you do. But this era of consumerism has led increasingly to review of the doctor's work by laymen and other physicians alike. And as those outside the mental health profession become more knowledgeable, increasingly the psychiatrist will be called to account for his diagnosis and treatment. More careful, thoughtful scrutiny of his methods and results presents a worthwhile goal. But in the meantime, getting there and getting care depend heavily upon you.

Psychoanalytic and Psychodynamic Theories

The psychoanalytic approach traces the origin of mental illness to early traumatic experiences repressed (buried) by the child when they occur, but which return to haunt him later in life. Analysts believe that all illness exists on a continuum running from bad to worse. Everyone has a few symptoms which make him a little neurotic. What distinguishes psychotics is that they suffer from a whole lot of what bothers neurotics just a little. But the cause of neurosis and psychosis alike is the same: early experiences. And you know whose fault they are!

The reaction suffered by a small baby left in a residential nursing home has been suggested as a model for all depressions. Observers noticed that when separated from their mothers, foundling home babies first seem to despair, but later become detached from their nurses and generally indifferent to their surroundings. Because this attitude resembled the withdrawal of depressed adults, theoreticians concluded that the cause of adult depression was also the loss of a loved one. But anyone could see that not all depressed patients had suffered a recent loss, so it was necessary to postulate a more distant one like the death of a parent years before. If only the child had been able to mourn his loss (who says he didn't?) he would not have become depressed later. So psychiatrists began to regard the task of therapy as reliving that traumatic event by talking about it time and again until the depression dissipated.

The Freudians and their followers actually deserve the credit, such as it is, for the invention of bereavement as a cause of depression. They view the psyche in terms of ninteenth-century physiology: conscious and unconscious portions of the personality battering each other through the ebb and flow of psychic energy (libido). The depressed patient withdraws his libido from a lost love object such as the dead mother or divorced spouse and invests a portion of it in his own ego (which you can roughly equate with the conscious self). The bereaved person has thus identified himself with the lost love object and finds himself in the anomalous position of melancholically mourning the loss of his own ego! After this bit of intellectual broken-field running, the try for the point-after is anticlimactic. The psychoanalysts conclude that mania is a "defense mechanism" against depression. The ball is fumbled for a turnover.

Variations on the parental perfidy theme concern anger or hostility turned inward. For example: the patient, mad at mother for making him too dependent as a child, cannot appropriately express his hostility if she inconsiderately dies. So he bottles up his feelings and his rage turns inward, producing depression. (But recent studies of grief have found substantial differences in the quality of bereavement and depression. Endogenous depression is more intense than grief reaction, is more likely to result in retardation of thought or action, lasts longer, and is more likely to lead to suicide. People who have suffered both bereavement and endogenous depression can easily tell them apart. They are not the same process at all.)

Parents are a sorry lot. Blamed on the one hand for meddling in their children's lives, they are just as likely to catch it for not "parenting" enough. Neglect and abandonment, particularly through the agency of divorce, have also been implicated as causes of psychosis. Now, no one will deny that divorce, sickness, or any other trauma which tangles the normal thread of childhood can lead to disturbed behavior, lower grades in school, or anxiety symptoms. But it is quite another matter to suggest that because Mom and Dad split up when Junior was in knee pants, he developed clinical depression years later. In fact, the diverse factors leading to divorce may themselves account for the illness. For example, divorcees are more likely than average to have mental illness—even *before* the divorce. A sick, divorced parent could transmit his illness to his child by, say, heredity. Divorce may be only a symptom of psychiatric illness, not its cause.

All of the psychoanalytic theories share a common fault—they generate few testable hypotheses (analysts use data to illustrate theories, not to test them). You have never seen an ego or measured a libido, and you never will. No one has, because they are hypothetical constructs reified by the scratchings of a thousand pens. Using concepts like these a theory can be tailored to fit any batch of facts to any desired conclusion without bringing us a millimeter closer to discovering the real cause of anything. Because of the heavy investment of time necessary to complete a single psychoanalysis (four hours a week for two to seven years), no analyst has completely treated more than a few patients who have any one illness. Hence, the second criticism of analytic theories of psychosis: they are based upon life histories of so few people that the conclusions reached may not apply to most patients. Take for example the Freudian theory that paranoia is caused by the fear of latent homosexuality. This little gem was devised from the analysis of a single patient—whom the psychiatrist never even met in person. The entire argument was constructed from the patient's memoirs, published years after he had become psychotic. Despite the doubtful quality of such evidence, the notion persists that the roots of schizophrenia lie embedded in the soil of homosexuality.

SOCIAL AND CULTURAL THEORIES

Social strife and the economic environment provide more fertile fields to be tilled by those who seek to uncover the roots of psychosis. Through the years sociologists have proposed many ways society might lay the groundwork for mental illness. Early in this century, the doctors who treated *dementia praecox* noticed that many of their patients came from the "lower classes." Later, careful epidemiological studies confirmed that schizophrenia is concentrated in the poorest and most disorganized sections of cities. Right away some psychiatrists jumped to the logical conclusion: poverty, crime, and social disorganization must cause schizophrenia. So now we are told it is society's fault, and if only we would spend the time and money necessary to eradicate poverty, we could also eliminate much of mental illness. But as you must begin to suspect by this time, there are other ways to look at the facts.

Some time ago the theory that schizophrenics "drift" to the lower strata of society drifted into view. The reason these patients gravitate to the working (and unemployed) classes is that they do not adapt well at higher levels. This theory offers us the social phenomenon as an effect, not a cause, of the illness. Happily, it also offers testability, a quality so often absent in the theories we have previously discussed.

For a long time sociologists have known that children normally have about the same socioeconomic status (SES) as their parents. So if schizophrenics do come from low SES groups, we would expect their fathers to have low SESs, too. But when researchers made this comparison, the patients ranked considerably below their fathers. We can only conclude that schizophrenic patients do drift to society's lower echelons—and that yet another environmental "cause" of schizophrenia has drifted around the bend.

You may not like this hypothesis—a lot of doctors don't, either. After all, it admits of no possibility for cure by manipulating social and economic factors. But even if we knew that certain life experiences regularly precipitated manic-depressive disease or schizophrenia, would we change the way we behave? For years we have known that drunken driving contributes heavily to the highway death toll, yet we have done little to prevent it. And Dr. Elliot Slater, one of England's foremost psychiatrists, has pointed out that although cigarette smoking increases the death rate from lung cancer and heart disease, this knowledge has not made a dent in per capita cigarette consumption. A plan for avoiding disaster only works if you're willing to follow it.

For many years some doctors have claimed that the stresses of industrialization and urbanization can cause mental illness. But you could have heard the same arguments over a century ago from physicians who thought then that mental breakdowns were on the rise. This they attributed to the competitive nature of the social environment and to the increased personal responsibility which they believed characterized the 1850s. This argument has two parts: (1) the incidence of mental illness has increased (2) due to stress. Although part two is nearly impossible to prove or disprove, part one has been evaluated with some facts.

Some thirty years ago, a team of epidemiologists thoroughly studied records from all Massachusetts mental hospitals for the preceding century. Sure enough, there *had* been a significant rise in the number of patients admitted for mental disorder. But patients *over* the age of fifty accounted for nearly all the increase. These people suffered from senile brain disease, not from the endogenous psychoses. Why were more old people being admitted in the twentieth century? Because modern families are less willing to care for senile relatives at home, as did families during most of the 1800s. As for manic-depressive disease and schizophrenia, the illnesses which would account for the majority of patients under the age of fifty—no evidence of any change in prevalence over the past century or more.

Even though we cannot demonstrate that stress has produced more psychosis overall, stressful life events could still lead to mental breakdown in individual patients. This statement encapsulates an argument which psychiatrists have carried on for years over the precipitating events hypothesis. People naturally try to explain everything logically, so when a mental breakdown occurs we tend to examine the events in the patient's earlier life for a possible clue to cause. And where we seek, we are likely to find. Olive Bard, whom we met in chapter 7, blamed her depression on the insulting remarks she thought she had made. Like her, about half of all seriously depressed people find something on which to blame their moods, though some have to dig pretty deep to find it. They cheated on their income tax years ago, or they did not return the change when undercharged at the grocery store. Or (this really happened), one man said he began to feel low when he learned his dog had ticks! And often a careful history turns up symptoms of depression beginning *before* the supposed precipitating event.

But some changes are of greater consequence and cannot be dismissed so casually. Any of us would regard as significant a life event like moving, changing or losing a job, marriage, divorce, the birth of a child, or physical illness. But it has never been proven that someone who has been so traumatized stands a greater chance of psychiatric illness than someone who has not. When scientists use our old friend, the controlled study, to investigate the significance of life events in causing psychiatric illness, they can demonstrate no consistent findings.

Of course, certain life events may be enough to make some people who are already sick seek treatment. Every psychiatrist is familiar with the man who was ill for many years but avoided hospitalization until his wife died. Her death had nothing to do with causing his illness—it simply left no one to look after him. Stopping maintenance drugs can be another steppingstone to the hospital for a schizophrenic or manic-depressive patient who has previously done well. These examples may seem trivial, but they do represent the reason for admission in a significant number of psychiatric patients.

What about traumatic events of greater calibre—a soldier serving in a war zone, for example? Surely the effects of stress on mental health will be found in combat veterans. But a study which compared Vietnam veterans with soldiers who had never served in combat found no differences either in terms of later legal problems or emotional maladjustment. The author of this article pointed out quite correctly that the conclusions of controlled studies often differ remarkably from impressionistic reports. The latter may be heavily biased by the author's own beliefs or by political motives. And this judgment can be applied equally well to many other studies which purport to show how your relative's environment can lead to his breakdown.

For the acute "good prognosis" psychoses or for some depressions, however, we can make a somewhat better case for the importance of stress. Rhoda Crews' reactive depression (chapter 7) was undoubtedly initiated by a series of these life events. Changes in hormone levels may also tip the balance toward depression or psychosis, and either the months following childbirth or the days preceeding a menstrual period can occasionally produce a depressive or paranoid psychosis. These illnesses usually begin suddenly and last briefly, and they nearly always resolve completely. But in most cases we can only speculate about the role of life events in the development of psychiatric illness; believable precipitants occur in too few cases, and too many different events have been claimed as precipitants for us to swallow this theory whole.

The Moral Model

According to this model, symptoms do not come from illness at all, but from habits learned by imitating parents. In any case they are unacceptable and need to be changed. Treatment is by exhortation ("C'mon, hold yourself together!") and by behavior modification (see chapter 18). In the past, this model has led to excesses of treatment such as whipping and chaining people to walls, practices now generally frowned upon.

Applied to affective disorder and schizophrenia, the model survives only in a few limited senses. For example, some people believe that ECT works because the patient needs to be punished. (Ridiculous: a study showed that depressed patients who thought they were being treated but were only anesthetized and then allowed to awaken did not recover.) Even recently, depressed patients have been "treated" by forcing them to do menial tasks like scrubbing the floor with a toothbrush to try to make them turn hostility outward. Sheer inhumanity!

But the hardiest survivors of the moral model are the attitudes that so many people harbor to some degree toward their mentally ill relatives. A notorious example: despite the fact that alcoholism is now largely regarded as a disease, anyone who has lived with an alcoholic begins to suspect, reasonably or not, that the patient "could help it if he wanted to." And until they have been taught otherwise, many relatives secretly believe that depressed patients, too, need only pull themselves together and forswear self-pity. The real misfortune occurs when the patient adopts the same point of view and blames himself for not trying harder to improve. In all, the moral model appears nearly useless for affective disorder and schizophrenia.

THE CONSPIRATORIAL MODEL

Somewhat similar to the moral hypothesis, the conspiratorial model regards psychiatric disorders not as illnesses but as normal reactions to intolerable living situations. Schizophrenia is not a disease but a breakdown in human relationships resulting from massive failure of communication. One of the most voluble exponents of this point of view, British psychoanalyst R. D. Laing, suggests that the "illness" actually is in the family (read "society" if you choose), not the patient. The family elects one of its members "it," then insidiously drives "it" mad. Schizophrenia is a coping mechanism of the mind, a special strategy to enable the individual to live in an untenable situation. The psychiatrist who tries to treat the schizophrenic is actually conspiring with the family to perpetuate the myth of the patient's insanity.

To try to refute these claims of the antipsychiatrists, as they have been called, is futile. These deeply politicized theories are embraced as tightly as the tenets of any religion and offer no testable hypothesis for study. Debate leads quickly to shouting matches from which no truth can emerge.

SUMMING UP

By now you know that a lot of people have given an enormous amount of thought to the etiology of mental illness. If you think that much of their work has been hastily or carelessly considered, you are wrong. For perhaps the strongest trait of the environmental exponents is an earnest dedication to their patients and to their theories. As one husband put it, "What impressed me was the infinite care with which her first doctor built a case describing me as the cause of her schizophrenia. He couldn't have taken greater pains if he'd been handling nitroglycerin. Trouble is she really had manic-depressive disease." Which shows that even if you nurture a theory with all the care in the world, it will not produce a fruitful harvest unless you fertilize it with facts. And often lacking fertilizer, the field of psychiatry flowers with as many unquestioned answers as unanswered questions.

12.
What Causes Psychosis: Biological Theories

The remaining model of psychiatric illness—the medical model—has always been overshadowed by the glamour of the intellectual theories we have just discussed. This model does not strive for elegance of philosophic logic, but is developed from its basis in scientific data. It assumes that mental illness really does not differ from physical disorder except in its location; careful diagnosis is of the utmost importance. Although no laboratory tests have yet been developed to define mental illness in an individual, those who subscribe to the medical model believe that it is only a matter of time before this, too, becomes possible. In this chapter we will examine the theories of those scientists who argue that mental illness is not always logical—sometimes it is biological.

Scientists have looked hard for biological theories of mental illness, and until quite recently, the search has been unproductive. If anything, early organic theories were even sillier and more speculative than the psychological and environmental theories we have already discussed. If a Greek physician in the time of Hippocrates, around 400 B.C., told an anxious husband that his-wife's depression was due to too much black bile in her system, who could say he was wrong? Some primitive cultures blamed mental illness on evil spirits which infested the patient's head. The treatment, worse than the affliction to judge by skeletal remains found in ancient grave sites, was by trephining—boring holes in the skull to release said demons. Noxious substances accumulating in the blood have also been implicated in mental illness for centuries, and cupping (drawing blood to the skin by a vacuum) and bleeding have hastened many a sufferer to an untimely death. At one time, schizophrenia was thought due to an accumulation of poisons in the body from infected teeth, spawning a tide of increasingly wealthy dentists who vigorously plied their trade upon a distracted clientele. The near-epidemic of extractions led to a generation of toothless schizophrenics whose delusions and hallucinations remained totally unaffected by the "cure."

Because they have found no consistent abnormalities in the nervous systems of most psychotic patients, scientists have been reduced recently to examining the blood, sweat, and tears (as well as cerebrospinal fluid and sundry excreta) for clues. Over the years an army of researchers and technicians, heeding their rallying cry, "No twisted minds without twisted molecules," has repeatedly sifted the fluids and tissues of the brain for abnormal proteins or hormone imbalances. From time to time one or another proclaims victory, only to learn later that no one could duplicate his results. Discoveries which at first seem highly significant almost invariably prove upon more sober examination to be a fluke of faulty laboratory technique or due to some previously unnoted peculiarity of the patients sampled.

A recent example was the flurry of interest shown in DMPEA, a chemical related to the psychotomimetic (hallucination-inducing) drug mescaline. Found first in the urine of schizophrenics, this substance produces a characteristic pink spot on a sophisticated laboratory test called a chromatogram. The fact that this pink spot was not found in the urine of non-schizophrenic controls caused enormous excitement in the scientific world, for here might be the first laboratory test which could differentiate psychotic from nonpsychotic patients. But as always before, these high hopes were dashed when other researchers could not confirm the results. Later, pink spot was attributed to nothing more complicated than the dietary use of tea (the kind you drink, not the kind you smoke!) by the schizophrenic patients. When non-schizophrenics drank tea, they also excreted DMPEA into their urine. The use of this common beverage had not been controlled during the earlier investigation.

Within the past ten years, other investigators claimed that the key to the schizophrenia puzzle was a peculiar inability to metabolize copper. This hypothesis was linked to the supposed finding of an abnormal protein fraction in the blood of schizophrenics, called ceruloplasmin. While this research was going on, still another group of workers reported finding certain antibody sites in the brains of schizophrenics, implying that the psychotic patient actually has developed an allergy to his own brain! But alas, like the other biochemical theories which have had their day, neither of these has been upheld by further research, and both have sunk into near-oblivion.

But winning the prize for single-mindedness of purpose and sheer ingenuity is the work of a midwestern research group which has spent years studying the sweat of schizophrenics. They collect samples by encasing their subjects in plastic bags and turning on the heat; then in the laboratory they inject an extract of the sweat into spiders, inducing the tiny weavers to spin erratic webs. The theory that this substance lies close to the root of schizophrenia surfaces in the scientific and popular press from time to time, and it has not yet been adequately disproven. But if historical precedent is upheld, it will be only a matter of time before it, too, proves made of gossamer.

HEREDITARY ASPECTS

A century ago novelists wrote of "hereditary taint" in relatives of the mentally ill and everybody regarded families so afflicted with open suspicion. More recently scientific theories of hereditary (genetic) influence in mental illness have been suspected as antihumanistic because they seem to leave no hope for treatment. But despite prejudice both by scientific and popular writers, researchers have pursued the genetics of mental illness to the point where today this discipline provides the most solid and coherent body of information available.

Before we can say that any illness is genetic, we must first decide whether it occurs in families of patients more often than in the general population. But determining the prevalence of any illness in the population at large is no mean feat in itself. You cannot just walk into a supermarket and ask the first hundred people coming through the checkout line whether they have ever had a breakdown. What if mentally ill people don't go to super-markets—your figures will be too low. You could make a door-to-door survey, but even this may be inaccurate—the psychiatric patients may have been locked up in institutions, or they may have moved to a different neighborhood. Or maybe they don't like to answer doorbells.

Even assuming that you have conquered the horrendous problems of sampling and accessibility, the age of your subjects when you interview them poses still more difficulties. If you count young people, you may count them at a time before they fall ill, falsely lowering your estimate. But try to solve this problem by interviewing only older people, and you miss those who died early, perhaps by suicide.

The solution to all of these objections is the arduous method of cohort interview: studying all members of an entire population born between specific dates. Because Americans are such a foot-loose lot, this method would be virtually impossible here, but it has proven feasible in Iceland, where few people emigrate and where careful birth, census, and death records have been kept for centuries. Using these records, Professor Tomas Helgason, in the 1950s, undertook the backbreaking job of following up all people born in that country from 1895 to 1897. This meant knocking on doors all over the country, visiting hospitals and retirement homes, and interviewing relatives of those few people who had left the country. He also talked with the surviving relatives of those who had died and obtained whatever records he could to determine the cause of death and whether they had ever had mental illness. So with a Herculean effort he arrived at population figures for psychiatric disorder which are among the most accurate of any available today.

His findings, confirmed by researchers in other countries, should be familiar to us by this time—we have already quoted his prevalence figures in chapters 7, 8, and 9. In most areas of the world, about 0.8 percent of the general population—eight of every thousand people, male and female—will develop schizophrenia if they live out their normal life span. For affective disorders the figures are higher. Around 4 percent of the general population will have an affective episode serious enough sometime to warrant treatment. But only about a quarter of these (one percent of the whole population) will actually develop manic-depressive disease.

With these figures in mind, let us see what having a mentally ill relative does to one's chance of developing a similar psychiatric illness, which is shown approximately in Table 3: For one thing, relatives of manic-depressives are more likely to become ill than relatives of patients with schizophrenia or with unipolar affective disorder—about twice as likely, as a matter of fact. But this does not mean that genetic factors necessarily play a more important role in bipolar disease. Some illnesses which are determined en-

Table 3
Approximate Family Risk of Mental Illness

	Affective Disorders Bipolar	Unipolar	Schizo- phrenia
First-degree relatives			
Mothers	20%	15%	5%
Fathers	15%	10%	5%
Sisters	20%	15%	9%
Brothers	15%	10%	9%
Daughters	20%	15%	12%
Sons	15%	10%	12%
Second-degree relatives	5%	4%	2%
General population	1%	3%	1%

tirely by heredity show up in a relatively minor proportion of relatives—it all depends on how the disease is transmitted. We will discuss that subject in due course.

Just as in the general population, women are more likely than men to develop affective disorder, but the sexes are equally likely to become schizophrenic. Nobody knows why men less often become depressed, so of course *everyone* has his own theory. Some thought that because our macho culture frowns on weakness in its men, they are less likely to give in to an illness and seek psychiatric help. But this theory has been proven dead wrong by population studies like those of Professor Helgason's which do not depend for their figures on patients coming to the doctor to be treated, yet show the same sex ratio. Another theory holds that female sex hormones have something to do with allowing depression to become manifest; still other physicians believe that the deficit of depressed males is somehow accounted for by the surplus of male alcoholics—perhaps depression and alcoholism are simply different manifestations of the same illness.

A third important fact from the table: the closer the genetic relationship between a patient and his relative, the more likely that relative is to become ill. For convenience, let us speak of relationship in terms of classes. Parents, children, and brothers and sisters of a patient are all first-degree relatives, and they have the greatest chance of developing a similar illness, whether it be schizophrenia or affective disorder. Grandparents, uncles, aunts, first cousins, and grandchildren we call second-degree relatives, and so on. Although any degree of relationship theoretically carries with it some increased risk for illness, in practice only first- and second-degree relatives have a risk much greater than the average for the general population.

So far, all that we have really learned is that mental illness does run in families. How it passes from one relative to another (transmission) forms the basis for the enormous controversy which we began to discuss in chapter 11: do the genes contained in sperm and egg vest a child with illness from conception, or does he acquire this tendency later through the influence of the environment? In brief: which to blame, nature or nurture? Although we cannot hope to distill the oceans of ink which have been spilled on either side in this often acrimonious debate, we will at least attempt to give a brief account of the genetic evidence. Because the scientific storm has centered upon the schizophrenic disorders, the bulk of this discussion will concern them. But identical arguments apply to the affective disorders, and, where available, genetic evidence will also be mentioned for this condition.

Twin Studies

One of the best ways to separate the effects of environment from those of inheritance is to study multiple births. About one in every ninety childbirths is multiple and the vast majority of these are twins. But twins themselves come in two varieties, and the comparison of mental illness in the two types of twins provides a beautiful exercise in logic and arithmetic which gives us valuable information as to how disease is transmitted from parent to child.

Two out of three sets of twins are the fraternal, or two-egg type. This means that these children, born at the same time, develop from two eggs fertilized by two separate sperm cells, resulting in people who are genetically no more alike than nontwin brothers or sisters. Two-egg twins can be either same-sex or opposite. The remaining type of twins, called identical or one-egg, form from the division of a single egg after fertilization by a single sperm cell. The two children which result (necessarily always same-sex) carry identical genetic material.

Any condition which is 100 percent genetic should appear in both members of an identical pair: that is, identical twins will be *concordant* for the trait. Because fraternal twins are less alike genetically, more fraternal pairs will be *discordant* for any trait which is genetic. Most sets of twins, whether fraternal or identical, are reared in the same home by the same set of parents, so the environment should not help determine any difference in concordance rate in a genetic disorder between one-egg and two-egg twins. In this natural experiment, we would say that the effects of nurture are held constant.

Now "all" we need to do is find a large number of twins who have, say, schizophrenia, then examine their co-twins for the presence or absence of the same disease. If schizophrenia is not a genetic disorder, the fraternal co-twin of a schizophrenic should be as likely as an identical co-twin to develop the same illness. But if genetics plays an important role, identical co-twins will have a higher concordance rate. (Figure 12.1 diagrams the logic of the study.) Now we have a simple exercise in arithmetic: count the co-twins who are ill, and compare fraternals with identicals.

Despite the difficulty you would expect of finding twin pairs in which at least one of the members is psychiatrically ill, this study is of such importance in determining etiology that it has been done some eight or ten times in the past several decades throughout the world. And the results have been remarkable for their consistency. Although the magnitude of the difference depends upon the age of the twins, the seriousness of the illness, and

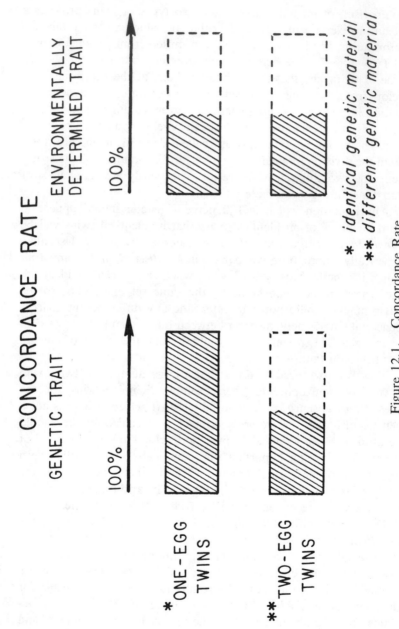

Figure 12.1. Concordance Rate

other factors, on the average the concordance rate for identical twins is about 60 percent. Identical twins are five times as likely to be concordant for schizophrenia as are their fraternal twin counterparts. And the fraternal twin of a schizophrenic is no more likely to develop the illness than is a nontwin sibling. Clearly, the genetic hypothesis receives strong support from studies as consistent as these.

Despite this evidence, critics continue to take pot shots at twin studies. Identical twins look more alike and their behavior tends to be more similar than fraternal twins—maybe they really are reared more similarly, too. If so, environment could *still* account for the higher concordance rate in one-egg twins. This argument has been partly answered by a variant of the twin study method— the examination of that phenomenal rarity, identical twins reared apart.

People are so wonderfully diverse that if you only look hard enough you can find nearly every conceivable experiment of nature. Yet the phenomenon of a set of identical twins separated at or near birth, brought up completely apart—sometimes not even knowing that the other exists—and at least one of whom has schizophrenia is so rare that over the past several decades only sixteen pairs have been reported. But even this small sample holds the power to test the idea that similar environments account for the high concordance rate in identical twins. If this were the case, we would expect that separate rearing would lower the concordance rate in these genetically identical twins. But when all such cases are carefully investigated and counted, ten of the sixteen co-twins (62.5 percent) also have schizophrenia. This concordance rate does not differ substantially from that for identical twins reared together, and it offers further strong evidence for genetic transmission.

In another natural experiment which occurs from time to time, the effects of genetics and environment are separated by the process of adoption. This was best exploited a few years ago by Dr. Leonard Heston, who, with a lot of luck and a tremendous amount of work, found and interviewed the children of women who had been hospitalized for schizophrenia. As infants, these people had been adopted and reared by nonschizophrenic parents. As adults, Dr. Heston tirelessly tracked them down and interviewed them. He compared these subjects to a control group of children of non-schizophrenic mothers; these controls also had been separated from their mothers at birth. This test of the effects of nature versus nurture yielded striking results. Whereas 11 percent of the experimental subjects had developed schizophrenia as adults, none of the controls with similar childhood environments (adoption) but without the risk of schizophrenic heredity became ill.

Adoption studies have been nearly impossible to do in this country because of the traditional reluctance of agencies to divulge their information, even to scientific investigators. So most foster care studies have been done in Europe, particularly in the Scandinavian countries where adoption records have been carefully kept for decades and are accessible to investigators. Without exception, these studies have also found more schizophrenics in the biological relatives of patients than in their adopted families. The theory of genetic transmission has been supported for schizophrenia by every type of genetic study thus far devised.

Affective Disorder

You can mention genetics in the same breath with depression and run less risk of a fight than you do for schizophrenia. The debate, if less acrimonious, has also been less interesting. The contribution of genetics to the development of manias and depressions has been so generally accepted that relatively few studies have been needed to prove it. In part this derives from the high prevalence of illness in close relatives of manic-depressives, making inheritance more visible and therefore more acceptable. For another thing, affective symptoms seem so much more understandable than schizophrenic symptoms—everyone has felt happy or sad at times, but few among us have had delusions or hallucinations. So complicated psychological/philosophical theories are not necessary: mechanistic (genetic) explanations are quite adequate.

Whatever the reason, arguments against a genetic etiology for affective disorder seem hardly to have arisen. But the few twin studies which have been done clearly demonstrate the importance of genetics: identical twins are four to five times more likely than fraternal twins to be concordant for these conditions. The data for affective disorder have been somewhat confused by a lack of studies distinguishing between bipolar and unipolar cases. Where the distinction has been made, the monozygotic co-twins of bipolar probands are nearly twice as likely to be concordant as their unipolar counterparts—72 percent versus 40 percent. (In neither bipolar nor unipolar groups did the dizygotic co-twins' concordance rate exceed 15 percent, about what we would expect for nontwin siblings.)

With further refinement of clinical methods and even more careful genetic investigation, we will probably find genetic subgroups of unipolar and bipolar affective disorder. "Blue genes" may come in several styles, as one wag put it. A start in this direction has been made at the University of Iowa by Dr. George Winokur, who has identified two subgroups of unipolar depression: late-onset patients, whose illnesses begin after the age of forty and whose ill relatives have affective disorder; and early-onset patients who may have relatives with alcoholism or personality disorder as well as depressions. Whether this dichotomy can withstand the test of time remains to be seen. But distinctions like these provide a hope for more accurately identifying clinical subgroups, allowing psychiatrists to more carefully tailor treatment to suit the needs of their patients.

Schizo-affective Psychosis

As we discussed at length earlier, physicians often disagree about what schizophrenia is or who has it, which probably accounts for the slow progress in the field of genetics of schizophrenia. After all, how could you learn anything about the cause of abdominal pain if you could not tell appendicitis from ulcers? But geneticists now know that which has been clear to careful clinicians for years —schizophrenia and affective disorder are distinct, separate illnesses. Relatives of schizophrenics have schizophrenia; manic-depressive disease "breeds true," too. For example, there are no known cases of identical twins where one had schizophrenia and the other had bipolar disease. Increasingly, scientists have used this genetic distinction to help tease apart the mass of schizophrenic patients into good and poor prognosis subgroups.

Using the criteria we discussed in chapter 10, the late Dr. Michael McCabe and his coworkers in St. Louis identified a number of patients with either good or poor prognosis schizophrenia. Then the close relatives of these patients were interviewed by a psychiatrist who did not know to which group the index patient belonged. (Researchers call this the "blind interview technique," and use it to eliminate their personal bias from their findings. Without it, even the most conscientious scientist may be tempted to slant his interview to support the theory he is trying to test.) The interviews completed, they broke the code and found that 13 percent of all relatives in both groups had a major psychiatric disorder. But the type of illness sharply differentiated the two groups.

In relatives of poor prognosis patients, schizophrenia outnumbered affective disorder three to one. For the good prognosis group, the figures were exactly reversed: affective disorder was found three times as frequently as schizophrenia. Because mental illnesses do run true to type within families, these results provide strong evidence that good and poor prognosis schizophrenia are actually different disorders. And the good prognosis group (as we noted before, sometimes called "schizo-affective schizophrenia" because these patients often have depression or elation as a part of their clinical picture) is genetically closely related to manic-depressive disease.

They may actually be manic-depressive patients in disguise, a suggestion made by Dr. Winokur after studying patients with schizo-affective disorder. Not only did these people have the usual symptoms of affective disorder—depression, elation, suicidal ideas, sleep disturbance, appetite loss, to name a few—but they also suffered from delusions and hallucinations typical of schizophrenia. In short, a difficult group of people to diagnose: are they really schizophrenics with an overlying depression, or does their craziness only cover the basic affective disorder? Winokur used genetics to help settle the question by interviewing relatives of these confusing patients. A considerable proportion of the relatives were ill themselves, but most did *not* have schizophrenia, nor even schizo-affective disease. Instead, most had rather typical "garden variety" manic-depressive disease. It is the great tragedy and shame of American psychiatry that these people who are probably best thought of and treated as manic-depressive so often incorrectly receive treatment for schizophrenia alone.

For both affective disorder and schizophrenia, heredity clearly plays a highly important role, accounting for half or more of your relative's illness. But of course this leaves the other half (or less) of the tendency to illness unaccounted for. Obviously, environmental factors must play some sort of a role. But what sort?

Child-rearing practices, according to recent studies, account for but a tiny percentage of the variability—5 to 10 percent, but no more. But the environment can include conditions in the uterus before birth, too, and some scientists suspect that the development of psychosis may depend in part upon events which affect the unborn child. Poor nourishment of the fetus or toxic chemicals swallowed or inhaled by the mother are only two of the possible mechanisms which could trigger the development of psychosis. Later on in life, the prolonged heavy use of stimulant drugs such as amphetamines have produced psychoses in some people, a small proportion of whom go on to develop an illness which looks similar to paranoid schizophrenia.

As we discussed in the previous chapter, we cannot say what environmental factors definitely are relevant to the development of psychosis, but they must be there. Much of the future in terms of understanding these illnesses, and of learning ways of controlling and preventing them, will depend on discovering how heredity interacts with environment to produce illness.

TYPE OF TRANSMISSION

It may upset you to learn that your relative's illness is genetic. Does this mean that you or your family are doomed to illness yourselves? What are the chances that any given relative will become sick with a similar illness? The answers depend largely upon the manner in which the genes responsible for illness are passed from one generation to the next.

First of all, genes. Genes are those tiny bits of protein which carry the information needed to direct the development of the characteristics of your body. Whether you will have a big nose or brown eyes, a high IQ or manic-depressive disease—all this information is contained in the genes present in each of your cells. Genes are grouped together on long strings called chromosomes, of which every cell has twenty-three pairs. So each one of us has two sets of genes for every inherited characteristic, and one gene of each pair was derived from mother and one from father. The number of these genes required to produce a given characteristic depends upon the "strength" of the gene involved. The accompanying diagrams should help you understand this explanation.

Certain genes are dominant in their action. That is, only one of the pair of dominant genes is needed for the trait to be expressed. Because the gene is dominant, every affected person had at least one parent also affected, and one-half of all children born to an affected individual will also have that trait (Figure 12.2). An example of a dominantly transmitted illness in human beings is Huntington's chorea, the ultimately fatal neurological disease which affected folk singer Woodie Guthrie. Although relatives of patients with affective disorder and schizophrenia are often ill themselves, the proportion affected (see Table 3) does not even approach 50 percent. Therefore, theories which propose a major dominant gene as the etiology must postulate something called *incomplete penetrance* (imperfect expression) of the gene—presumably due to another gene which prevents the first one from fulfilling its manifest destiny. This all becomes rather confusing, rendering a single dominant gene unpromising as the explanation for any psychiatric condition.

In the second type of transmission—*recessive* transmission—both genes of a pair must be "abnormal" for the trait to be expressed. Someone who has one normal and one abnormal gene will carry the trait without actually becoming ill. A patient with a recessively transmitted disease (phenylketonuria, mental retardation due to the inability to metabolize certain types of protein, is a good example) must have two abnormal genes, one derived from each parent, both of whom are carriers. As Figure 12.3 shows, the chance that any of their other children (brothers and sisters of the patient) will also have the characteristic is one in four. But the child of the patient with a recessive illness will never become ill unless the patient marries a carrier, a relatively rare event. Therefore, one of the hallmarks of the recessive transmission is that the siblings are affected far more often than children. From Table 3 you can see that in neither schizophrenia nor manic-depressive disease do affected siblings outnumber children.

DOMINANT GENE TRANSMISSION

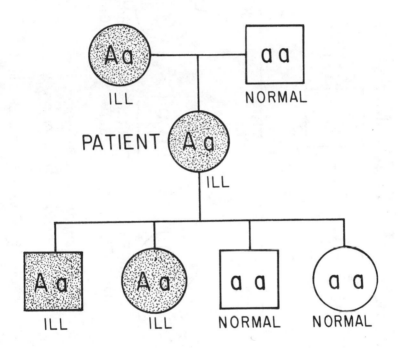

Figure 12.2   Dominant Gene Transmission

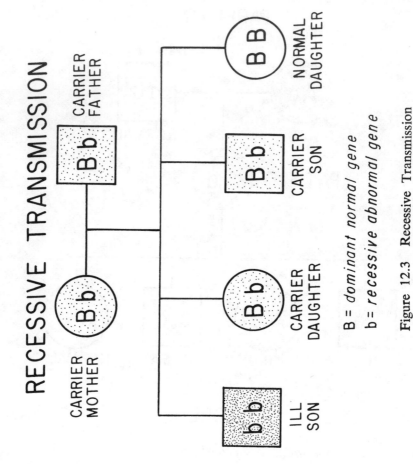

Figure 12.3 Recessive Transmission

164

This discussion has made no distinction between males and females. The twenty-two pairs of chromosomes considered so far (called autosomes) occur equally in the two sexes, and the types of transmission we have discussed affect men and women equally. But in the remaining pair of chromosomes, the X and Y (sex) chromosomes, the sexes do differ. Females have two X chromosomes, and males one X and one Y chromosome (beginning genetics students get this advice on how to tell the sex of a chromosome: pull down its genes!). Although the Y chromosome determines that the child will be a boy, it is relatively empty of genes. So genes occurring on a male's lone X chromosome are not paired, and any abnormal gene carried here will always be expressed (Figure 12.4).

A peculiar pattern of inheritance results from this "X linkage" in which women carry the characteristic but are rarely affected by it—they need two of the relatively rare recessive X-linked genes to have the illness. But they do transmit the condition to their sons, who require only one of these genes to be ill. Fathers can pass the trait on to their daughters, but because they donate only a Y chromosome to their sons no male ever inherits an X-linked trait from his father. Figure 12.5 illustrates this criss-cross pattern of inheritance where the trail appears to jump from mother to son to granddaughter to great-grandson. Examples of X-linkage include red-green color blindness and hemophilia, the bleeding disease which affected so many royal families in Europe.

Recently Dr. George Winokur made interesting observations suggesting that some cases of manic-depressive disease may be controlled by an X-linked gene. Studying families in which two generations were affected by bipolar disease, he found that ill mothers passed the trait to their sons or to their daughters, but ill fathers only transmitted it to their daughters. The absence of ill father–ill son pairs clearly suggested X-linkage. Further supporting evidence was obtained by studying the association between bipolar disease and red-green color blindness, which is known to be carried on the X chromosome. Nine families have been found in which both conditions occur, and in virtually all members color blindness and manic-depressive disease are distributed as if carried on the same chromosome. We still do not know whether

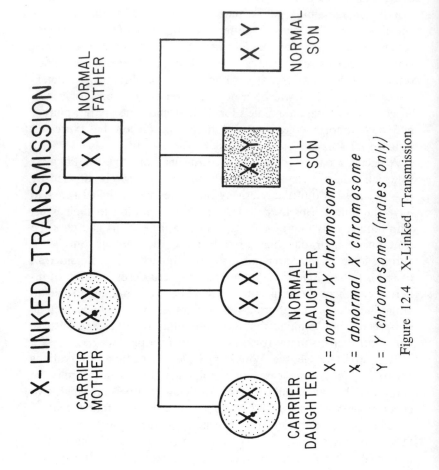

Figure 12.4 X-Linked Transmission

"CRISS-CROSS" INHERITANCE IN X-LINKED TRANSMISSION

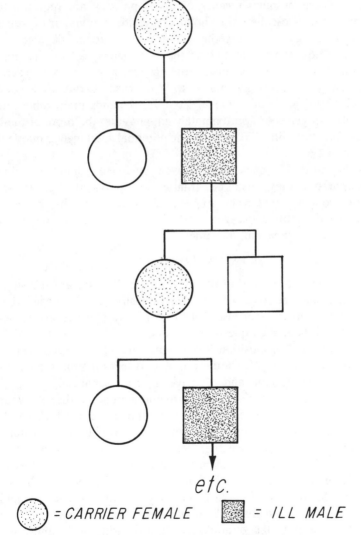

etc.

= CARRIER FEMALE   = ILL MALE

Figure 12.5   "Crisscross" Inheritance in X-Linked Transmission

X-linkage holds true for all cases of manic-depressive disease, but it certainly seems a likely candidate for some. In any event, neither unipolar depression nor schizophrenia is inherited this way.

In the remaining type of transmission, *polygenic* transmission, several (perhaps many) genes of equal potency are required to overcome the so-called threshold—the critical number of genes which must gang up together before the patient becomes ill (Figure 12.6). Beyond that point, the more genes present, the more abnormal the patient becomes. Intelligence, although not exactly a disease ('tis only folly, not sick, to be wise) serves as a good model of polygenic inheritance. Your IQ depends upon inheriting a number of genes of approximately equal value; the more of these genes you start with, the higher your potential intelligence quotient (Figure 12.6).

Although it has not yet been proven, evidence is increasing that schizophrenia may also be transmitted polygenically. If so, we can conclude that when someone does develop schizophrenia, the genes probably came from both sides of the family, neither of which should scapegoat the other.

Genetic Counseling

With evidence increasing that psychiatric illnesses are transmitted genetically, relatives of patients naturally are concerned that their own children may also fall ill. And psychiatrists are sometimes asked the loaded question, "Should we have children at all?" —a complicated proposition indeed, and one which depends upon a number of factors. We should probably discuss it from the standpoint of schizophrenia and affective disorder separately.

If either you or your spouse has manic-depressive disease, your children could also become ill. The risk hovers around 15 to 20 percent for each child, so even if you have two children you stand a better than even chance that neither of them will be affected.

But besides the risk, we should consider what you would really be risking. Suppose your child does develop either unipolar or bipolar affective disorder—how seriously ill might he become, and will it interfere with his life? As we have already pointed out in chapters 7 and 8, the outlook for these conditions is uniformly good. He may have only one episode, and even if he should have

POLYGENIC TRANSMISSION

AVERAGE PARENTS

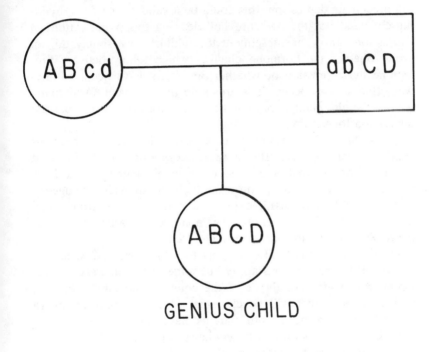

GENIUS CHILD

ABCD = *dominant genes for high intelligence*
abcd = *recessive genes for low intelligence*

Figure 12.6   Polygenic Transmission

multiple attacks, he can anticipate long periods of normal life between. And the medicines developed over the past twenty years can quickly treat later attacks, or they may be able to prevent future episodes altogether. To deny your child his life and yourself the joy of having a child simply because he could develop a treatable illness does not make good sense.

Two other factors sometimes worry prospective parents: the possible stressful effects of childbearing and child rearing on an already depressed mother; and the competence of a depressed mother *or* father to rear a child. If we knew that having children did precipitate depression, this could be a valid reason for remaining childless. But the data are not clear on this point. Although depression can occur subsequent to childbirth, we simply do not know whether the hormone changes which follow delivery precipitate the depression or whether one might have occurred anyway. If one does occur, it is treatable in any event. And many women would gladly endure the discomforts of a postpartum depression for a baby.

As to the ability of the psychiatrically ill parent to rear his child, we can at least offer a satisfactory opinion. Although it stands to reason that a depressed or manic parent might have trouble caring for his offspring when he is ill, no evidence suggests that the children of manic-depressive patients suffer from overall lack of effective parenting. Again, no real reason for manic-depressive parents to fear having children.

Do the same considerations apply to schizophrenics? Well, yes and no: the considerations apply but some of the answers are different. As in affective disorder, the chances that any child of a schizophrenic parent will develop that illness are only about 15 percent—50 percent if both parents have the disease. But the quality of life for that minority will be rather substantially affected. This child stands a substantial chance of spending much of his adult life under psychiatric care. He may never be able to marry or to hold a job and he could end his days in an institution, considerations which may well deter many patients from having children of their own. Also, schizophrenic men and women are much more likely than manic-depressives to have trouble caring for children. And although inadequate child rearing cannot by itself produce schizophrenic offspring, the child raised by a psychotic parent who is intermittently hospitalized might well grow up with some problems relating to other people.

Of course, these comments apply only to "poor prognosis" schizophrenia. A parent who falls ill suddenly, has marked depressive or manic features or other characteristics of a "good prognosis" disease (see chapter 10) may well have a variant of affective disorder. His children, if they are ill at all, will probably have typical depressive disease, not schizophrenia. So any patient who has fully recovered from an atypical psychosis should not be discouraged from bearing and rearing a family. This question is one which you would want to discuss thoroughly with your physician before allowing it to affect your life.

But suppose Diathesia, your second cousin from East Nowhere, suffered from mental illness—of any type—what are the chances then? You can see from Table 3 that the more distant the patient's relationship to you, the smaller are your chances of being similarly affected. Speaking practically, there is no point in worrying about anyone more genetically distant than a first-degree relative. Scientists estimate that any baby has a 6 percent chance of a birth defect of some kind, but this does not deter most people from plowing right ahead and having children anyway. Neither should the "likelihood" of schizophrenia in a distant relative.

TRANSLATION

The problem of transmission of psychosis from parent to child has begun to yield to scientific inquiry. But how is the genetic disposition translated into the mental illness? The scientist's job is to forge a logical chain of evidence between your relative's inheritance and the onset of his clinical illness. Unfortunately, our present state of sophistication leaves a number of links lying about loose on the ground. And in fact we cannot even be sure how many of these links actually belong in the chain.

Scientists would like to discover a logical causal sequence like those which have been discovered for other medical illnesses. The sequence would start with a defective gene causing an abnormality of one of the brain enzymes, those complex protein molecules which catalyze (speed up) the rate at which the body converts food to energy. The next step: this enzyme deficiency alters the available amount of certain chemical substances vital to normal brain functioning. Cellular activity is affected, in turn producing the depression, psychotic thinking, or abnormal behavior which complete the chain. But techniques for directly studying brain enzymes have only recently become available, and the field of neurobiochemistry is still in its infancy. Nonetheless, some advances have been made.

Affective Disorder

Over the past decade or more, a group of scientists at the National Institute of Mental Health in Bethesda, Maryland, has been largely responsible for developing a model which explains many aspects of both mania and depression. Let us look at this model now, with the help of the accompanying diagrams.

The brain is, after all, nothing more than a highly specialized tangle of nerves. Everything that we sense, think, or do comes about on the basis of the complex communications between the nerves in the brain. As tightly packed as brain cells are, they do not directly touch each other, but are separated by a few thousandths of a millimeter of the fluid which cushions and bathes the entire nervous system. Impulses travel from one nerve to the next not by sparks of electricity like lightning, but by a chemical reaction.

Figure 12.7a shows two nerves in their resting state. In the storage granules of the nerve on the left is contained norepinephrine (NE), the neurotransmitter manufactured by the body and kept in readiness at the ending of the nerve. Across the way (the space between the nerves is called a *synapse*) is a receptor site located on the next nerve to be stimulated. When the NE molecule occupies this receptor site, it stimulates the nerve on the right to send off its own electrical impulse, continuing the message on its journey through the brain. In Figure 12.7b, a nerve impulse has come to the foot process of the first nerve, causing the storage granule to release its supply of NE into the synapse. Only a fraction of a second later (Figure 12.7c) one of the NE molecules has occupied the receptor site on the second nerve ending, stimulating it.

Once the neurotransmitter has done its work, the receptor site releases it (Figure 12.7d). Some is washed from the intercellular

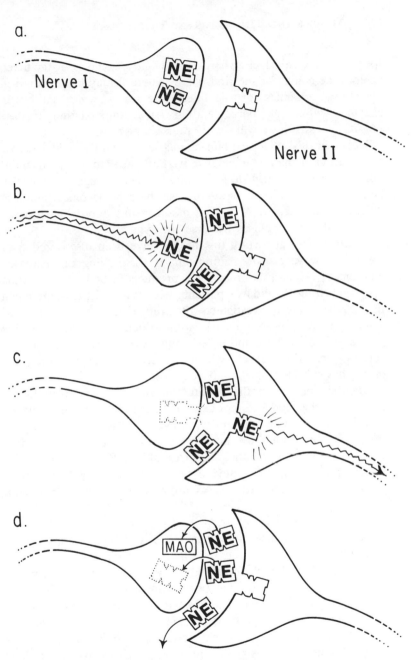

a.

Nerve I

NE
NE

Nerve II

b.

NE

NE

NE

c.

NE

NE

NE

d.

MAO

NE

NE

NE

Figure 12.7   Nerve Function

space and destroyed elsewhere in the body; some is again taken up into the ending of the first nerve, where it may be re-stored in the storage granules for use later. The rest is destroyed by an enzyme within the nerve ending called monoamine oxidase (MAO), of which we will say more in chapter 14.

How can this model explain manic-depressive disease? Suppose that the job of the nerve synapse we have just studied is to maintain its owner's mood. If too few impulses get through this synapse, he feels depressed; if too many impulses pass, he becomes euphoric, "high," or too happy. A normal mood results only when just the right number of impulses traverse the synapse.

Several facts supporting this model have been discovered over the past few years. Most important is the finding of decreased amounts of NE and its breakdown products in body fluids (urine and cerebrospinal fluid) of patients with severe depression. When these patients are reinvestigated after returning to a normal mood state, the levels of NE have also returned to normal. Patients with mania often have more NE than normal in their urine and cerebrospinal fluid, levels which decrease to normal when the mania has subsided.

Even coupled with the genetic information we have already mentioned, this model cannot explain all the facts known about depression. It is too simple and will have to be modified or revised in the future. Within the next few years we may discover that other neurotransmitters help control affect. But right now this system provides a reasonable explanation of many facts and a reasonable theoretical framework upon which to base treatment.

Schizophrenia

Because biochemical hypotheses are testable, scientists have naturally tried to find one to explain schizophrenia. Recently, dopamine (DA), a chemical which acts as a neurotransmitter in some parts of the brain, has been proposed as the culprit.

One bit of evidence has to do with the amphetamines, drugs which act as stimulants to the brain much like the caffeine in your cup of coffee. These substances not only can worsen a schizophrenic's psychosis, but normal people who take a high dose of these drugs sometimes develop an amphetamine psychosis which looks just like paranoid schizophrenia. How does this happen? The amphetamines release DA from storage granules in the brain (Figure 12.8a), in turn stimulating the nerve on the other side of the synapse to fire more frequently. Some scientists now believe that a similar mechanism may underlie naturally occurring schizophrenia.

A second line of evidence has been developed from studies of how neuroleptic drugs (chapter 15) exert their antipsychotic effects—probably by occupying receptor sites, thereby blocking DA from entry (Figure 12.8b). Those neuroleptics which most powerfully block DA receptor sites also have the strongest antipsychotic effects. Whether these findings will eventually prove yet another blind alley in the maze of schizophrenia research we will know only with the passing of time. Thus far, they have provided some very interesting straws in a powerful wind.

Emphasis on heredity and biochemistry occasionally causes a sense of futility about the future for the mentally ill, whom some people envision plodding lockstep, willy-nilly, to their foreordained fate. But these fears about biology's tyranny over the individual are groundless. The most notable modern example is that of phenylketonuria, which years ago inevitably led to mental retardation. But once its hereditary biochemical basis was discovered, it became possible to diagnose affected children within hours of birth and to place them on a special diet which allows normal development. When the biochemical deficiency is found for schizophrenia, similar preventive measures may prove effective for this illness as well.

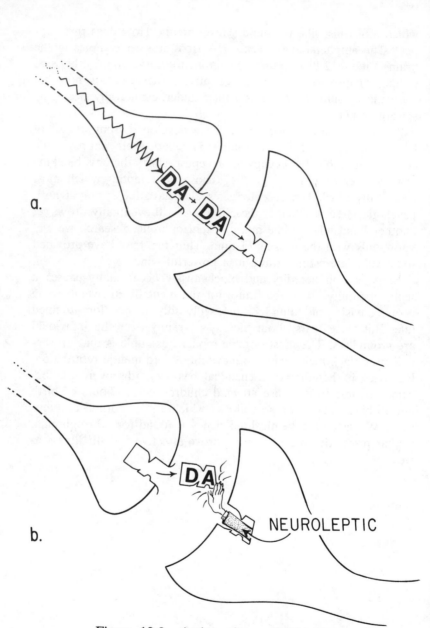

Figure 12.8   Action of neuroleptic drugs.

13.
Suicide:
The Final Solution

With its potential for final tragedy, the suicide attempt poses a psychiatrist's most difficult challenge. Any miscalculation in his evaluation or management and he may lose a patient, and the patient his life. So any physician who deals with suicidal people values the help of relatives and friends who can provide both the information and the manpower needed to see the patient safely through this difficult time. The trouble is, many relatives find the prospect of suicide too painful to face, so they ignore the circumstances leading to it. When an attempt finally comes, it often catches them unprepared. If this has happened to you, it means neither that you care less nor that you are stupid—thoughts which can haunt anyone who has been surprised by an attempt. But you do need to learn some facts which can help you work with the psychiatrist to prevent a replay of this drastic finale to mental illness.

We won't use the term suicide to mean activities like cigarette smoking, drunk driving (usually), or trifling with the wife of your neighbor who was a middle linebacker for the Packers. Although everyone acknowledges the risk in these activities, they are undertaken without the intent to die. Suicide is simply acute, intentional self-destruction.

Through history, it has been regarded from a changing perspective. That which we now regard with horror was considered honorable by the ancient Romans, who preferred skewering themselves upon swords to the disgrace of defeat in battle, a philosophy which persisted to the present century in the Japanese Samurai. Primitive societies believed suicidal behavior signified an infestation of devils, and our own traditional view of suicide as sin comes from the Sixth Commandment, "Thou shalt not kill." In more puritan times, this attitude resulted in some unbelievably harsh, repressive measures against suicides and their families, whose possessions were confiscated, whose children were ostracized, and to whom burial in hallowed church ground was denied. But about two centuries ago we began to recognize suicide as a sign, not a sin—a sign of sickness, to be treated, not exorcised. Not a disease itself but more than just another symptom, suicide stands alone in terms of its consequences for the patient and his family. So we will devote a chapter to suicide and suicide attempts, considering symptoms, diagnosis, treatment, and management together.

Factors in Suicide

According to official figures about twenty-five thousand people kill themselves each year in the United States. But because it still bears the stigma of moral wrongdoing, suicide is so vastly under-reported that the real figure is probably three times as great. It accounts for about one percent of all deaths in this country, where it now ranks as the eleventh leading cause of death. Better record keeping might promote it to seventh or eighth. High as these figures seem, we are no worse off than average, and much better than some: three and one-half times as many West Berliners as Americans kill themselves, on a *per capita* basis.

People who complete suicide differ in important ways from those who merely attempt it, even beyond the obvious difference in outcome. So we must always specify carefully which group we are discussing.

Happily, the numbers themselves differ greatly. Suicide attempts are eight to ten times more common than completions—and for adolescents the ratio may be as high as one hundred to one. Suicide attempters are *not* simply "completed suicides gone wrong." Many do it to seek attention, not death, and clearly they should not be lumped in with those who seriously intend to die. Without careful education it can be difficult to tell the difference between the frivolous and the sincere attempt. So with the ratio of attempts to completions running eight or ten to one, it is small wonder that people adopt a ho-hum attitude toward suicide attempts. Understandable, but this kind of thinking can catch you napping.

Sex

The sex ratios in both suicide attempts and completions are striking, and different. For completed suicides men outnumber women three to one, but for attempts the ratio is the reverse, women predominating by the same margin. Why the discrepancy? The fact that twice as many women as men see psychiatrists has been well established and suggests that women are better able to talk out their feelings, rather than acting them out violently. Our society frowns upon men crying, and the same taboos may also cause those of the so-called stronger sex to "tough out" emotional distresses until they become so overwhelming that death seems attractive. Women more often use suicide attempts to advertise for help before it is too late.

Partly for this reason, partly because she hates to be disfigured even in death, a woman usually chooses less lethal means, such as drug overdose and wrist-cutting. A man will prefer firearms or leaping from heights (one, rescued from an open manhole into which he had leaped, wryly guessed he had tried to commit sewercide). Finally, hormones may contribute to the discrepancy between the sexes, or to differences among women. During pregnancy, for example, a woman is only about one sixth as likely to commit suicide as at other times.

Age

Age is also an important factor. Suicide attempts are much more common in younger people, completions relatively uncommon. With advancing age the likelihood of completed suicide also increases, rising steeply after the age of forty-five. This is not to say that young people never kill themselves, which does occasionally happen. In the fifteen- to nineteen-year age group, suicide forms the third leading cause of death (it is actually not all that frequent except by comparison—few teenagers die of anything). On college campuses it is the second leading cause of death (next to accidents), and even an occasional little child will kill himself. But older people are generally more likely to fall victim than are the young.

Marital Status

A stable family environment best protects against suicide. Single people are somewhat more likely than married people to kill themselves, with widows and the divorced most susceptible of all. A recent loss such as divorce or death of a spouse can make a patient particularly vulnerable, as may other reasons for feeling empty—unemployment and retirement, for example.

Social Factors

Suicide is democratic—it spares no social or economic group. Some professional people are especially prone to it, however, with physicians ranking near the top. (Some writers allege that psychiatrists are more susceptible than other physicians; recent research has proved that this is only a vicious rumor.) Pharmacists and dentists rank even higher on the list than physicians; for reasons which are probably cultural, whites are five times more vulnerable than blacks.

Mental Illness

In 1845, the French psychiatrist Esquirol pointed out that suicide can be due to psychiatric illness. It was a good idea, but way ahead of its time. Even now, in the latter part of the twentieth century, people (doctors, too) rarely connect suicide with mental illness, instead associating it with various real or imagined life stresses. Over the past few years, however, scientists have clearly established that nearly all suicide attempters and completers have serious psychiatric illness. And the type of illness sharply differentiates those two groups.

People with primary depression stand the greatest chance of committing suicide; this diagnosis can be made in about half of all those who do it. Of course, most severely depressed people never even make an attempt, and only about 15 percent eventually take their own lives. Although manics rarely ever kill themselves while euphoric, remember that they can rapidly shift into the depressive phase of their illness, at which time they become vulnerable. Overall, the bipolar patient is at least as likely as the unipolar to commit suicide—no room for complacency here.

Alcoholism contributes the next highest percentage to suicide statistics. About a quarter of all completed suicides have had the serious drinking problems we discussed back in chapter 2. The daily social problems an alcoholic faces lead to alienation from family and friends and to ever-diminishing self-esteem. Small wonder then that as they reach the end of their financial and psychological resources, many of these unfortunate people decide to "take the easy way out." This likelihood increases considerably when alcoholism complicates an already-existing depression or psychosis.

Schizophrenics constitute a smaller proportion—probably under 10 percent—of all suicides, but only because schizophrenia is less common than depression or alcoholism; probably around 10 percent of all schizophrenics do kill themselves. These people are particularly vulnerable when they are young and have been ill only a short time. The impulse to die comes during an acute attack of illness when they realize that something is incredibly, perhaps incurably, wrong and to continue the struggle with psychosis seems futile.

Can the tendency to suicide be inherited? The example comes to mind of Ernest Hemingway, who killed himself with a shotgun some years after his father had shot himself with a revolver. But the suicide is only a symptom of the predisposing psychiatric illness, which does have a genetic basis. The symptom itself cannot be inherited. Even if a close relative commits or attempts suicide, feel reassured that this does not constitute a "taint" which predisposes you or your family to the same fate. In fact, suicide is one of the more preventable problems we encounter in psychiatry.

IDENTIFYING SUICIDE RISK

Now we can sketch a picture of the person most likely to commit suicide. Because he has been recently divorced or widowed, this middle-aged white man lives alone. He has become increasingly depressed over the past several months, and since he lost his job he has had little to do but sit around the house and indulge his already heavy drinking habits. Of course, plenty of people who do not fit this typical profile may also stand at considerable risk for suicide. Just because Cousin Maria is a young, married, and totally abstemious Chicana is no proof against an attempt at self-harm, providing that other predisposing factors (like depression) are strong enough.

The presence of several of these factors together suggests the need for special alertness. A previous suicide attempt also conveys greater risk, and you should be especially concerned if it was a serious one either medically (endangering life or limb) or psychologically (he really wanted and expected to die, or he took pains to insure that he would not be discovered in the act). Finally, if your relative has the means to carry out a successful attempt (his gun collection or hoard of sleeping pills) you should also revise upwards your estimate of risk.

Although stress without an underlying psychiatric illness seldom leads to suicide (the suicide rate actually dropped in England during the blitz), a stressful event such as a family argument may provide "the last straw" for someone who has had suicide on his mind. But this is not to say that the stress itself caused the suicide. One day in the park, for example, a pigeon dropped its calling card squarely on the head of a seriously depressed postman. Sighing deeply he muttered, "Even the birds . . ." and a short time later leaped from a building to his death. Just as bird droppings did not cause this man's suicide, families should not hold themselves responsible for suicides or attempts in their relatives. When a tragedy does occur, it invariably happens despite the best efforts of family and friends, not because of them.

Suicide intent is almost always a transient, even fleeting state of mind. Cousin Pete awakens one morning to realize that he cannot control his drinking, and he becomes despondent. Uncle Henry's future seems suddenly gloomy and hopeless on the day that he returns to find that his wife has left him, taking their children with her (or leaving them with him). Lois Downing had struggled on for months before the apparent hopelessness of her situation crystallized into plans for suicide. But what each has in common with virtually all other suicidal people is the potential for complete recovery, if alert relatives intervene and competent physicians begin treatment. (Contrary to logic, terminal or chronically debilitating illnesses form only a small percentage of either attempted or completed suicides.)

The problem with suicide is, of course, that once it has happened, there is little you can do to pick up the pieces. But a suicide attempt, plan, or idea is quite different—it offers you another shot at solving the problem, for whether the patient intended his suicide attempt to end fatally or as a cry for help, it conveys an important message of *some* kind. Both you and the doctor should regard it as a statement of serious distress, an attempt to communicate thoughts or ideas which your relative has found too unacceptable to express otherwise.

Regarding attempts as communication has a lot of practical value, particularly once we dispel the foolish notion that "those who talk about suicide never do it." This hoary story has been debunked more often than the Colonel cooks chicken, yet it keeps returning to affect the way people deal with their suicidal relatives. For one thing, it requires considerable mental gymnastics to convince yourself that Uncle Henry, always a model of stability and common sense, could ever *really* do anything foolish like that. But for any of a dozen reasons Uncle Henry has changed—temporarily his self-esteem has plummeted and his usually excellent judgment has given way to darker thoughts at which he may only hint. Obviously, your only safe course is to regard every statement of suicide intent as serious, every gesture as genuine, until the psychiatrist assures you that your relative does not have an illness associated with high suicide risk (primary affective disorder, schizophrenia, alcoholism). Until this point has been firmly established, you simply cannot afford to regard any communication about suicide as less than deadly serious—you could be dead wrong.

Many severely suicidal people *do* talk before an attempt— perhaps two-thirds of those who have actually gone on to kill themselves. And most have told several people, often including their physicians. But even when faced with broad hints of impending tragedy, families and doctors as well are often reluctant to take the bull by the horns and ask about suicidal ideas. They think they will only distress the individual further or will put ideas into his head. These fears are totally unjustified. If he really has been having morbid thoughts, your relative will probably feel relieved at bringing them out into the open; your uncritical acceptance of them will help to lessen his embarrassment and encourage further "unburdening." But like pregnancy, you cannot solve suicide by ignoring it.

Nor can you depend upon your relative to clearly, unmistakably state his intentions. It takes little special insight to recognize bald statements like "I've decided to take poison" or "I bought a gun today to shoot myself." All you need then is the courage to act. But to "hear" some of the less obvious signals of distress requires careful listening and sensitivity. "You'd all be better off if I were dead," "It all seems so useless," "I just don't feel that I can go on," and "There's no hope left for me" are all statements which can be easily overlooked, particularly if you fear upsetting your relative with further questions or if you are afraid of his answers.

In communicating suicide intent, actions sometimes speak softer than words. For example, if Grandpa wills his body to science at age eighty it may seem perfectly natural, even altruistic—but it could be that he has become abnormally preoccupied with death. In one group of people who donated their bodies to a medical school, a substantial number actually committed suicide. Distress may also be noticed, but more often goes undetected, in those who set their affairs in order by making wills, giving away their possessions, or by attending church faithfully for the first time in years. One university professor systematically divested himself of all research, administrative, and teaching responsibilities before taking home a large bottle of lethal barbiturates from the laboratory where he had worked. These and other subtle changes in behavior will escape the attention of the doctor, who does not know his patient's routine. It must often be left to the family or friends (or attorney) to observe, to draw conclusions, and to take appropriate action.

But even the best observer in the world cannot infer danger from a suicide communication when there has been none. Nearly 40 percent of those who kill themselves tell no one of their plans; death comes as a complete surprise to everyone. Young schizophrenics particularly fall into this category, like the twenty-year-old boy who, the day he was released from a month-long stay in a psychiatric hospital, was helping his father clean out the garage, came across a loaded pistol, picked it up, put it casually into his mouth, and squeezed the trigger, killing himself instantly. Other patients may become so preoccupied with the hopelessness of the situation that without clearly realizing what they are doing, they make attempts upon their lives.

Ardetha Roper indignantly denied death wishes or suicidal ideas when she was admitted to the hospital, but because her doctor knew that people with agitated depressions can suddenly become desperately irrational, he put her on "suicide precautions" anyway. Later, her guardian nurse sitting just outside the door, she hanged herself with a loop of her bathrobe sash thrown across the top of the door. Vigorous resuscitation literally restored her to life. A month later, successfully treated for her depression, she walked out of the hospital well and happy.

WHAT SHOULD YOU DO?

Once you have picked up cues which make you suspect your relative of harboring designs on his life, your next step should be the logical one: go ahead and ask him about them. You will not be putting ideas into his mind, only giving him a chance to ventilate his feelings, perhaps helping him to better understand himself. And your inquiries will reassure him that someone he loves knows and cares. If he tries to put you off with jokes or an air of wounded dignity, he may simply be denying his own frightening thoughts. Then, and particularly if he has depression, alcoholism, or schizophrenia, keep a close eye on his mood and a little later ask the same questions again—you may get further on the second or third try.

You should act on your suspicions the moment they arise. In suicide prevention the "stitch in time" phenomenon is all-important. If you sit around debating whether Mom is either too sensible or too chicken to kill herself, you may learn to your sorrow that she is not. So, if your suspicions have become aroused, rouse your psychiatrist, from a sound sleep if necessary. (Because he has had more experience than you in this area, you may find his alarm greater than yours.) His experience in distinguishing those who are likely to make an attempt from those who are not will enable him to decide what steps may be necessary.

After you have carried your fears to the doctor and he has made his recommendation, follow it. Few things frustrate a psychiatrist more than to listen to your concerns, to become enough concerned himself to recommend hospitalization only to hear you say, "Oh no, he couldn't take that!" Stuff and nonsense—of course he can take it! He may not last long without it. The psychiatrist who deals with serious mental illness every day becomes pretty conservative. He knows that in any given case the chances are 95 percent or better that the patient will not commit suicide. But no psychiatrist can tolerate the possibility of suicide in *any* of his patients, let alone five out of every hundred, so he tends to err on the cautious side. In the hospital your relative will be watched day and night—can you assure the same degree of safety at home?

If hospitalization is simply impossible, other potentially life-saving steps should be taken. Although locking up, disabling, or removing firearms from the house seems a pretty obvious measure, a surprising number of people neglect this simple stratagem. The doctor may ask you to monitor your relative's medicines, keeping large quantities of potentially lethal drugs like antidepressants and sleeping pills under lock and key. Or he may prescribe only a small number of pills at a time—as little as a half-week's supply of antidepressants, for example, trying to hold down the risk when these drugs must be in the house. And while you are at it, you might as well discard the forest of old prescription bottles which grow in the average medicine cabinet—no point in courting disaster with outdated, unneeded pills.

Right up to the final moment, the suicidal patient remains ambivalent. Usually he does not really want to die at all, only to be relieved of his intolerable burden. A genuine death wish is usually short lived. There are psychiatrists among us (particularly Thomas Szasz) who would have you believe that suicide is an act of free will, and that someone who decides to do away with himself should be allowed to proceed. But the mind which conceives of suicide is not free at all, but rather a prisoner of mental illness.

Once this shackle has been cut away and the patient returns to mental stability—the nearly invariable outcome—he feels immense gratitude towards those who helped preserve his life. With affection and careful attention, you will be able to bring your relative through his crisis to the point where he can, if grudgingly, agree with Dorothy Parker's dour reflection:

> Razors pain you;
> Rivers are damp;
> Acids stain you;
> And drugs cause cramp.
> Guns aren't lawful;
> Nooses give;
> Gas smells awful;
> You might as well live.[1]

Part III
Doing: Treatments and Management

14.
Drug Treatment I: Antidepressants

MID-STATE PSYCHIATRIC HOSPITAL
Progress Notes—Lois Downing

Feb. 21. 28 y/o m/w/f[1] transferred from ICU[2] with barbiturate and carbon monoxide poisoning three days ago. Now alert, oriented but withdrawn, tearful, offering no spontaneous conversation. History from husband of several months depression. Will begin Elavil 50 mgs. daily, increase rapidly.

Feb. 23. Sleep improved on Elavil 100 mgs. q.h.s.[3] but patient spends much time staring out window; little spontaneous conversation. Admits to marked feelings of guilt: "They should have left me in the car." Affect generally dull, but she becomes tearful as she mentions "the harm I have done my family."

Feb. 25. On Elavil 200 mgs. q.h.s. patient complains some of dry mouth, but sleeps soundly all night. She takes a dull interest in visits from her husband, smiled at flowers he brought. Has begun to discuss her feelings prior to suicide attempt: inadequacy as mother, nonfulfillment in homemaker role; "nobody understands or cares."

Feb. 28. Over the weekend, marked improvement. Now she wears makeup, smiles frequently, and speaks spontaneously. Insight has improved, and she has begun to speak of depression in past tense: "I just kept feel-

---

[1]Twenty-eight-year-old married, white female
[2]Intensive Care Unit
[3]Each bedtime (q = each, h.s. = hour of sleep)

ing worse and worse. No matter what happened. I couldn't see any good in it. It was all so worthless."

Mar. 1   This morning, metamorphosis! Lipstick, eye shadow, and hair styling have transformed Mrs. Downing into a butterfly. She smiles readily, takes an active part in ward meetings (elected chairman). In talking with other patients, she has learned that her depressive feelings were by no means unique, and although she now regrets making a suicide attempt, she has lost her delusional guilt and feelings of worthlessness. "I've really got a lot to live for." Beginning to consider plans for discharge—"Bored with hospital."

Mar. 3   After an overnight pass with her husband, she returns this morning cheerful and confident she can take up where she left off. Her husband has hired a part-time housekeeper until her strength improves. In a conference with patient and husband this morning, biochemical theory of depression explained again; importance of taking medication regularly each day emphasized. Discharged on Elavil 200 mgs. q.h.s. Return to office in one week.

Prognosis: Excellent!

Before 1940, the outcome of Lois Downing's illness might have been less happy. In that year, American psychiatrists started using electroconvulsive therapy (ECT), at last affording effective treatment to patients with severe endogenous depressions. Before then a doctor could use wet sheet packs to calm his patients, hot baths to relax them, straitjackets to contain them, and sleeping draughts to sedate them. In fact, he could do almost everything but treat their depressions, so patients often spent months (sometimes years) in hospitals awaiting spontaneous remissions.

ECT changed this dismal outlook for tens of thousands of patients, but in the minds of psychiatrists it also fanned the spark of hope for a drug which might help as much as electricity without its side effects. The psychostimulants like dextroamphetamine (sold on the street as "speed") temporarily improved energy and mood, but after a few hours or days the patient "crashed," becoming more depressed than ever. Then in the 1950s researchers testing medicines to treat tuberculosis noted that some of their patients, understandably depressed as they languished in sanitariums, became suddenly more cheerful when treated with a new drug, Marsilid.

It was only a short step to realize that this and other monoamine oxidase inhibitors (named for the way they affect brain enzymes) could help depressions in nontubercular patients, too. Although Marsilid soon fell from use because of serious side effects, several of its less toxic relatives gained rapid popularity. And late in the same decade, a whole new class of antidepressants, the tricyclics, came into use. Then it was off to the races, with new variations introduced every year or two. We will discuss the second class of drugs first, as it is far more widely used today.

The Tricyclic Antidepressants

These drugs, so named because of the three-ringed chemical structure of the molecule, have now been used for two decades. Use by hundreds of thousands of patients has established an unsurpassed record of effectiveness: about 75 percent of patients with primary depressions[4] like Lois Downing's recover when treated with adequate doses of these drugs. Even those patients most helped by the medicine take five days to two or three weeks before obtaining real relief. The drug has a long way to go, after all, from the intestine to the blood stream, metabolized by the liver, then to the brain where it must alter enzymes and other chemicals before it can begin to return mood to normal. Even then relief takes several days, so the time from starting therapy to feeling well again may be anywhere from one to six weeks. Antidepressants do not affect mood in people who are not depressed. Nor do they act like a pep pill to make you feel better than normal—so people looking for a chemical high do not abuse them.

The doctor can choose from a variety of tricyclics, each with a slightly different chemical composition formulated by the drug companies to give it (they hope) an advantage in selling their product. Table 4 lists the tricyclics currently available in this country, along with the trade names under which they are marketed. Because each of these can effectively treat primary depression, you might think that pure happenstance (or whichever pharmaceutical

---

[4]Depressions which develop secondary to other psychiatric illnesses (alcoholism, neurosis, personality disorders, schizophrenia) and reactive depressions respond poorly to antidepressants, which in secondary depressions may be no more effective than sugar pills.

Table 4
Tricyclic Antidepressants

Generic Name	Trade Name
Amitriptyline	Elavil, Endep, Amitril, Limbitrol
Doxepin	Sinequan, Adapin
Nortriptyline	Aventyl, Pamelor
Desipramine	Norpramin, Pertofrane
Imipramine	Tofranil, SK-Pramine, Presamine
	Imavate, Janimine
Protriptyline	Vivactil

salesman most recently visited the doctor's office) dictates the use of a particular drug. Not true. When the doctor chooses his medicines with the common side effects in mind, he seldom has to give additional sleeping pills or tranquilizers. And in psychiatry as in all of medicine, the fewer pills a patient must take, the less chance for harmful side effects, toxicity, or drug dependence.

The most important of these factors is the tendency to cause drowsiness (hypnotic effect) of several tricyclics. The doctor uses this side effect to help the patient who has insomnia—he might just as well take a medicine which will help him sleep while it treats his depression. The drugs on the list are arranged in order from most hypnotic to least, so either Elavil or Sinequan might be used to help the sleepless depressive. He can usually take his entire daily dose at bedtime without losing antidepressant effect—the mood-elevating effect of all tricyclics lasts at least twenty-four hours. Once-a-day administration also decreases the chance that he will forget a dose or neglect to take his medicine altogether.

If your relative paces back and forth in agitation or if anxiety incapacitates him, treatment with the more hypnotic tricyclics at the top of the list may also allow him to avoid tranquilizers. But if he sleeps *too* much or if his depression has caused his speech or body movements to slow down, he will probably feel better with a less sedating drug from lower on the list. The hypnotic effect can persist into the next day to produce undesirable drowsiness at work or at school. Your relative will feel it most during the first few days after he starts taking medicine, though if the first doses are small enough he may not be bothered at all. But if he is, he should not drive a car or operate dangerous machinery until the drowsiness subsides. If he feels drowsy more than a few days, either the dose should be reduced or a new medicine tried.

As with virtually any psychiatric drug, alcohol can add significantly to the sedative effect; if two drinks normally make him drowsy, one drink plus antidepressants or tranquilizers may do the job. Anyone who takes psychiatric drugs should therefore decrease his drinking (and not, as many do, omit a night's dose of medicine because they plan to drink).

Nearly everyone who takes a tricyclic complains of dry mouth, for drying of all mucous membranes is a common sign indicating that the medicine has begun to affect the nervous system. (Lois Downing's doctor used this symptom to judge when he had prescribed a high enough dose of medicine). The dryness can be disagreeable, but you can help by giving your relative gum to chew, hard candy to suck, or something soft to drink. Later, after his mood has stabilized, his physician may be willing to decrease the amount of medicine slightly.

Drying of the intestinal tract can result in fierce constipation. Although this side effect may help those who have had diarrhea as a symptom of depression, it can sometimes be virtually disabling. If the simpler home remedies like prune juice and bran flakes don't help, the doctor may suggest a stool bulk expander like Metamucil or laxatives of varying strengths, starting with milk of magnesia.

Blurring of vision and difficulty urinating occur much less often and have the same significance: the medicine is working. Blurred vision can be a problem for those who must do close work, but it poses no serious hazard; a slight decrease in dose may help. But urinary retention does more than just annoy—if it persists, the bladder can become painfully, even dangerously, distended. Decreasing the dose of medicine ultimately cures this problem, but this takes time and meanwhile emergency catheterization may be necessary to relieve pressure. Should urinary retention occur, you should call the doctor immediately.

Side effects are funny; they can work either way, so opposite reactions are sometimes blamed on the same drug. Sometimes it even seems your doctor is "covering" himself when he discusses them with you. For example, although people usually become sleepy when they take Elavil, occasionally it causes wakefulness instead. Or consider this scenario:

Patient: I've been having trouble with my appetite.
Doctor: Well, Tofranil sometimes stimulates appetite, so you gain weight.
Patient: I mean, food tastes funny and I don't want to eat.
Doctor: Yep, that's Tofranil.

Nearly any side effect can occur with any medicine, and even physicians who have practiced for years hear about new side effects nearly every week. Your relative will undoubtedly develop some of these unwanted symptoms. Most of them are harmless, but you should check them all out with the doctor anyway. Keep a list, if necessary.

Other side effects which occasionally crop up include skin rashes, nausea, dizziness, jitteriness, and tremors, to name only a few. Not serious in themselves, any of them can become bothersome enough to demand a reduction in dose or even a change of medicine. Although mild memory loss ("Where did I put those damned glasses—I just had them in my hand!") is fairly common and generally not too troublesome, more serious confusion can occur. Actual disorientation, even psychosis, can affect anyone, but particularly older people or those who have had previous brain injury. Then, discontinuing treatment becomes mandatory.

Although these drugs have never been proven harmful to a developing fetus, they have never been proven safe, either. An unborn child probably would not be harmed if its mother took antidepressants, but because we cannot be sure, pregnant women should not take these drugs. Depressions in pregnancy can be handled nicely by other methods which are safe for the baby (chapter 17).

One problem many patients fear above all others is weight gain, and for good reasons. Some people who take antidepressants develop ravenous appetites and threaten to grow out of their clothes during the first few weeks of treatment. We don't know exactly why this happens—although the medicine may actually change the way the body metabolizes food, it may more simply stimulate appetite directly. Whatever the cause, the best treatment is to diet—

weight control pills risk interfering with the system in the brain responsible for the depression in the first place, the same one being manipulated by the antidepressants. The doctor can suggest a *sensible* program of slight caloric restriction that your relative will be able to adopt as a long-term measure, eschewing crash diets that he will give up on—with a vengeance! He may also gently recommend some exercise.

Two effects of tricyclics are particularly worrisome—although both occur rarely, one is potentially common. Any of these drugs can lower the "fit threshold" in a very small number (under one percent) of patients, resulting occasionally in a grand mal seizure. This unwelcome occurrence can be terribly frightening at the time, but it does not mean that the patient has epilepsy or will continue to have convulsions once the drug has been withdrawn. Should the doctor decide he has to go ahead with the medicine anyway, he will protect the patient against further seizures by giving an anticonvulsant drug.

The second serious problem with antidepressants is that they are lethal. Indeed, these drugs are among the most dangerous of any used in medicine. A fatal overdose of tricyclics can be as low as 1,000 mgs.—less than a week's supply for many patients—and twice that amount can kill nearly anyone. Fortunately, though depressed patients often have suicidal ideas they seldom implement them with antidepressants. They simply do not guess that a drug designed to relieve their misery could put an even quicker end to it in another way. Your physician may insist on safeguards to prevent access of severely depressed patients to more than a one-day supply of drug at a time. The rest of the medicine you should keep under lock and key.

Whether antidepressants can set off a manic attack has been debated for years without satisfactory resolution. Antidepressants do not elevate mood in normal people, nor can they raise the mood of a depressed patient above its normal level. But occasionally someone taking antidepressants will move from depression right through the normal range and off into manic behavior much like Gilbert Grant's (chapter 2). When it does happen, no one can say for sure whether the medicine was at fault or whether the patient would have become manic anyway—after all, this event is more likely to befall someone with a past history of mania. No matter: when it does (rarely) occur, the doctor readily controls it with other medicines.

MONOAMINE OXIDASE INHIBITORS

These drugs, abbreviated MAOI, first appeared in the late 1950s, but quickly lost favor to the generally more effective tricyclics. Although doctors seldom prescribe them today, MAOIs should be kept in mind for the severe depression which responds poorly to the tricyclics or for one accompanied by a lot of anxiety. A clinical vignette may do more to describe the use of these drugs.

Noah Steam had never been an exciting personality, but he had always gotten by. Average grades in college had somehow netted him a good engineering position in the aviation industry, where he had proven himself imaginative, though far from aggressive. In fact, his chronic lack of self-confidence—the dominant feature of his adult personality—had caused him to turn down several promotions to positions of leadership in his company. Now, at forty-five, he had reached a sort of "mid-life crisis." Over several years he had become increasingly depressed, anxiety-ridden, and even more retiring, qualities which had not yielded to two years of weekly psychotherapy. By the time he consulted his second psychiatrist, Noah had withdrawn from his family, had lost interest in sex, and often entertained ideas of suicide. "I feel better knowing it's there if I need it," he explained.

During a brief hospitalization, he easily tolerated 300 mgs. a day of Elavil. Sleep improved and his thoughts of suicide no longer seemed so imminent, but his depression continued. Thereafter he spent his fortnightly office visits obsessively mulling over a detailed diary of his personal inadequacies. A month of this and his psychiatrist had had enough.

"Mr. Steam, I'm not satisfied with your progress," he said midway through one session. "I'd like to take a gamble, if you're willing." He explained that a drug change might produce greater improvement than had been made before, but that because the new medicine should not be given together with the old, there would be a tapering-off period followed by a week of no medicine at all. During this week he could become much more depressed and might even need rehospitalization.

"Well," murmured Noah, "I guess it's worth the chance." He smiled crookedly. "It's not much of a life anyway. And if it gets too bad, there's always my old standby."

Over the next three days Noah tapered off his Elavil, and a week later he was back in the office. On no medicine, his depression had worsened and once again insomnia plagued him, but his suicidal ideas had not worsened. His doctor gave him a prescription for the MAOI Nardil and a diet list to follow, telling him that a few foods could interact harmfully with the medicine. With the warning to call should he experience dizziness or fainting spells (the major side effects of the medicine), he ushered Noah out the door.

Noah returned two weeks later, his manner changed. Now he leaned back comfortably in his chair, a half-smile playing across his face. His diary of complaints nowhere in evidence, he described the changes he had noted in a strong, clear voice. His mood and self-esteem had so improved that he now demanded and received attention and respect at work, and he talked confidently of heading up a new project being developed by his department. His interests had improved also: now he participated regularly in Scouts with his son and sex with his wife—almost to a fault.

"Sometimes I think she doesn't quite like the new me." He complacently rolled a cigar between thumb and fingers. "I used to be so docile that I'd do about what she wanted. Now, after all these years I'm making some demands on *her,* and I guess it takes some getting used to."

Of course, the response is not always (or even usually) as spectacular as this, but it happens often enough to warrant a trial of MAOIs in patients with long-standing anxiety-laden depressions. The drugs available include phenelzine (Nardil), tranylcypromine (Parnate), isocarboxazid (Marplan), and nialamide (Niamid). The MAOI pargyline (Eutonyl) has only been approved in this country to treat high blood pressure, but it too has antidepressant properties and has been used in patients who have both problems.

As his doctor mentioned to Noah, the most frequent side effect of these drugs is dizziness due to sudden drop in blood pressure. Known as orthostatic hypotension, it happens when a person stands up and the blood rushes to his feet. It can lead to fainting spells and may require lowering the dose, although the patient can sometimes solve the problem by getting up more slowly than usual or by wearing support stockings.

A more dangerous, though fortunately less common reaction

to the MAOIs is quite the opposite—sudden onset of severe high blood pressure. The patient experiences this as excruciating, throbbing headaches, which can occasionally lead to strokes. This reaction is usually due to interaction of the drug with tyramine, an organic compound contained in certain foods. Even though far fewer than one percent of all patients could have such a reaction, all patients are placed on a diet when they start one of these drugs.

This diet is not onerous. It mainly prohibits foods prepared by the aging of protein—sour cream, yogurt, and any aged cheese must be avoided (cottage and cream cheese are allowed). In addition, certain foods naturally contain high amounts of tyramine and must also be omitted: chicken livers (no problem for most people), raisins, dried figs, and pods of broad beans (lima, soybeans and cowpeas); steak sauces, red wine, beer, anchovies, pickled herring, and yeast extract. Chocolate and coffee should be used moderately, and all cold remedies should be avoided. The low tyramine diet should be followed from the day the patient starts his medicine and should be continued for two weeks after he stops. Obviously, if severe headaches occur at any time during treatment, the doctor should be notified immediately.

Combined Therapy

Before Noah's doctor prescribed Nardil, he made sure he had been off the tricyclic antidepressant long enough to eliminate it from his system. He took this precaution because of several published reports of patients who took the two types of drug together, resulting in severe attacks of high blood pressure, some leading to strokes or death. Ample reason for caution! But the psychiatrist who treats many depressions sometimes finds himself in the difficult position of recommending the same combination of drugs he avoided a few weeks before. With a little effort we can resolve this seeming contradiction.

A few depressed patients respond poorly to all other forms of treatment, including tricyclics, MAOIs and shock treatments, but do improve when they take the two types of antidepressants together. These people, many with depression so long-standing it seems part of their personalities, regard the possible risk of combined treatment as negligible compared with the certain agony of continued and otherwise incurable illness. When a doctor starts the two antidepressants together in small doses and carefully watches for blood pressure change, he rarely has trouble. But the patient and his family must be advised that even a slight potential for difficulty exists.

WHY DO THEY WORK?

Medicine abounds with treatments which work, but no one knows why. Aspirin, for example, has been prescribed by four generations of physicians who have not known how it kills pain and lowers temperature. Psychiatrists, surely no better off than other medical specialists, also must often use treatments empirically—that is, *because* they work they continue in use while research into *why* they work goes on. Innumerable double-blind studies which compare antidepressants to placebo (sugar pills) have shown that tricyclics and MAOIs both help patients recover from depression. But how?

This question has been partly answered in the past ten years through numerous experiments with slices of brain in the laboratory and studies of body fluids of patients actually being treated. We can understand the best theory as to how drugs work if we refer again to a diagram of the two brain cells which are trying to communicate with each other (see Figure 14.1). Messages do not pass from transmitting nerve I to receiving nerve II because I lacks sufficient norepinephrine (NE) to jump the synapse. You will recall that monoamine oxidase (MAO) is an enzyme which quickly inactivates some of the NE released from storage granules. Although the purpose of this mechanism is to rid the normal brain of unneeded NE, in a depressed person who lacks sufficient NE anyway, the action of the MAO causes wastage. The MAOIs, not surprisingly, work by inhibiting MAO so it cannot destroy the neurotransmitter. MAOIs allow the transmitter manufactured by the brain to be used more efficiently.

The tricyclics also work by increasing the supply of brain NE, but these drugs go about their job differently. As you can see from the diagram, the tricyclics block reuptake of NE into nerve I, which the brain normally does to conserve NE once it has been used. Less uptake means more NE available in the synaptic space to

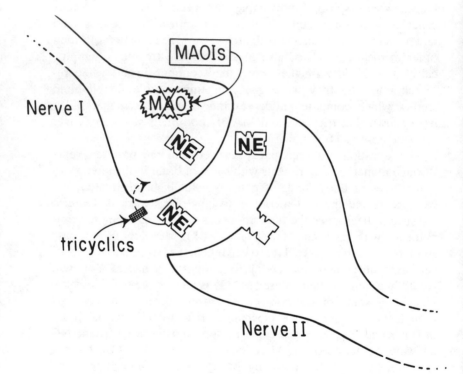

Figure 14.1   How Antidepressants Work

stimulate the receptor site of nerve II, and the patient feels less depressed. The chemical and psychological end result is therefore the same, no matter which antidepressant we use. Only the location within a neuro-synapse distinguishes the actions of these two classes of drugs. You should clearly understand, however, that this scheme is only a theory, not established fact. When we finally learn the complete story, probably within the next generation, it will most likely follow this general plot outline, although the details may vary and a whole new supporting cast may have been introduced.

THE ART OF PILL-PUSHING

By instinct and training physicians are a cautious lot (be glad). When your relative starts taking antidepressants it will usually be with a small amount—25 or 50 mgs. of Elavil at bedtime for a night or two to check for side effects. Finding none, the doctor will raise the daily dose gradually (perhaps over a week or two) to a level determined by the onset of side effects (usually dry mouth or drowsiness) or by improved mood. Most patients need doses from 150 to 200 mgs. a day; a few require higher amounts yet— 300 mgs. or more in rare cases.

The most common error patients make with antidepressant medicine is giving up too soon. They should take 200 mgs. a day or more for three weeks before calling the experiment a failure. For their part (and this is by far the more common mistake), physicians err by prescribing too little medicine. Time and again the consulting psychiatrist sees patients taking 75 mgs. a day of a tricyclic who, partly treated, now sleep well but still have frequent crying spells and guilt feelings. Often these remaining symptoms can be fully relieved by doubling, tripling or even quadrupling the dose. One of the saddest stories in psychiatry, one which need never occur but often does, concerns the depressed patient who for months has been treated with a piddling dose of a medicine which in proper strength has the power to relieve all symptoms.

Once started, how long should an antidepressant be taken? To this complicated question we have as yet no truly scientific answer. The key lies in the fact that no antidepressant cures depression in the same sense that penicillin cures pneumonia or surgery (sometimes) cures cancer. As we have seen in the diagram, the medicines artificially elevate the amount of NE until the brain spontaneously recovers its ability to manufacture and store the stuff. So antidepressants serve only as a crutch to use until recovery takes place. But how long will that be? This varies tremendously with the individual patient, but because the average endogenous depression lasts anywhere from six to twelve months, withdrawing or decreasing medicine before several months have passed invites recurrence of symptoms. So the doctor usually continues the therapeutic dose for at least three or four months before attempting to back off. Then he will reduce it gradually, watching for recurrence of symptoms.

What about long-term side effects? Again, we simply don't know for sure. We do know that some patients have safely taken antidepressants for years but the possibility that trouble could develop makes doctors cautious about prescribing *any* medicine for long periods of time. The probable benefits of the medicine must be balanced against possible harm, a judgment easy to make in the case of chronic depression. Here, the value of treatment is so evident and the chance of harm so slight that, when informed that such a risk exists, patients invariably choose to be treated.

15.
Drug Treatment II: Antipsychotic Drugs

A generation ago, schizophrenics occupied half the hospital beds in this country, and a psychiatrist's options in dealing with them were tightly limited and thoroughly unsatisfactory. He could prescribe barbiturates or bromides, which calmed but did not control the psychosis and which could even produce psychotic symptoms of their own. Or he could use wet sheet packs or the straitjacket, but these "soft chains" did little for the patient's psychosis (or, you can imagine, for his disposition). In 1954, Thorazine burst upon the scene, changing all this.

Its discovery actually was a glorious accident on the road to a new surgical preanesthetic, a drug intended to keep patients calm before surgery without rendering them unconscious. When Thorazine proved equal to this task, psychiatrists quickly realized it might have applications in their field. There, too, it enjoyed immediate success, allowing chronically ill patients to return home or to lead less strictly supervised lives. As the population of mental hospitals declined for the first time in decades, the race to discover new drugs with similar actions began. With nearly a score of these drugs now on the market they rank among the most used (and abused) in psychiatric practice.

At least a part of the problem has to do with their popular name: major tranquilizers. Because they tranquilize highly disturbed, agitated schizophrenics, physicians and patients alike often assume that they also calm patients who suffer nothing worse than simple anxiety. Later we will see just how wrong this assumption is, but for now let us begin calling these drugs by a better name, the *neuroleptics*. Psychiatrists coined this term (from the Greek *neuro* = nerve and *lepsos* = to seize) to sharply distinguish these drugs from minor tranquilizers (chapter 16) and from other drugs which have antipsychotic properties.

Neuroleptics do calm agitated patients. You see this effect almost immediately after an injection and within a few minutes of an oral dose. But the second characteristic of these drugs is even more important—to relieve the symptoms of psychosis. In adequate doses over a sufficient period of time—anywhere from a week to three months—delusions and hallucinations gradually melt away, leaving only the ghostly memory of absurd thoughts and irrational behavior. Even profoundly tangential speech improves to the point that the patient can once again "talk in a straight line."

MID-STATE PSYCHIATRIC HOSPITAL
Discharge Summary

Name: Lyonel Child
Admitted: 12–21–78
Discharged: 2–17–79

History: This 25 y/o s/w/m[1] was admitted with a chief complaint of "They told me to do it." History of a lifelong seclusive, schizoid personality insidiously developing auditory hallucinations and delusions of persecution. Sheriff's deputy picked patient up after he fired shotgun into house of the girl he thought jilted him (no one hurt—she wasn't home).
Physical Examination: Healthy male; normal neurological.
Mental Status on Admission: Youthful appearing, unshaven, he sat nervously on edge of chair, eyes darting about the room. Little spontaneous conversation; when questioned, replied appropriately, but frequently stopped in mid-sentence, cocking his head as if listening to something. Affect bland and unchanging as he described voices in the air which instructed him to "kill her." Deluded that others knew his unspoken thoughts and plans; delusions of reference (winking and hand gestures had special meaning for him). Orientation intact and sensorium clear. Insight into illness nil, judgment very poor by history.
Laboratory Data: Blood count, urinalysis, chest and skull x-rays all normal.
Treatment: Prolixin 10 mgs. per day for one month, then switched to Prolixin Decanoate 25 mgs. intramuscularly every two weeks. Daily psychotherapy was brief and supportive, and

encouraged him to take medicine and return for visits when discharged.

Hospital Course: During initial three-day evaluation without drugs, patient remained seclusive and suspicious and continued to have blocking of speech. No change through first week on drugs, during which he continued to have infrequent hallucinations. He then spoke less and less about his hallucinations, and his speech lost its halting quality. Affect remained stiff for first month, but he later relaxed and began to smile appropriately and showed increasing modulation in his voice. During the first two weeks on medicine, he remained utterly convinced that staff members and fellow patients would purposely walk in front of him to try to "trip him," or winked or gave other signs to annoy him. By the fourth week, the frequency of such occurrences had diminished, and thereafter he admitted that they may have been imagined. By discharge, he was substantially symptom-free and had insight that he had been ill and the judgment to know he needed medicine.

Final Diagnosis: Paranoid schizophrenia.

Condition at Discharge: Greatly improved.

Disposition: Discharged to parents' home, to return every two weeks for Prolixin Decanoate shots.

Fortunately for him, neuroleptics vigorously attack the very symptoms that most bothered Lyonel Child. His delusions yielded completely, though the drug required several weeks to do the job. And his psychotic withdrawal—sitting alone in his room for months brooding about "his" girl—eventually remitted, too. Hallucinations didn't bother Lyonel much, but they did Anthony Yelle (chapter 9)—for him, the neuroleptics proved a godsend, at last quieting the clamoring cacophony of voices spun out of his diseased mind. Generally, hallucinations of all types respond well, though, like Anthony, a few severely ill people remain ever aware of the dull rumbling of voices somewhere in the background. The uncooperativeness (negativism) which so many patients develop as they become locked in the grip of illness also responds well to drugs, as do disorders of the form of thought (tangentiality, blocking, and other sorts of loose associations).

Disorders of affect present problems even for those big guns of the therapeutic armamentarium. Miles Brodeur's silly inappropriateness will probably improve with treatment, but his affect may never completely return to its premorbid level. It may be left forever slightly blunted or stiff, not so you would pick him out of a crowd as mentally ill, but enough that those who knew him before would recognize the difference if they stopped to think about it.

Type of affect usually does not change much with neuroleptics. For example, they won't budge most depressions and can even do real harm if misused for this purpose. And although many physicians treat anxiety with neuroleptics, this symptom can be better handled with other drugs (chapter 16) which have far fewer serious side effects.

In fact, the only affective abnormality regularly helped by the neuroleptics is mania. For the patient whose severe euphoria and talkativeness constitute a threat to the serenity of the neighborhood and to the sanity of his family, the neuroleptics are essential. When he finally entered the hospital, Thorazine quickly quieted even the bumptious Gilbert Grand (chapter 2), and within three days he lost interest in the grandiose scheme for a transcontinental railway.

DRUGS

An "ideal drug," if there were such a thing, would do everything you wanted it to do and nothing you did not want it to do—and it would be cheap. Because this ideal is unattainable (or, as science fiction writers sometimes suggest, suppressed by the pharmaceutical houses as unprofitable), we must accept compromise. No drug (with the lone exception of lithium) is cheap, so the compromise is always between the wanted and unwanted effects. The doctor constantly asks himself the question, "How can I help my patient the most while harming him the least?" From Table 5 you can see that he has a wide variety of drugs to choose from. And these drugs differ in important ways.

One of the most important features differentiating the many neuroleptic drugs is the dose required to treat a given patient. (This amount varies nearly a hundred-fold—if 100 mgs. of a drug in the high dose group are required for a given effect, 10 to 25 mgs. will produce the same effect in the middle dose group, and 1 to 5 mgs. in the low dose group.) But other factors also go into

Table 5
Neuroleptic Drugs Available in the United States

	Generic Name	Trade Name
High Dose:	chlorpromazine	Thorazine
	chlorprothixene	Taractan
	mesoridazine	Serentil
	promazine	Sparine
	thioridazine	Mellaril
Medium Dose:	acetophenazine	Tindal
	butaperazine	Repoise
	carphenazine	Proketazine
	loxapine	Loxitane, Daxolin
	molindone	Moban, Lidone
	perphenazine	Trilafon
	piperacetazine	Quide
	thiopropazine	Dartal
	triflupromazine	Vesprin
Low Dose:	fluphenazine	Prolixin, Permitil
	haloperidol	Haldol
	thiothixene	Navane
	trifluoperazine	Stelazine

matching a drug to a particular patient, notably genetics. The rate at which the body absorbs, metabolizes, and excretes medicines is at least partly determined by heredity, as several studies have recently proven. So if someone else in your family responded well to Prolixin, for example, the doctor may choose that drug to try first on your relative.

Probably the commonest cause for medicine failure is that the patient simply does not take it. Half or more of schizophrenic outpatients refuse to swallow their pills, "cheeking" them and later spitting them out. This trick has been so universally practiced that physicians even encounter noncompliance with drug prescription in their hospitalized patients. Because what he does not swallow cannot help him, drug refusal often mystifies his relatives. But it makes perfect sense to the patient. Lacking insight that he is sick, he sees no need for pills in the first place. And if he is paranoid as well, drug refusal may seem the only way to protect himself.

To combat this problem, a few years ago drug companies developed a long-acting neuroleptic which can be given by injection every two to four weeks. The medicine, Prolixin Decanoate, is released so slowly into the bloodstream that therapeutic blood levels of the medicine are maintained even though the patient never actively "takes pills." Another advantage: the injectible form requires far fewer milligrams to control symptoms than does the oral form, decreasing chances of serious long-term side effects.

Whether in oral or injectible form, experience with the individual schizophrenic or manic patient determines the dose necessary, and the range varies greatly. A severely manic patient may require up to 2000 or 3000 mgs. of Thorazine per day to keep him calm enough to tolerate even on a locked hospital ward. But for symptom-free maintenance in a schizophrenic patient, 100 mgs. a day may suffice. Because the presenting symptoms can be serious, the psychiatrist usually starts with a higher dose than will eventually be necessary for maintenance. Symptom control in schizophrenia and mania often takes up to several weeks, and if he gradually increased the dose as he does with the antidepressants, it would drag out the treatment process far too long. Once he has controlled the worst of the symptoms, he can decrease the daily dose (often on an outpatient basis) to the smallest amount which will keep the symptoms from breaking out again.

SIDE EFFECTS

As with the antidepressants, the choice of drug often depends upon which side effects the physician wants either to employ or to avoid. Any drug can produce virtually any side effect, so many of those previously mentioned for the antidepressants (blurred vision, skin rashes, dry mouth, constipation, urinary retention) may also occur with the neuroleptics. But several reactions are more or less specific for the neuroleptics, and sometimes they can be predicted by the dose category to which the drug in question belongs.

The high dose neuroleptics more often lead to low blood pressure (the orthostatic hypotension that produces dizziness and fainting spells we discussed a few pages back), so older patients and those with a history of blood pressure problems may do better on a low dose drug. The high dose drugs are also famous for producing drowsiness, so the doctor may use them when he wants to calm an excited patient quickly or to help him sleep. (As with nearly all psychiatric drugs, neuroleptics stay in the body a long time, so an entire day's dose can usually be given at bedtime without losing effectiveness. Although some drugs come in time-release capsules, this conveys a real advantage only to the manufacturer, who can sell them for more.)

Any of the neuroleptics can infrequently cause epileptic seizures, which should cause you to call the doctor right away—they are more frightening than dangerous, but he will want to take steps to prevent any further convulsions. Thorazine can increase sensitivity to sunlight to the point that some patients must take extra precautions against sunburn. Two items on the positive side: knowledgeable drug abusers almost never use neuroleptics—like the tricyclics, they just do not produce a satisfactory high. And, unlike the antidepressants, neuroleptics rarely prove lethal, even in massive overdose. About the only way a potential suicide can succeed with these drugs by themselves is to swallow so many he succumbs from simple gluttony.

But the neuroleptics have another group of side effects all their own—neurological complications which, though they bother some patients to the extreme, are rarely dangerous. It will pay you to learn about these four neurological syndromes, for they occur fairly frequently, yet even physicians sometimes fail to recognize and treat them correctly.

The first of them, pseudoparkinsonism—the most common of the lot—we have already encountered in Emanuel Trimmer. He was the pathetic old gentleman in the nursing home with the persistent back-and-forth "pill-rolling" tremor in his hands and a stiff, mask-like facial expression. Had we asked him to walk, we would have noticed his short, shuffling gait and the difficulty he had moving his foot forward for the first step. This condition was named for its resemblance to naturally occurring Parkinson's disease, due to degeneration of cells (usually for reasons which are unknown) in the base of the aging brain. But when caused by neuroleptic drugs, this uncomfortable and disfiguring condition can affect people of any age. Although any of the neuroleptics can produce pseudoparkinsonism, the low-dose drugs are far more likely than the others to have this effect. So, for any patient who has naturally occurring Parkinson's disease, his psychiatrist will prefer to use one of the high dose drugs instead.

Discontinuing the offending drug is the obvious treatment of choice for this or any other neurological side effect. (You may recall that in Mr. Trimmer's case neuroleptics were really not indicated at all—prescribing them in the first place was a ghastly mistake.) But if neuroleptics must be used despite pseudoparkinsonism, the physician may prescribe an antidote—any one of several antiparkinson drugs which can help diminish the severity of the symptoms. These include biperiden (Akineton), benztropine (Cogentin), trihexyphenidyl (Artane, Pipanol, Tremin), diphenhydramine (Benadryl), procyclidine (Kemadrin), and amantadine (Symmetrel).

Neuroleptics can also cause a jerking of the muscles known as acute dystonia, spasms which occur suddenly, without warning and within a few days of starting treatment. They may cause the patient's head to jerk to the side and his eyes to roll up; his breathing becomes labored, and his muscles develop painful cramps. Once again, low-dose drugs more often cause acute dystonias, and, as with pseudoparkinsonism, treatment is with one of the drugs listed above, some of which may be given by injection for immediate relief.

The dystonias can be quite frightening, and patients complain loudly of them. No wonder, then, that many physicians have fallen into the habit of automatically prescribing antiparkinson drugs whenever they give neuroleptics. But like so many habits which serve as substitutes for thinking, this one too can land your relative in trouble, because the antiparkinson drugs themselves can cause side effects, notably dry mouth and heat intolerance. So with only a fraction of patients (under 10 percent) ever developing neurologic side effects, the antidote should be prescribed only when symptoms arise to demand it.

The third neurological complication encountered, again particularly with low-dose neuroleptics, is akathisia—severe restlessness, especially of the feet and legs, which makes the sufferer unable to sit still more than a few seconds. He shifts from one foot to the other as he tries to make himself comfortable, but finds no relief save in pacing. Sadly, physicians sometimes mistake this side effect of medication for agitation or anxiety, which they then try to cure with more of the same drug which originally caused the problem. Of course, the proper treatment (if the neuroleptic cannot be discontinued) is an antiparkinson drug.

The remaining neurological complication is a bad one. Tardive dyskinesia refers to a peculiar group of tic-like muscle twitches and convulsive movements, particularly of the face and mouth, which afflict a very few of those who take heavy doses of neuroleptic drugs for several years. The movements themselves are not painful—indeed, patients rarely seem to notice them at all. But in severe cases, the flicking of tongues and facial grimacing can be incredibly disfiguring and a source of embarrassment to the family, if not to the patient. There is no truly satisfactory treatment for tardive dyskinesia—the antiparkinson drugs help little, if at all. Sometimes increasing the very drug which caused the condition overloads the circuits to decrease the dyskinesia, but in the long run this "treatment" may actually make the condition worse. Until more research produces neuroleptics which do not cause tardive dyskinesia, this uncommon side effect is a risk which must be accepted in treating patients who truly need antipsychotic drugs. But the risk can be minimized if doctors will only take greater care in prescribing neuroleptic drugs.

As of this writing, and probably for many years to come, we cannot predict how long a chronically ill patient must continue to take medicine. The issue can be decided only through experience with individual patients. Some patients will require continuous treatment to prevent symptoms from developing, but many others can be given drug holidays of varying lengths. For them, medicine may be needed only during the week days, leaving the weekends drug-free. Others may be able to go without for a month or two before restarting treatment. Such dosage schedules require the fullest cooperation of relatives, who must be ready to act quickly if symptoms reappear. When successful, drug holidays help the patient to become less dependent upon both drugs and doctors, boosting his self-esteem. And reducing the chances of tardive dyskinesia and other long-term side effects provides an additional benefit.

HOW DO NEUROLEPTICS WORK?

An excellent question which, like so many in psychiatry, we cannot answer clearly yet. Our best guess is a theory based upon another theory, the dopamine (DA) hypothesis of psychosis we mentioned in chapter 12. If an oversupply of DA does cause delusions and hallucinations, these symptoms should be suppressed by drugs which somehow interfere with transmission of nerve impulses across the synapses where DA acts as the transmitter. And sure enough, a number of different studies have shown that the neuroleptics block the receptor sites for DA, probably by physically occupying them so the DA cannot enter (Figure 6).

How does the neuroleptic get into the receptor site? Probably by trickery. The shape of Thorazine, for example, is similar to DA, and this physical resemblance may serve as the passkey to the DA receptor space. Years in the future when we have learned the whole secret of the effectiveness of the neuroleptics, this theory may prove only its skeleton.

COMBINATION DRUGS

Two pills on the market for several years are nothing more than combinations of a low dose neuroleptic (Trilafon) and a tricyclic antidepressant (Elavil). They were designed for patients who have depression with anxiety/agitation and have achieved wide acceptance with heavy advertising. A few patients appear to respond better to two drugs than to either the antidepressant or neuroleptic given alone. But the main reason for the popularity of these combination tablets is that too few physicians realize that agitation which accompanies depression usually responds well to the antidepressant alone. Most depressed people need the antipsychotic effects of the neuroleptic no more than they do its side effects.

Some doctors use these combination medicines as substitutes for careful diagnosis in patients who present symptoms of both psychosis and depression. But the most common problem lies with the amount of antidepressant in these tablets. They contain

10, 25, or 50 mgs. of Elavil, doses established before physicians realized just how much tricyclic a really severe depression requires. Doctors usually prescribe four tablets of the lower dose combination drug a day—and for most people 100 mgs. of Elavil is only a bare starting dose. If your relative takes these tablets for a severe depression, he may have to swallow a serious overdose of a powerful and potentially dangerous neuroleptic in order to get enough antidepressant. Although combination drugs may sometimes provide a well-diagnosed and stabilized patient with his exact medication requirement, he usually receives rather more, or less, than he and his physician have bargained for.

16.
Drug Treatment III:
Drug Potpourri

Every once in a while along comes a drug which approaches our ideal of efficacy, safety, and cost. Aspirin and penicillin are two notable examples; although they don't help everybody and occasionally they can do real harm, the ratio between helping and hurting is enormous—and they are cheap. So far, the closest psychiatrists have come to this ideal is lithium carbonate.

LITHIUM

Lithium has been around for a while—since the world was made, in fact. It is the only current psychiatric drug which is an element (one of the basic building blocks of the universe, like hydrogen, oxygen, and carbon). In ancient times, the Greeks treated excited and depressed patients with mineral waters which may have contained lithium, but not until the 1800s was the substance identified and named for rock (Greek: *Lithos*), in which it is found. In 1949, an Australian physician named Cade, experimenting with guinea pigs, fortuitously discovered lithium's power to control excitability. But it took another twenty years before the drug came into common use for mania in this country. Because lithium is an element, it cannot be patented, making it one of the least expensive drugs on the market; you can fill a prescription for an average month's supply for five or ten dollars.

Lithium is neither an antidepressant nor a neuroleptic; it is a mood stabilizer in a class by itself. Why it works no one knows for sure, although everyone has his theory. But the fact that it controls manic-depressive disease better than any other treatment has been well established over the years. As Dr. Cade learned just a generation ago, its greatest use is in the treatment and prevention of manias.

"It was really a weird experience," said Gilbert Grand, as he and his wife sat in the doctor's office. "I was awfully excited —not really happy, though I remember saying that I never felt better in my life. It was more of a nervous compulsion to keep talking and doing things. But I didn't really have any fun because I felt so damned uncomfortable. Then there were a couple of days I don't remember much of anything, because that oaf of a nurse kept hitting me with shots of Thorazine. It knocked me out for a while, but when I woke up my mind would still be racing."

The doctor laughed. "She had to do that or you'd have kept the entire ward stirred up twenty-four hours a day," he said. "What happened after you started on lithium?"

"I didn't really notice anything for the first several days— not even any drowsiness. But pretty soon the plans I had made for that railroad began to seem less important to me, and then just plain silly. And as that damned, driving excitement left me and my mind stopped racing, I could talk at a normal rate and pay more attention to other people. And that's the way it's been since I've been out. Right, honey?" He patted her arm affectionately.

"He's certainly been more even-tempered since he's been home. And a lot more understanding about why I can't accommodate him," she added, smiling as she touched her swollen abdomen. "But I think we'd better be getting back to the hospital, anyway."

"What's the problem?" Gilbert asked. "I had my lithium level checked already this morning. It was right on the money."

"Not for you—for me," she replied. "It's about that time. I've had two pains since we've been sitting here talking."

Hurriedly, the doctor wrote a prescription for lithium and handed it to his patient.

"Thanks, doctor," Gilbert said as they shook hands. "You know, it's great to be excited about something really exciting, without being delirious about it!"

This vignette illustrates the two most common uses of lithium: treatment of acute mania, and protecting against it in the future. When the psychiatrist saw that neuroleptics alone could not control Gilbert's excited behavior, he added lithium. This drug does more than just keep the patient quiet—Thorazine can do that, but often without stopping the manic flow of thought. (One patient had to be so heavily sedated with Thorazine that he literally hadn't the strength 'to get out of bed. But he could still move his lips, and when the nurse put her ear close to his mouth, he whispered his ideas about how he could improve the hospital. His grandiosity had not been touched by the conventional drugs.)

Not so with lithium, which does not sedate the patient but calms *all* the symptoms of mania we have previously discussed. This usually occurs within the first week of treatment, sometimes quite suddenly—a patient thoroughly psychotic when he goes to sleep may awaken in the morning normal. As mood normalizes, social life stabilizes. The patient can once again hold a job and live harmoniously with his family, and if he responds really well, he may be able to avoid further hospitalizations and other medicine altogether. Unfortunately, lithium is not as magical when it comes to conjuring away depression. Although either bipolar patients with depression or depressed patients with bipolar relatives may respond to lithium alone, those with unipolar depressions (who make up the majority of patients) are seldom helped.

Effective though lithium can be in treating acute mania, preventing further attacks of mania and depression is really its more important action. Over three-fourths of the bipolar patients who take it find that lithium can stabilize their previously incapacitating mood swings, in effect chopping off the peaks of elation and filling in the valleys of depression. But only pathological mood swings are eliminated—they can still feel the normal highs and lows of mood which we all have occasionally. So once the doctor has controlled the mania, he and his patient must choose: to maintain or not to maintain?

When your relative begins prophylactic lithium treatment, he signs up for a long hitch—it works only as long as he takes it. So his choice depends on how sick he has been. Although he will never become addicted (lithium makes a very unsatisfactory and highly lethal drug of abuse), should he discontinue it he may become manic all over again—full throttle. So if he wants to hold his lifelong mood swings at bay, if he wants to head off further closely spaced or incapacitating attacks, he faces a lifetime of treatment—a small price to pay, for him.

But what about the patient who has suffered only one or two relatively mild attacks, perhaps spaced years apart? No point for him in taking pills year after year if another attack may not occur for a decade. His physician may only continue lithium for a few weeks, gradually reducing it after the acute attack subsides. Several other factors will influence the decision, including the severity of each attack, frequency of attacks, your relative's age, and whether he has other medical problems. In any case, the doctor will want to discuss thoroughly the pros and cons of continued treatment with all concerned (you included) before you agree on how to proceed.

If it is so enormously successful, why *not* use lithium in every suspected case of bipolar disease? For one thing, this medicine is more difficult to give than average: you can't just pop pills until you feel better. Nor can the doctor tell whether he has prescribed the correct dose just by talking with his patient. Instead, he must measure the drug concentration in the blood by ordering a special test called flame photometry—routine blood tests do not give this information—which reports the blood level in milli-equivalents per litre (mEq/l). The therapeutic level of lithium ranges from 1.0 to 1.4 mEq.l. To get there, a patient will usually start on three 300 mg. capsules or tablets a day, and the effect on his blood will be measured every two or three days (weekly if started as an out-patient). The doctor adjusts the dose gradually as dictated by the blood levels, until he reaches the therapeutic range.

If your relative does require long-term maintenance therapy once the acute attack has subsided, his doctor will shoot for a lower blood level—in the 0.8 to 1.2 mEq/l range. But once his level has stabilized on a consistent dose, he will need to have his blood tested only once every month or two. And if he is like most manic-depressives, that will be plenty often to go to the psychiatrist, too. Most bipolar patients neither need nor want much psychotherapy.

Perhaps because lithium is such a simple (in fact, elementary) substance, it produces far fewer side effects than many other drugs used in psychiatry today. Nausea occasionally causes problems, but taking the tablets with meals usually helps. Now and then a patient complains that his mouth tastes funny or that he cannot tolerate the flavor of certain foods. (On his fiftieth birthday, one patient who had taken lithium for several weeks announced that he could "no longer stand the taste of goldfish." His psychiatrist was still trying to recover from his surprise when the man explained, "They used to be my favorite cracker!")

People with kidney trouble sometimes do not excrete lithium rapidly, so it can accumulate to dangerous levels unless they take special precautions. For this reason, doctors should always obtain a blood test of kidney functioning upon starting treatment. The doctor will also recommend that the patient not try to limit salt (if there is too little salt in the body, the kidneys will also retain lithium to try to compensate). If a low-salt diet must be prescribed for other medical purposes, even more careful observation of blood levels than usual will be necessary. And because lithium occasionally interferes with thyroid functioning, an occasional patient will develop an unsightly but benign enlargement of the thyroid known as goiter. So the doctor will also obtain a blood test for thyroid functioning at the beginning of treatment and once a year thereafter.

Another problem: sometimes a patient complains that lithium works too well, that it takes away the highs which he used to enjoy so much. But he usually agrees that the fun of the high is not worth the tortured lows which inevitably follow, and he continues his medicine. Potentially more serious is the case of the writer or poet who believes the drug stifles his creativity. "It holds me back," one young composer complained after two months of treatment. True, during that period he had written little, but neither had he been rearrested for playing shuffleboard nude on a crowded shopping mall. As time goes by, the muse returns, and most of these people find that their new-found self-discipline enables them to be more creative, not less.

In the last very few years a new concept in treating bipolar patients has crept into public acceptance—the lithium clinic. Still available in only a few major cities, either public institutions or private psychiatrists run these clinics, which offer patients the chance of quality maintenance care with the added qualities of convenience and economy.

Lithium clinic patients meet every month or two. Before each session, their blood is drawn to check its lithium level, and the results are made available to them the next day. (Many states prevent laboratories from releasing results to patients, but the doctor can pass on the laboratory values.) Then they have a group therapy session, usually educational in nature, with a psychiatrist or social worker, following which each patient spends a few minutes privately with the doctor. He checks each one for side effects, asks how his mood has been and whether it has been stable, and prescribes additional medication for depression or hypomania if necessary. And he hands out bottles of lithium (usually cheaper than pharmacies can provide it). Here is one-stop shopping—the supermarket approach to psychiatric care.

Despite its tremendous value for manic-depressives, lithium is not the answer for everyone. Some whose manias are arrested by lithium nevertheless continue to have occasional depressions of varying intensities—these from time to time must be treated with antidepressants. Others have mild hypomanias which also require supplementary treatment. Fortunately, lithium can be taken safely either with antidepressants or neuroleptics, as well as with the antianxiety agents, which we will discuss next.

Antianxiety Drugs

The antianxiety (anxiolytic) drugs, sometimes called minor tranquilizers, are important to your relative for two reasons: what they can do for him, and what they cannot. Too bad that too many physicians have trouble distinguishing between the two. These drugs have neither antidepressant nor antipsychotic activity. So what is their place in psychiatric treatment?

In medicine, the name of something does not always describe its purpose, but in this case the term is quite apt. These drugs often effectively relieve the anxiety that occurs either alone or with other psychiatric symptoms. When anxiety accompanies depression, antidepressants usually can control both symptoms. But occasionally fears and worries so bedevil a patient that additional treatment seems warranted. Then the anxiolytic agents may be necessary for a few days until the antidepressants can do their work.

Antianxiety drugs should never be used as the main treatment for depression or psychosis. (If more doctors would learn this, fewer patients would waste time, money—and sometimes their lives—on pills which cannot possibly help.) But because so many patients complain first and most of anxiety, doctors do often treat it alone, forgetting to dig deeper for the underlying depression or psychosis. This leaves the patient feeling a little less tense but as depressed as ever—or perhaps more so, because the anxiolytics act as "downers" in some people. Given to psychotic patients to treat their apparent anxiety, the anxiolytics leave delusions and hallucinations untouched, perhaps even unrecognized.

A number of drugs, some so commonly used that they have become household words, fall into this class. The first six listed (Table 6) belong to the family of drugs called benzodiazepines.

Table 6
Anxiolytic Drugs

Generic Name	Trade Name
chlorazepate	Tranxene, Azene
chlordiazepoxide	Librium, Librax, Libritabs, Menrium, A-poxide, SK-Lygen
diazepam	Valium
lorazepam	Ativan
oxazepam	Serax
prazepam	Verstran
hydroxyzine	Vistaril
meprobamate	Miltown, Equanil

Because these drugs alone among the anxiolytics felicitously combine high effectiveness with minimal danger, they deserve special comment. Each of them has a long duration of action in the body, making once-a-day dosage quite practical (one of them, Tranxene, has recently been marketed in a once-a-day dose given at bedtime). Because all benzodiazepines have some sedative action, giving the entire dose at bedtime may help the still-insomniac depressed patient sleep, yet leave a substantial amount of the drug in his body the next day to relieve anxiety. Of course, giving medicine this way may take away the sense of control the patient feels when he takes a smaller amount of the same drug as needed several times during the day. (One woman said she took the same dose of Librium in the morning as at night so she could maintain her "equal-librium.") Because the body eliminates these drugs over a period of several days, the patient feels no abrupt "drug let-down" or withdrawal symptoms, so he does not become addicted. Although many people take tranquilizers who should not, heavy abuse of the benzodiazepines occurs infrequently.

While on the subject of anxiety, we should mention (only to condemn) the over-the-counter (OTC) tranquilizers advertised in the various media and sold without prescription for relief of "simple nervous tension." The constant harangue of latter-day medicine-show men and electronic hucksters urging people to Compoz their Quiet World by popping a downer of any sort poses several problems. As ever, the most serious of these is ignoring the depression, alcoholism, or other psychiatric disorder for which the anxiety only fronts. Then, treating a symptom and ignoring the illness can be an error of cosmic proportions.

A second objection to these drugs lies in their contents. Many supposedly safe OTCs contain one or more potentially toxic drugs which can generate confusion or psychosis of their own. Bromides, once widely sold as sedatives and still present in preparations like Miles Nervine and Bromoseltzer, are famous for their ability to create a psychosis where none existed before. Because OTCs can be purchased without prescription, they are particularly susceptible to abuse, as the user finds he must forever increase the dose to achieve the same effect.

Perhaps the strongest argument which can be made against either physician- or patient-prescribed drugs for anxiety is the way our society increasingly relies on pill-popping to solve its problems (over 43 million prescriptions written for the benzodiazepines in 1975). For a definite, diagnosable psychiatric disorder medication may be valuable, even mandatory. But trying to eliminate every vestige of anxiety—every emotional pang—smacks of Soma, the panacea Huxley devised so his creatures could escape their *Brave New World*—"A dram is better than a damn" was their rallying cry. (And now, God help us, a compound for the relief of pain called Soma has actually been marketed, hundreds of years ahead of schedule.)

A certain amount of nervous tension has its value—it encourages us to strive harder to achieve. If we could eliminate all anxiety, satisfy all drives, we would probably spend all our time lying about in hammocks waiting to be fed. The psychiatrist only tries to blast the boulders out of the road of life, but pebbles and stones and the remaining loose rock fragments will still be there. We must learn to deal with these by looking to self, not substance, to regulate our subjective experience of day-to-day life.

HYPNOTICS

Although nearly everyone endorses the value of sleeping soundly, scientists have never proven that mental patients recover faster if they sleep better. And hypnotics (sleeping pills) present practical and philosophical problems similar to the anxiolytics. The value of a good night's sleep has also been much ballyhooed in the popular press, particularly on radio and television. Here is another case where focusing on the symptom sometimes overlooks a severe underlying mental disturbance. When doctors recognize the underlying disorder, they often can cure the insomnia without special pills. But in our current far-from-perfect medical world, physicians so often prescribe "sleepers" that every mental patient and his family should know something about them.

The first drug listed (Table 7), Dalmane, is also one of the newest. It provides the most natural sleep with the least potential for serious side effects. Dalmane belongs to the same family (benzodiazepines) as Librium and Valium, and, like its relatives, it has little addiction potential and has not led to deaths from overdoses. Of all the hypnotics in use today, it promotes the type of sleep most like natural sleep. If a sleeping medicine must be used, this is certainly the one to try first. The remaining drugs on the list, which is arranged roughly in decreasing order of safety, might be tried if Dalmane proves ineffective (and if giving minor tranquilizers, antidepressants or neuroleptics at bedtime likewise does not produce satisfactory sleep). Several of the drugs mentioned here, though, deserve special comment.

The barbiturates hold the dubious honor of anchor spot on the

Table 7
"Sleeping Pills"

Generic Name	Trade Name
flurazepam	Dalmane
methyprylon	Noludar
ethchlorvynol	Placidyl
ethinamate	Valmid
triclofos	Triclos
methaqualone	Quaalude, Sopor Parest
chloral hydrate	Noctec, Beta-Chlor, Felsules, Aquachloral
glutethimide	Doriden
Barbiturates*	
amobarbital	Amytal, Tuinal**
aprobarbital	Alurate
phenobarbital	Eskabarb, Luminal
talbutal	Lotusate
pentobarbital	Nembutal, Nebralin, Pento-Del
butabarbital	Butisol
mephobarbital	Mebaral
secobarbital	Seconal, Seco-8, Tuinal**

*Plus a plethora of preparations combining barbiturates with other drugs to be sold as remedies for headache, intestinal complaints, and tension.
**Tuinal contains amobarbital and secobarbital in equal parts.

list. Among the first "tranquilizers," for a long time psychiatrists had little other than these deadly drugs to calm agitated patients. Unfortunately, many physicians still have not kicked the barbiturate habit, despite the fact that they are so dangerous they deserve virtually no place in modern psychiatric treatment.[1] They work by depressing the nervous system, meaning that they reduce the general electrical activity of the brain so it does not work as well—and its owner feels sleepy, slowed down, and sad. These unfortunate effects can worsen an already depressed mood, adding to the patient's illness rather than treating it.

---

[1]However, barbiturates also have marked anticonvulsant properties, so are legitimately used in treating epilepsy.

Because barbiturates also depress activity in the brain stem centers which control respiration and heartbeat, even a relatively minor overdose can be a pretty serious matter, sometimes resulting in death. And as if these problems were not enough, the barbiturates are frequently abused and often lead to addiction. Finally, we have recently learned that they increase the rate at which the body destroys useful drugs such as the antidepressants, thereby reducing their effectiveness. Competent clinical psychiatrists have often (and recently) argued that the barbiturates are as effective as the benzodiazepines and cost far less. Whereas the prescription price is unarguably low, in terms of overdose, addiction, and side effects the true cost of these drugs is high indeed.

Other drugs on the list have some of these same drawbacks. Quaalude has enjoyed a certain popularity with drug abusers looking for a new "downer" and has been traded heavily on the black market. That old standby chloral hydrate (the principal ingredient of the Micky Finn, it has been used since the 1870s) has a low safety margin between effective therapeutic dose and lethal overdose. Doriden invites abuse and addiction and can be fatal in overdose, which, to top it off, is almost impossible to treat. Hardly a drug of choice for the occasional insomniac, yet doctors continue to dispense them by the carload.

STIMULANTS

Stimulants (also called psychostimulants) do just that: they stimulate (increase the excitability of) the nervous system. Most Americans start out the morning with a cup or more of the stimulant caffeine, the habituating effect of which you note quickly on those days your percolator breaks and you get off to work without it: you just don't feel right. You feel similar effects with the other stimulants, too, drugs like the amphetamines (Dexedrine, Dexamyl, Benzedrine) and methylphenidate (Ritalin). Taken by mouth, they almost immediately improve the depressed patient's sense of well-being. So why not simply prescribe direct stimulants for all depressions and have done with it?

We can understand the answer best with the now-familiar diagram of our nerve synapse in the brain (Figure 16.1). You will recall that the tricyclic and MAOI antidepressants act by inhibiting,

HOW AMPHETAMINES WORK

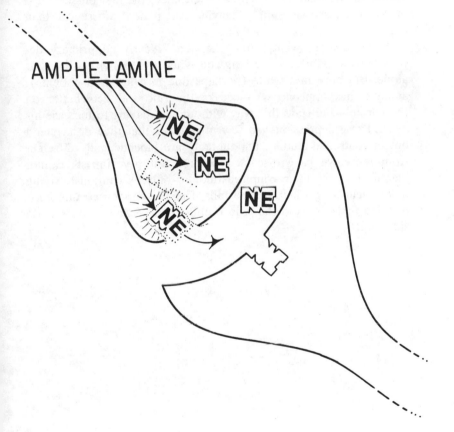

Figure 16.1   How Amphetamines Work

respectively, reuptake and destruction of norepinephrine (NE) at the synapse (chapter 14). So each of these drugs makes the brain use more efficiently what little NE it does produce during depression. But the psychostimulants act by simply releasing stored NE. Temporarily, more of the neurotransmitter is available in the synapse, and the patient feels better. But because the usual mechanisms of NE destruction remain unchecked, the first burst or two of NE exhausts the supply, leaving the patient worse off than before.

At least, that's what usually happens. Nearly all primary depressions do poorly in the long run when treated with stimulants alone. But once in a while (perhaps one in a hundred patients), along comes someone who breaks the rule and gets better on Dexedrine—and stays that way without ever having to increase his dose. These depressions, so few in number that they don't stand out in controlled studies, undoubtedly are biochemically different from those we have discussed before. But psychiatrists cannot identify them by their symptoms alone—only by cautiously trying a stimulant drug when all else fails. But the antidepressants *must* be tried first, to avoid the twin pitfalls of drug abuse and serious side effects.

17.
Convulsive and Other Physical Treatments

Probably no other aspect of psychiatry has made people more suspicious or distrustful of its practitioners than electroconvulsive therapy (ECT). Because no one really understands why it works, it seems more than a little like witchcraft. To the layman, anyone who believes he can cure psychosis by producing a convulsion with a jolt of electricity to the head may need some shrinking himself —hence, movies like "Shock Treatment," in which Lauren Bacall portrays a psychotic psychiatrist who sadistically electrifies a succession of people far healthier than she. That she ends her days a patient in her own mental institution seems almost too good for her or, by implication, for any other doctor so inhuman as to assail his patients with legions of Reddy Kilowatts. So bad has its press become that even psychiatrists have written articles implying that ECT "fries the brains" of its victims. Let us try to put some of these arguments and rebuttals into perspective.

If you guessed that convulsive therapy was discovered by accident, you are either a good guesser or you have begun to realize that most of psychiatry's advances came about through luck, or the lack of it. Nearly half a century ago, some doctors believed that patients with naturally occurring epilepsy did not develop schizophrenia—that somehow the convulsions prevented the onset of delusions and hallucinations. Now we know that epilepsy in no way protects against schizophrenia (in fact, one type of seizure, temporal lobe epilepsy, even increases the chances of schizophrenia). So for the wrong reasons psychiatrists began to

229

look for a way to easily and safely produce convulsions artificially, on command. They eventually discovered that a weak (140 to 160 volts at a few milliamperes) electrical current passed through the patient's skull for a half second or so caused all his brain cells to discharge simultaneously, producing a rhythmic jerking of his muscles—exactly what happens in an epileptic seizure, except that involuntary tongue-biting and urination do not occur.

Since its introduction in this country in the late 1930s, the basic form of this treatment has not changed at all. What has changed is the safety and comfort with which doctors give it—and its indications for use. When any new treatment comes along, it is tried on every disease from alcoholism to zoophobia, and so it was with ECT. But it (quickly) became apparent that although some schizophrenics improved briefly following ECT, depressives responded much more dramatically and often recovered completely. A patient who only a week before had begun to saw off his head with a table knife soon played cards sociably on the ward. A depressed woman who thought she had killed everyone in the world laughed and joked with the attendants after her third treatment, and a few days later went home well.

At least a part of ECT's bad press through the years can be laid to the early practice of giving treatments without anesthesia. But the scenario of the patient who cowers under his bed while hairy-armed goons approach with crackling electrodes has gone the way of cupping and leeches. Now, he is first put to sleep with a rapidly acting anesthetic, so he feels and remembers no more of the actual treatment than a surgical patient recalls of his appendectomy. And another medicine briefly paralyzes his muscles, so the treatment now produces only a mild twitching instead of the full-blown seizure which used to fracture bones from time to time. To get a better idea of how ECT is given, let us look over the doctor's shoulder as Olive Bard receives her treatment.

"Come on in, Miss Bard, it's your turn," says the nurse from the door of the waiting room. Dressed in her own pajamas and slippers, Olive Bard walks into the treatment room. She climbs onto a wheeled stretcher and lies down on her back. Her psychiatrist stops writing in her chart to greet her. "Let's see, this

is your third treatment, isn't it? How are you feeling by now?"
"Oh, better," she replies. "I don't feel so guilty now. It's funny. I can remember feeling guilty, but I can't figure out why I felt that way. I'm still kind of depressed, though."

"You have shown a lot of improvement, but you have a way to go. But how about the treatment itself? Does it bother you?"

"Oh, I just come in here and lie down and go to sleep," she replies. "I don't know anything more about it until I wake up afterwards in the other room."

"Well, there's no question but that you're a lot better. A few treatments more and we'll have you out of here and back at work."

The anesthesiologist cleans her arm with alcohol and inserts a small needle into one of the veins made prominent by the tourniquet above her elbow, which he then releases. One after the other, he quickly injects three solutions: atropine to stabilize her heartbeat and to keep her respiratory system from secreting too much fluid; Brevital, the anesthetic which puts her to sleep within a few seconds; and as her eyelids flutter shut, succinyl choline to relax her muscles. Stepping to the head of the table, he places a ventilating mask over her mouth and nose and squeezes a basketball-sized rubber bag several times, forcing air into her lungs. As her muscles become partly paralyzed, they twitch slightly throughout her body. A minute later, he gives the go-ahead. "She's ready," he says, removing the mask from her face and inserting a soft rubber bite plate between her teeth.

Now the nurse places the two electrodes—each a quarter-sized silver disc attached to a wooden handle—against either side of Miss Bard's head, just above her ears. From each disc a wire snakes back to an electrical apparatus about the size of a table model radio. The nurse nods her head that all is ready.

The psychiatrist pushes a button on top of the box, producing two clicks half a second apart. Olive Bard's toes curl downward and her body stiffens for several seconds until a rhythmic twitching of arms, legs, and face replaces the initial tension in her limbs. A few seconds later, she lies quietly.

"Just right," the psychiatrist comments as the anesthesiologist begins once again to bag-breathe the patient. For another minute or two he will continue to breathe for her, until the effect of the muscle paralysant wears off and she can once again breathe on her own. Then they will wheel her into the recovery room next door where a nurse will carefully watch her respiration, pulse, and blood pressure until she awakens fully, twenty or thirty minutes later. Then it will be time for breakfast.

This description should make clear the remarkable simplicity of ECT. But deciding who should receive these treatments is not quite so simple a process. It requires some discussion.

About 80 percent of seriously depressed patients improve substantially when they receive ECT—5 or 10 percent more than those who receive the most effective antidepressant drugs. Most likely to respond is someone who is emotionally well until he becomes acutely and severely depressed—he will almost surely return to his good premorbid personality. Past history of response to ECT also (as one might expect) predicts good outcome for a second course of treatment, as does a history of depression in a relative who has recovered with ECT (called "living better electrically" by less reverent psychiatrists).

Curiously, the most seriously depressed patients respond quickest and best to ECT. By her third treatment, Olive Bard had already forgotten her ruminative delusions, although she remained somewhat depressed for another four days. Another woman started ECT after antidepressants had failed to relieve her withdrawn and totally mute condition. When she even refused to eat for several days, her doctor nearly started to feed her intravenously. Instead, he ordered ECT. When she awakened from her first treatment, she smiled and ordered breakfast. Although most patients do not respond quite so rapidly, families often describe the effects of ECT in these very severe cases as close to miraculous. The average patient needs six to twelve treatments before he recovers completely from depression, with the average about eight. Even if there has been no improvement by the fifth or sixth treatment, it is best to continue, because some patients only begin to show progress when well into the series.

Only a few conditions other than depression call for ECT. Occasionally a severely manic patient cannot be controlled with medicine and must be given electric treatments, which were used extensively and effectively for mania for years before lithium and the neuroleptics came along. ECT can actually save the life of an occasional manic, interrupting the constant day-and-night activity which threatens death from exhaustion. Catatonic schizophrenics like Wilma Freese (chapter 9) sometimes can be blasted out of their mute, withdrawn posturing by ECT when drugs prove unavailing. And you could make a convincing argument for trying ECT in almost any newly-diagnosed schizophrenic, particularly if he is young and has "atypical" features which suggest affective disorder (see chapter 10). But for the noncatatonic schizophrenic who has been chronically ill for many years, ECT adds little to the treatment program other than expense. Of course it's a gamble— perhaps fewer than one schizophrenic in ten will really improve with ECT. But when the alternative is long-term illness, possibly with prolonged confinement, even long odds seem better than no odds at all.

A generation ago psychiatrists used ECT liberally. Now that most depressed patients can be helped with drugs, it is usually relegated to second choice, but several situations continue to demand it.

The most obvious indication is high suicide risk. The psychiatrist has no practical way to guarantee the safety of any patient really determined to end his life—except to control the illness. And despite years of intensive research, psychopharmacology has yet to yield a drug which works quite as quickly or as surely as ECT. Often, one or two treatments will erase all thought of suicide in even the most deeply depressed or psychotic patient. When risk of suicide is the reason for considering ECT, it should be started right away, before it is too late. Or if drugs have already been tried unsuccessfully, ECT may turn the trick, particularly in a previously normal person who has developed delusions or hallucinations.

Sometimes ECT should be used first because it is safer than drugs. For example, certain forms of severe heart disease could make your relative especially susceptible to the side effects of tricyclics. Exposing him (particularly if he is elderly) to a potentially toxic chemical twenty-four hours a day may prove too great a strain on his body. But ECT is all done in the hospital, under the careful supervision of two physicians. The only medicines involved stay in the patient's system but a few minutes—if he responds well, he may not need maintenance treatment which could cause trouble later on.

ECT is so safe that it can be given during pregnancy (when drugs should not be given because of the slight chance they could cause fetal malformations)—even in the ninth month of pregnancy it does not precipitate delivery. It can be given in the face of nearly any imaginable medical or surgical ailment, and can be as effective for octogenarians as for adolescents. Even the fractures of spine, arms, and legs due to osteoporosis (softening of the bones), which used to cause trouble once in a while, now have been eliminated by using succinyl choline. Recently a woman who had already fractured her back in a fall caused by drug-induced dizziness had eight ECTs, with her back continuing to heal during the procedures. But though these treatments can be given despite nearly any physical ailment, the doctor will want to know about any medical problems your relative may have so he can prevent complications. Accordingly, the work-up before shock treatments always includes a complete physical examination, electrocardiogram, and X-rays of the chest and back.

Does ECT pose any dangers? "Danger of what?" Of death? Sleep and death have long been associated in religion, philosophy, and literature, causing even mentally well people to recoil at the prospect of being "put to sleep" (they do that to unwanted dogs). To be perfectly candid, anyone who undergoes general anesthesia, even if it lasts only five minutes, accepts a tiny but definite risk that something could go terribly wrong. But the chance of death from ECT is so slight (perhaps 1 in 100,000 treatments) that it pales in comparison with risk of suicide in severe depression. And most patients feel only too happy to assume this vanishingly small risk to rid themselves of the disabling symptoms for which they have sought treatment.

Most other side effects are minor and quickly resolved. Immediately after treatment, patients occasionally complain of headache, but no worse than a medium hangover, and treatable with aspirin. ECT itself is painless, but the first couple of treatments sometimes produce muscle stiffness due either to the seizure itself or to the temporary paralyzing effects of the succinyl choline on muscles. And beginning about the third or fourth treatment, most patients complain of memory loss which persists to the end of the series. If he has quite a lot of confusion, your relative may become distraught that he cannot even remember your visits from one day to the next. Disconcerting and occasionally embarrassing, this memory loss is easier to accept if you bear in mind that it usually heralds improvement in the patient's clinical condition.

The memory loss from ECT has been publicized enough to merit a few more moments of thought. True enough, most people do forget events which take place during the two or three weeks of treatment. That period will remain only a sketchy memory—your relative may forget an anniversary or find that he cannot place the names or faces of people he met while in the hospital. But inconvenient as it is to lose memory ever, the recollections of a psychiatric hospitalization are usually nothing to brag about. And if he forgets how he felt before his treatment, so much the better. More important, his basic capacity for forming and recalling new memories will not be damaged by ECT. A few days after the last treatment, he will begin to sort through his confusion to recover his past memories up to the time of hospitalization, and he will once again be able to absorb and retain new information.

In recent years, unilateral ECT has partly solved even the temporary loss of memory. When electricity is applied only to the nondominant side of the brain (that half of the brain which is *not* responsible for thinking and memory—the right side in all right-handed and many left-handed people), the same type of convulsion and the same antidepressant effect usually obtain, but with considerably less memory loss and confusion than when both sides are shocked. Patients who can ill afford even temporary severe memory loss—students for example—can be treated effectively and returned to work more quickly with unilateral treatments.

Unilateral ECT may also be useful in a course of treatment called maintenance ECT. Occasionally a patient responds well to treatment but relapses within a few weeks. For him, treatment may be extended past the time of discharge from hospital by giving him occasional "booster ECTs," first weekly, then gradually extending the interval between treatments until even monthly treatments are no longer necessary. With unilateral boosters the patient can continue to work or attend school, even on the day he goes into the hospital for his treatment.

So you can reassure your relative that there is only the tiniest chance imaginable that any serious or lasting unwanted effects will come of his ECT and that the potential for improvement is great. Because he feels frightened, confused, perhaps depressed or psychotic, he may need your help in deciding to have ECT. But in reassuring him about the safety of this procedure, try to avoid the mistake one doctor made when his patient asked if she would be able to play the piano after her treatment. "Of course you will," he said. "That's wonderful, doctor," she gushed, "I never could before."

Controversy

ECT is highly effective and about as safe as medical treatment can get. So why has it received such a miserable press over the past two decades? The intense, often vituperative objections of some people (including not a few psychiatrists) largely flows from the distrust we all feel of that with which we are unfamiliar. Some probably fear the side effects which used to be a problem, but now rarely occur. Others object to using any treatment when they do not understand how it works. This does not mean that they are more ignorant than the rest of us—in truth, no one knows exactly why ECT works. One hoary theory held that it satisfied the depressed person's so-called need to be punished, but this is certainly wrong. In psychiatry's neolithic age, before the turn of the nineteenth century, mental health experts punished patients more than adequately by flogging, chaining, and other therapeutic indignities —without improving their depressions or psychoses a bit. Besides, today ECT is so innocuous that many patients awaken from the anesthesia not realizing that they have already been treated. The most sensible theory is that with electrical stimulation, nerve endings (see Figure 4) become once again able to produce norepinephrine in normal quantities.

But one of the criticisms leveled against those who administer ECT is, unfortunately, all too often entirely warranted. Some psychiatrists *are* guilty of running "shock factories." For several years popular and scientific media have appalled readers with stories of psychiatric hospitals which specialize in ECT, often shocking 50 percent or more of patients, with or without proper indication. This compares with an average ECT rate of perhaps 10 or 15 percent in acute care psychiatric hospitals nationwide and suggests that some psychiatrists use electrotherapy in lieu of diagnosis—easily as reprehensible as prescribing penicillin for all infections, or operating on all stomachaches. This style of "therapy" is mentioned only to be condemned; no treatment should ever be given without first carefully considering diagnosis.

In fact, one of the questions you might ask in looking for an acute care hospital for your relative might be, "How many patients receive ECT here?" Regard any answer much above the 20 percent mark with as much suspicion as you would the reply, "We wouldn't *dream* of using *that* sort of thing!" Either extreme suggests an institution which has straitjacketed itself into (or out of) a particular mode of therapy, rather than tailoring treatment to fit the patient.

The considerable brouhaha over ECT raised in the past few years has resulted in legislative attempts to control or even to eliminate it altogether. For example, California recently passed a law requiring three consulting psychiatrists to agree that each patient's health and well-being *demands* ECT and that all other modes of therapy be exhausted before this treatment is given. The effect of this legislation has been to deny therapy to some patients who need it desperately, inasmuch as three psychiatrists can rarely agree on where to have lunch, let alone who should have shock treatment. But the law also proved a pecuniary windfall to the consultants, who are well paid for delivering themselves of opinions totally unnecessary for the patient's care. Even more recently, this law was declared unconstitutional by a state appellate court. But the same state legislature is now considering banning ECT for any patient under the age of eighteen, regardless of indications or medical opinion—another master stroke which would condemn some young people to chronic hospitalization until they age sufficiently to claim their civil right to treatment.

Under this government regulation, Eddy would have been in real trouble. Eddy was a depressed sixteen-year-old with a strong family history of affective disorder—his mother had been severely depressed during her late teens, and at age twenty, one of his brothers had received ECT for a serious depression. Outpatient treatment with medicine could not relieve Eddy's mounting illness. When he became psychotic, he was hospitalized. There he expressed the fear that his friends had conspired with the staff to plot against him. In his confusion, he tried to take off his pants in the middle of group discussion and spent most of his time whimpering for more medicine. He awakened from his first ECT stating, "Gee, I sure feel a lot better." After several more treatments, he was discharged; four years later he remains well.

Psychiatrists themselves know little enough about treatment. Lawyers and lawmakers, knowing nothing, should have the grace to keep silent.

PSYCHOSURGERY

When ECT fell under a cloud of distrust, psychosurgery was caught in a deluge. The term psychosurgery actually encompasses a number of different operations in which a surgeon actually cuts connections between the frontal lobes of the brain (the part just behind your forehead) and more posterior structures, thereby changing emotions. Of course, any procedure which actually damages brain tissue conjures up politicians conspiring to control men's minds in a power-play created to rule the world. The explosive arguments surrounding this topic have echoed to the floor of Congress, generating shock waves which still threaten to end this procedure by legislative fiat. But whether or not psychosurgery deserves the same fate as the great auk should be determined through research, not rhetoric. Fortunately, considerable data does exist on the subject.

As with most other treatments in psychiatry, those who first cut people's brains to try to help them some forty years ago tried it out on a variety of severely and chronically ill patients. Schizophrenics are sicker than anybody else, so they were particularly likely to receive the operation. And some did become more docile and easier to manage, but their disease process remained untouched, and they still required oceans of care. The advent of the neuroleptics finally sounded the death knell for the use of surgery in schizophrenia, particularly in this country.

This left two groups of chronically ill patients for whom psychosurgery is still advocated: chronic obsessive-compulsives and depressives. Patients with obsessive-compulsive disease have recurrent thoughts and actions which seem silly to them but which they cannot resist (see the case of Emanuel Trimmer in chapter 6). This condition is so rare that even busy psychiatrists see only an occasional case, so it need not concern us here. Fortunately, chronic depression so severe that none of the conventional forms of treatment can touch it is equally uncommon. But for those few patients who remain virtually immobilized despite drugs, ECT, and psychotherapy, surgery can be a successful last resort.

No one really knows how or why psychosurgery reduces obsessive-compulsive or depressive ruminations: the pressing of the surgeon's knife through a tiny band of fibers appears also to sever the pathway whereby certain emotions are carried from one part of the brain to another. Somehow or other this interrupts a vicious cycle of morbid thinking, leaving the patient free to concentrate on other, more productive matters. A number of careful follow-up studies have shown that people who receive this procedure suffer far less from severe depressions or obsessions than they did before surgery.

But what about side effects? Don't these operations have some pretty awful consequences for the patient, as well? Well, they can. Convulsions can crop up after any trauma to the brain, and up to a quarter of patients treated with psychosurgery do develop seizures. These can be controlled with drugs, however, and usually incapacitate the patient far less than his original illness. An occasional patient has died as the result of the operation, although this has become increasingly uncommon as surgeons have become more practiced.

Despite these uncommon but very real possibilities, the aspect of psychosurgery which has most horrified its opponents has been the possibility of personality change. True enough, back in pioneer days methods were crude: surgeons would crack the patient's skull and, in effect, go in with a shovel to see what they could dig out. This "technique" damaged a great deal of brain tissue and left some people unable to relate normally to others or to experience the usual variations in mood (flat affect). But the newer, more selective procedures have virtually eliminated this problem, while retaining their effectiveness in ridding the patient of disabling depression.

After several years of unremitting and totally incapacitating depression responsive neither to medicine nor to ECT, Mattie Grey finally received a cingulectomy (an operation which interrupts a tiny bundle of fibers called the cingulum and damages virtually no other tissue). Within days she returned home, functioning adequately and apparently recovered. She did well for several months, when her husband died. Fearing a recurrence of her suicidal depression, her psychiatrist hospitalized her briefly, but within a few days she had expended her tears and was discharged home with a diagnosis of "normal grief reaction." She has remained well since then.

DIALYSIS

Just recently renal dialysis has been used in a few medical centers for the treatment of schizophrenia. As with someone whose own kidneys have failed, the patient's blood is passed through an artificial kidney machine to filter out toxic substances. In the case of schizophrenia it is assumed that these circulating toxins enter the central nervous system and somehow produce psychotic symptoms. This still-experimental technique has not yet been adequately evaluated, but early reports suggest that it may prove helpful even in some highly disturbed chronic patients who fail to respond to conventional drug therapy. If further studies justify these early expectations, dialysis may offer hope to some patients who previously had none, and a shot in the arm (so to speak) for the increasing legions of psychiatrists who regard schizophrenia as a biological disease.

OTHER PHYSICAL METHODS OF TREATMENT

Until we finally devise the perfect treatment for psychiatric illness, imperfect methods will continually appear to plague us or please us. For the manic-depressive, lithium approaches the ideal in terms of specificity and effectiveness, but for convenience and safety it still leaves much to be desired. The situation is worse for schizophrenia, and worse still for personality disorders and the neuroses, and in all of these areas a procession of "new" treatments greets us yearly. Like the succession of worthless miracle anticancer drugs concocted from apricot pits or sheep semen, they are accepted eagerly by a public grasping straws to find relief from serious illness.

In the previous three chapters, we have discussed every type of treatment known to be effective. Before any new treatment is accepted, it must be evaluated in controlled trials which prove it superior to already established forms of therapy. We will now briefly mention a few methods which have not been evaluated satisfactorily, which have been evaluated and found wanting, or which have been superseded by other, more effective and safer means.

Insulin coma is the main example of the latter category. Psychiatrists in the 1930s discovered that seriously ill patients could be calmed, their psychoses abated by injecting them with insulin, lowering their blood sugar levels to produce a sort of artificial shock. Back in the old days, a series of these treatments did help many schizophrenics, but because of its unreliability and danger (when blood sugar stays too low too long, brain functioning may not return), this treatment method has been completely replaced by ECT and the neuroleptic drugs.

Diet plays a central role in two forms of therapy which have recently received considerable attention from the popular press. In orthomolecular (megavitamin) therapy, the patient eats enormous amounts of vitamins to compensate for a deficiency which some psychiatrists believe causes schizophrenia. Another small group of doctors believe that certain foods cause schizophrenia (the allergen theory) and claim successful treatment by systematically eliminating certain foods from the patient's diet until he recuperates (or starves). Do these plans work? So far, no one has adequately evaluated the allergen theory (most scientific psychiatrists give it little serious attention), but some early results are in from a Canadian megavitamin therapy study. The preliminary data suggest that, if anything, patients treated with high doses of vitamins fare slightly worse than controls given no medicine at all. Neither of these techniques can be recommended; the hope of cure which they appear to hold out to sufferers from schizophrenia is no more than a clutching at chimerical straws.

Electrosleep, during which the patient receives a mild continuous electric current delivered to his scalp, has also enjoyed some vogue, but evidence for anything more therapeutic than a mildly pleasurable tingle has been lacking. Biofeedback, a legitimately helpful treatment for tension headache, offers nothing of lasting value to the schizophrenic or manic-depressive. Acupuncture, a faddish treatment of physical disorders, has spawned a variant, staples in the ear. Used by a few psychiatrists to "treat" heroin addiction, this sorry practice will eventually probably be touted for other illness. In reality, it is nothing more than the basest quackery.

18.
Psychotherapy

Most books on psychiatry discuss psychotherapy first. After all, it is older than drug treatment, has more intellectual appeal, and wears the mantle of tradition. We have saved it until last for reasons which you will understand presently. But exactly what is psychotherapy? Actually, it is not *exactly* anything. The term "psychotherapy" is simply a convenient way of referring to the collection of ways people communicate to try to help one another. We will discuss some of these methods in this chapter.

When you consult your family doctor about those episodes of racing heart and shortness of breath and he tells you, "your heart is sound—you're just suffering from anxiety," he uses psychotherapy to reassure you. When the newlyweds down the block have their first spat and turn to their pastor for help, he *counsels* them—psychotherapeutically. And when Aunt Minnie encourages Manly to stand up to his father so he will feel better about himself, she uses *directive* psychotherapy (although its effect could prove less than therapeutic). Plainly, psychotherapy is not something mysterious or complicated done only by psychiatrists. It happens every day and comes in a variety of styles and sizes (and prices). It can be supplied by parents and psychologists, by barbers and bartenders.

Although psychiatrists have no corner on the psychotherapy market, all psychiatrists do use psychotherapy to some extent in treating patients. In fact, some psychiatrists and psychologists use psychotherapy so exclusively that they refer to themselves as "therapists," implying that nearly all of what they do is psychotherapy. But by the word "therapist" we understand two things: while it means one who treats, it also implies that the treatment produces improvement. But the mere implication of success does not suffice for the modern consumer. The skeptical patient properly demands that psychotherapy, like all other treatment modalities, be evaluated according to scientific principles and that it be used as the sole method of treatment only when the evidence suggests that it can help.

EVIDENCE

What evidence supports the value of psychotherapy alone in treating manic-depressive disease or schizophrenia? Plenty of psychiatrists claim they can successfully treat depressed patients psychotherapeutically. But anyone who has read chapters 7 and 8 can explain this easily enough: whether you treat them with psychotherapy or Pepsi-Cola, depressed patients get well anyway. Recovery is the natural course of these illnesses. The trick is to determine whether *any* treatment can improve upon the speed of natural recovery. And a collection of the studies supporting the value of psychotherapy as the principal treatment for depression or psychosis would qualify as a volume in the "World's Thinnest Book" series, shelved right alongside *Saving Your Marriage* by Henry the Eighth. In plain English, there is no such evidence. Psychotherapy simply does not work as the sole or main treatment for these conditions. But perhaps we have asked the wrong question. Let us instead ask, Can psychotherapy improve on the rate of recovery from mental illness using drugs alone?

A decade ago, a massive study carried out in California by Dr. Philip May virtually laid this question to rest for schizophrenia. He randomly assigned over two hundred patients to five different treatment groups, then watched them over the next two years. One group was treated with psychotherapy alone and one received only ECT. A third group was treated with neuroleptic drugs, a fourth received both psychotherapy and drugs, while the fifth group served as the all-important control. These last sixty patients were given no active treatment other than good nursing care and the warm supportive atmosphere of the hospital ward.

The results amply confirmed the faith modern psychiatrists have placed in the neuroleptic drugs over the past twenty years, for of those patients receiving drug therapy alone, 95 percent were discharged to return home. Compare this with the discharge rate for the control group, only 58 percent of whom returned home. Psychotherapy given without drugs failed utterly to improve upon this dismal untreated discharge rate.

But how did those patients who received both drugs and psychotherapy fare? Every bit as well as those who received drugs alone, but no better—and at the cost of several months' additional hospital stay. In this experiment, psychotherapy added nothing but expense to what drugs alone provided more quickly.

But perhaps there should be more to "outcome" than just getting out of the hospital. Most people have greater expectations for their day-to-day lives than the hope of one day flying over the nest, cuckoo-wise. And if psychotherapy can enrich the life of a patient while he recovers, isn't this in itself worthwhile? Here is a dimension to psychotherapy which the May study did not tap.

The competence of the therapists themselves provides the focus for a second criticism of the study. Every psychiatrist secretly believes that he is better at his trade than just about anybody else in the world, so each will be suspicious of any study of psychotherapy in which he did not provide the treatment. You can imagine the scorn with which many regard a study in which the psychotherapy was done by residents who had not completed their psychiatric training, some of whom had had only six months of experience under their belts. If only the therapist had been trained psychoanalytically, they argue, results favoring psychotherapy would surely have appeared. "After all," reasoned one world-famous psychiatrist in commenting on May's report, "seven years of analytic training must count for something!"

Fortunately, another recent study bears on both of these criticisms. Dr. Lester Grinspoon and his colleagues studied twenty hospitalized schizophrenics treated for two years by fully trained psychoanalysts: there can be no doubt as to the quality or intensity of the psychotherapy these patients received. Ten of the patients also received neuroleptics, while the other ten were given placebo, setting up on a small scale the critical portion of May's study of psychotherapy. How did it turn out? At the end of treatment, the patients given neuroleptics had improved while those on placebo had not. Not only could the authors find no evidence that psychotherapy had substantially affected outcome, they also could unearth little indication that it contributed to the quality of the patients' lives. In most cases the therapists had been unable to establish any sort of meaningful working relationship with their schizophrenic patients. Indeed, in half those given neuroleptics and in nearly all who received placebo, the patients did not even notice if their therapists left on vacation!

We cannot escape the conclusion that psychotherapy, whatever its intensity or the expertise required for it, is neither necessary or sufficient for the actual *treatment* of hospitalized schizophrenics. Drugs alone appear to do the job quite nicely. Later we will discuss the use of psychotherapy in managing these people, particularly when they become outpatients. But let us first briefly touch upon affective disorder.

The reasons for using deep (insight-directed) psychotherapy with depressed patients are good and plentiful—providing we accept the psychodynamic model for the development of affective disorder. The dedicated psychotherapist sees his job as helping the patient relive an early childhood loss such as the death of a parent, thereby getting it out of his system. Another purported task of psychotherapy is to teach the patient to avoid behavior which may precipitate depression. Because many psychiatrists believe depression results from hostility turned inward, they encourage the patient to direct his anger and hostility against those in his environment who deserve it. Usually meaning you, his family.

But most good psychotherapists admit the futility of psychotherapy as the principal treatment for primary affective disorder. Forcing someone who is severely depressed to "face issues" usually increases his feelings of worthlessness, as he finds once again that he cannot cope. Most therapists actually regard severe depression as a contra-indication to deep psychotherapy. Manics make equally poor candidates; after all, you have to catch someone before you can talk to him. Confronted with manic speech, therapists of all persuasions quickly find themselves carried away and buried by the avalanche of words.

Unfortunately, we cannot point to scientific proof that psychotherapy alone fails to treat the primary affective disorders. Before the 1940s, studies evaluating the effectiveness of treatment were poorly controlled, and investigators did not distinguish unipolar from bipolar illness. With the availability first of ECT, then of antidepressant drugs, medical treatment quickly proved so superior that scientists felt no need to demonstrate elegantly something which everyone already knew empirically. Nowadays the ethics of withholding treatment known to be effective poses real problems for those who would like to "do the studies right." In fact, it is questionable whether even the May or Grinspoon studies could have been done in the moral and political climate of the later 1970s. So we will have to be content with something negative— the knowledge that no studies exist proving that psychotherapy alone should be used to treat primary depressions or that psychotherapy between attacks can immunize against further episodes.

Many psychotherapists, taught that drugs "only treat symptoms," believe that psychotherapy must be used to get to the root of the problem. Critics of psychiatry claim that only the wealthy can afford "real" therapy, while the poor must get by with second best—symptomatic treatment with drugs and ECT. Ironically, the rich often receive treatment which is more elegant but less effective. Any of these same critics might reflect on which treatment he would prefer for pneumonia—a shot of penicillin from an intern in an emergency room, or having the country's most fashionable specialist sit at his bedside and hold his hand. Which would you choose?

WHY DO PSYCHOTHERAPY AT ALL?

We have found several excellent reasons for not using psychotherapy. Psychotic patients are too sick; it may actually delay (sometimes fatally) the use of more effective treatments; and drug therapy costs but a fraction of psychotherapy, yet leads to recovery in far less time.

Many patients simply do not *want* psychotherapy. Again and again, depressed people at first request it because they believe that is what one does for mental illness. But after two or three weeks of drug treatment have relieved the acute depression, their problems no longer seem sufficiently serious to warrant the effort and expense. One manic-depressive man complained of trouble finding a physician who would "just prescribe lithium." Incapacitated for several years by a disease which had not yielded to intensive psychotherapy, he had finally stabilized on this drug. Now, forcibly retired and moved to a new city, every doctor he had consulted "wanted to take me off my medicine and get to the bottom of my problem. All I wanted was someone who'd give me my medicine and let me alone!"

Again, why do psychotherapy at all? And if what we have said about it is right, how did psychotherapy become so popular in the first place?

Like many other therapies (leeches, for example), the talking treatment for schizophrenia and other illnesses became fashionable at a time when no other rational treatment was available. Since 1789, the time of Pinel, chains had been discouraged. Wet sheet packs and hot tub baths, though somewhat more humane than their ancestor the ducking stool, were not much more calmative. Psychotherapy ambled onto a field virtually devoid of competition for the mind of the schizophrenic.

Grounded in psychological theory, the intellectual appeal of psychotherapy virtually assured its wide acceptance. For if you regard the schizophrenic's hallucinated voices as an attempt to adjust to life's vicissitudes (chapter 11), then uncovering and talking out these traumatic events would seem not only logical but mandatory for a cure. If psychosis stemmed from Mother's double-binding messages, an early step in treatment *would* be to identify and extirpate these pathological roots. Psychotherapists hope to teach their patients to cope more effectively and appropriately with the frustrating life events which have led to the mental breakdown.

During the first four decades of this century, psychotherapy became so widely accepted that it spawned a peculiar and occasionally disastrous circular thinking. Because it was used for all illnesses, psychotherapy often took the place of diagnosis. Later, when more specific treatment *was* finally developed, many psychiatrists lacked sufficient diagnostic skill to employ the new methods effectively. So what did they do but continue to use psychotherapy as their primary mode of treatment, disparaging diagnosis as irrelevant.

The irony is that proper diagnostic criteria can identify groups of patients who respond poorly to drug therapy but who do fare better with psychotherapy. These patients have neither classical primary affective disorder nor schizophrenia, but they may suffer from secondary or reactive affective disorders (chapter 7), or from personality disorders or neurosis. Or they may simply have problems in their lives which they cannot solve alone. They neither require nor respond to ECT; drug therapy may only lead to addiction or overdose. Just as Rhoda Crews improved her life (her husband returned home) by acting upon the conclusions she reached with her therapist, so have countless others found relief through psychotherapy for their problems of living. Despite the fact that the enormous therapeutic strides of the past forty years allow psychiatrists to effectively treat the vast majority of their patients, no latter-day Panacea has yet conjured up a cure-all for every emotional problem. As in the rest of medicine, the treatment prescribed—whether pills, poultices, or psychotherapy—*must* depend upon scientific diagnosis and careful evaluation of outcome.

Which patient should receive psychotherapy in addition to their primary treatment? The answer: every patient. Therapeutic exchanges go on every day, and conversations between physicians and patients especially should be geared to treatment. For when someone consults his doctor he expects and deserves not only relief from symptoms but also a sympathetic hearing of his problems, and, he has the right to hope, compassionate understanding.

LISTENING AND UNDERSTANDING

The mental patient probably needs these two ingredients more than any others, but how likely is he to receive them? When he complains, "No one understands me!" he is probably quite right. Most of his family and friends have never before experienced deep depression, have never heard voices in the night calling them liars, cheats, or whores. Who can comprehend a parent so distraught that he wants to take his own life, or a friend whose emotions are so tangled he cannot even give you a civil "good morning"? But when it comes to frightening, incomprehensible thought and behavior, the psychiatrist has seen the elephant and heard the owl.

Through supportive psychotherapy he allays the patient's anxiety by placing his fears within the framework of prior human experience. He tells him that far from having a rare, even previously unknown ailment, his condition is so common that physicians know a lot about how to treat it. Immediately, even more quickly than an injection can begin to work, the reassurance "You are not alone" begins to calm the patient (and his family) and to provide the strength and support they need to weather the next few days.

But before he can be very reassuring, the psychiatrist must find out what he is up against. And to get there he employs his greatest single psychotherapeutic tool: listening. Patients and families hear and store up a tremendous volume of misinformation, and as treatment begins imaginations run riot with all manner of suppositions and superstitions about where the illness came from and where it is going. Rooting out these fears involves active listening on the part of the psychiatrist.

During the initial treatment session, while the patient is still acutely disturbed, the doctor will spend part of his time soliciting thoughts and questions from him and his family so their many misapprehensions can be laid to rest. Because he has treated hundreds of people with similar illnesses, the psychiatrist can ask questions about sensations and thoughts that you may not at first recognize as symptoms. These talks increase his understanding of the patient's condition while they strengthen the patient's faith that the doctor knows what he is talking about.

So develops *rapport*—good feeling which flows back and forth between doctor and patient. Its importance should not be underestimated. Obviously, the patient needs to trust his doctor so he will take his medicine, return for appointments, and talk freely about symptoms or side effects which crop up in the course of treatment. But the physician also needs to trust both patient and family. After all, he must rely on relatives to carry out his instructions, to continue at home treatment begun in the hospital, to provide the support the patient continuously requires. No doctor can treat vigorously when he worries that medicines will be taken improperly or that he will not be called should trouble develop.

All of this comes under the heading of *supportive* psychotherapy, the purpose of which is to do just that: support and reassure the patient. Therapy of this type cures no one, so it never shows up in recovery statistics. But it can help any patient, no matter how depressed or psychotic, to feel better temporarily. Even if reassurance has to be given all over again each day, the effect is well worthwhile. Time and again patients have claimed that the continuing reassurance from their physicians gave them the will to go on.

Every doctor does psychotherapy, whether he is a surgeon or a psychiatrist (except pathologists, whose patients have passed the point of conversation). But supportive psychotherapy hardly requires a physician; anyone trained and experienced in the care of psychiatric patients can be an effective psychotherapist. In the hospital, the task often falls to the nurse to provide minute-to-minute support for the more acutely disturbed. Psychologists, social workers, and mental health aids belong in this act; interchanges with family and friends can also be helpful, providing that those close to the patient can keep their own feelings from misdirecting a conversation which is supposed to be therapeutic.

Any time a patient's illness begins to interfere with his judgment, the therapist may use *directive* therapy to guide him through decisions which he cannot make himself. Take the decision to enter the hospital. Someone whose morbid thinking has paralyzed him into indecision may be totally incapable even of seeking the care he needs. Then the physician says, "I'm going to take this decision out of your hands—you should go to the hospital for a while." (Once there, the patient usually feels relieved that someone else can bear all the responsibilities while he rests.) But he may reach the doctor having already made decisions which he believes will help him feel better. Getting married or divorced, having babies, changing jobs, selling the old homestead—these are only a few of the maneuvers he might use to try to cope with mental illness. Then he must be told *not* to make any radical changes until he has improved. Even when the decision he has reached turns out to be the right one after all, a few weeks' delay seldom hurts. But more often, when the illness has been controlled he no longer feels the need to change.

As the patient improves, he needs less and less reassurance that he will recover; now psychotherapy can focus on more substantive matters. The therapist helps the psychotic patient test reality, at first stressing simple facts like the date and place so he can reorient himself to the real world. As his delusions and hallucinations diminish, he accepts the psychiatrist's assurance that they were only part of his illness, not real problems on which he must act.

With treatment well under way, the therapist begins *educational* (explanatory) psychotherapy in which he discusses the nature of the illness and reviews the signs and symptoms which led to the diagnosis. He explains the type of treatment he is using and why, need (if any) for maintenance medicine, and whether to expect a relapse or a minor recurrence of symptoms. By educating his patient about the illness, he prepares him for living with it in the future.

Still later, the original illness under control, the patient and his psychiatrist may return to some of the problems of living which they put aside earlier. Some of these will have melted away in the course of treatment, but others (looking for a job, learning to control temper better) become grist for the mill as doctor and patient enter the *problem-solving* phase of their relationship. Now they identify problems and put them into perspective in the patient's life, helping him arrive at solutions himself. As one wise psychiatrist put it, "The essence of psychotherapy is to distill the gallons of words the patient pours forth into a bracing tonic, then serve it back to him in a thimble."

FAMILY THERAPY AND OTHERS

While all this has been going on, the family has been (or should be) treated, too. Ideally, this is provided by the treating psychiatrist—he knows the patient and his background better than anyone else, so he has the best chance of giving sound advice. But another psychiatrist, or social worker, or psychologist may do as well, particularly if the interests of patient and family conflict. It may require one, two, or many face-to-face sessions, or it may be accomplished quite satisfactorily with a telephone call, but contact with the family is always important.

The first and simplest objective should be to tell everyone the working diagnosis, plans for treatment, and outlook for recovery.

This reassures the family while it comforts the patient. After being told that her husband's condition would be temporary, one wife sighed with relief and said, "I wondered what I would *do* if you told me he would always be like this." Doctors sometimes let the patient pass along the information to his family himself (it is easier for the doctor), but word of mouth is a notoriously unreliable vehicle for communication. Because patients often distort what the doctor says to fit their own psychological needs, there can be no substitute for direct communication between family and physician.

When someone they love falls ill, relatives naturally tend to blame themselves. When they do, talking with the doctor can set the record straight. He listens to their ideas and fears about their role in producing the illness, and often with a few words he can absolve them of guilt. With guilt and anxiety diminished, they do not have to cast anyone into roles of victim or villain, and they begin to see the patient in a new light. He becomes simply someone who is ill and needs care. Because they no longer blame themselves for his feelings, they can listen to him. And with listening they become more sensitive to his needs, able to cooperate more fully in his care.

At the same time individual psychotherapy with family members may be indicated to help them through the difficult period of a relative's illness.

> Enola Ranger's policeman husband had become increasingly depressed over the past several years. Not recognizing his depression as illness, he moved his family three times in as many years, believing that a change in jobs would relieve his feelings of low self-esteem. After several therapy sessions Enola felt better. She told the doctor how angry she felt with her husband for frequently uprooting his family. The psychiatrist helped her understand how normal these feelings were, and he offered her a better place (his office) to ventilate than her own living room, where her complaining had only further depressed her husband. The doctor also praised her for her excellent care of the couple's three small children, support which her husband had been unable to give during his depression.

Although a patient's own doctor may treat the relatives as well, sometimes he will refer them to another psychiatrist, particularly when the family situation contains such conflicts of interest that he cannot advise both parties impartially.

Still later, family therapy of a different sort may be indicated. Just as sickness can disrupt a family's cohesiveness, the recovery of the patient who has been ill for some time can change relationships between relatives. You may recall how puzzled and upset Noah Steam's wife became when he escaped his nearly lifelong meek submissiveness to become assertive and more demanding (chapter 14). To iron out such wrinkles in the fabric of a marriage, the therapist will sometimes request all parties to participate, including children or parents, depending upon who lives with the patient. With everyone present, he can better understand who does what, and to whom. Family therapy can help each person to understand and better appreciate the others' points of view and to make whatever adjustments seem necessary for a happier family life.

GROUP THERAPY

Over the past decade or two, group therapy has grown almost notoriously popular. Groups operate on the premise that if one head is no good, ten may be better. What is so positive about the group experience that people with widely diverse problems band together to try to find solutions? For one thing, group therapy uses the therapist's time efficiently, so it is economical for the patients. For another, it enables people to learn from the mistakes (and successes) of others.

Group members support one another by example rather than by exhortation. After attending several sessions while still hospitalized, one depressed man learned that other people have troubles, too. "Until now I thought I was just weak and that other people handled stress better than I do. Now I know that everyone else is just about as screwed up as I am."

But all sorts of people run all sorts of groups, so a warning or two may be in order. Although it takes considerable skill and experience to run a group well, little at all is needed to do it badly. And because group therapy has so recently become popular, governments have not yet gotten into the business of regulating them. Anyone who can read and write (plus, one suspects, a few who cannot) can hang out his shingle and practice, sometimes with disastrous results. The moral is to know your therapist. Check out his qualifications with your own doctor, or if necessary with your local medical or psychological society.

A second point to check is the character of the group itself. People who have something in common get along better together than those who do not, and group therapy provides no exception to this rule: people with similar illnesses have similar problems and benefit from each other's company. For instance, drug-treated schizophrenics do better with group therapy than those who are followed with individual psychotherapy. Groups have also proven useful for manic-depressive patients being treated with lithium. An hour spent with eight or ten people who take the same drug for the same disease brings out more problems and solutions than the much less efficient "one-on-one" psychotherapy. And because one of the psychiatrist's main jobs is to teach people about illness and how to live with it, he might as well do it with the efficiency of a classroom. Group education also appeals to the conservation-minded—its lower per-person cost can contribute to the greening of your pocketbook.

Behavior Modification

That human beings learn most of what they do hardly qualifies as a theory; it is a truism. In the past generation or two, psychiatrists have used theories of learning as the basis for a school of psychotherapy in which the therapist simply trains the patient to behave differently, hence more comfortably. He can do this in several ways.

He can reinforce (reward) desired behavior when it occurs, thereby encouraging the patient to try it again. A parent might use this principle to train his child not to wet the bed: a piece of candy in the morning for staying dry (often, praise alone works as well). The same technique has been applied to chronic schizophrenics who live in hospital settings. When their behavior improves, they are rewarded with tokens which can be redeemed for privileges. For example, each time one patient abandoned his usual tangential speech to talk coherently, he was given a poker chip with which he could later buy candy or a visit from his family.

Of course, these schizophrenic patients also receive neuroleptic drugs, which gives them enough control that they can profit from the behavior techniques. Although behavior therapy can be used as primary treatment for some conditions, schizophrenia and primary affective disorder are not among them. But the obsessions, compulsions, and phobias which sometimes accompany severe mental illness can be favorably affected by these means.

> At age twenty-three, Ima Quaker became severely obsessed with the idea that she would kill somebody younger and weaker than she. As fate would have it, her two-year-old son *was* smaller and weaker, so morning, noon, and night she fancied that she would stab or strangle him. In the hospital, her depression treated with Elavil, her obsessions continued to disable her for all other activity. The word "kill" kept arising unbidden in her mind, forcing aside all other thoughts. Then her doctor set her the task of writing "kill" ten thousand times on a pad of paper—daily. A few days and a ream or so of paper later she lost interest in the project and her fear of the word as well—the behavior treatment of *mass practice* had subdued her obsession. Encouraged, next she herself discovered how to use another technique, *paradoxical intention,* to treat the thought that she would strangle her child. She acted out this scene in fantasy, strangling for all she was worth the drainpipe which ran through her bathroom. The ludicrous spectacle she presented soon caused even her to laugh. Because she could not fear something she could laugh about, this symptom also disappeared. Within a few days, the rest of her obsessions departed, and she has remained well over the succeeding ten years.

Psychiatrists are an assorted lot, and in that diversity lies both strength and weakness. The value of having several potential solutions to a problem is that if one proves ineffective, another can be tried. Of the many techniques conceived by practitioners in the field, some meet with enough success to warrant trying again. Of these, only a few stand the test of scientific trials to become an accepted part of the standard therapeutic repertoire. But the drawback of so diverse a system is that it promotes some techniques which beyond placebo effect have no value whatever. Attractive packaging and enthusiastic promotion can lead the public to accept methods which have no basis in scientific theory and no substantiation in fact.

We have witnessed patients screaming primally, analyzed transactionally, meditating transcendentally, acupunctured pointlessly —all in the name of therapy. These techniques and countless others like them may help some people who have problems of living, but when applied to seriously ill patients who need medicine for recovery, they can do great harm. They should never be used as the primary treatment in schizophrenia and affective disorder. For someone whose defenses have already been weakened by psychiatric illness, encounter groups and marathon sessions can prove stressful enough to precipitate severe anxiety, depression, or even psychosis.

19.
Management I: Helping Your Relative

Our philosophy that the psychiatric patient's relatives need information so they can help him has led us to examine a lot of material about mental illness. At this stage, although your knowledge has increased considerably, you are probably still groping for the right steps to help your relative. In these last three chapters, we will provide you with some specific guidelines, for the care you provide at this point may spell the difference between success and failure of treatment. This is because the best diagnostician in the world cannot help unless your relative comes to see him, and the finest treatment will be useless if it is refused. You play the critical role in bringing your relative to treatment, in seeing that he accepts it, and in helping him to regulate his life while he is still ill and to readjust himself to the world once his health has returned.

HELPING THE DOCTOR HELP YOU

Let's say you have just realized that Aunt Minnie needs psychiatric help. Where do you go to get it? In chapter 6 we discussed the various sources of help to which you might turn, and you may want to review them now.

Your choice made, now it is time to get the patient to see his physician for the first time. How do you go about it? You may have to make the initial appointment yourself—severely depressed people often cannot make the decision to seek help, so they need some prodding. Someone who is psychotic will not realize how sick he is, and it may take some cajoling to get him to cooperate. Sometimes it helps to wait until the patient is feeling worse, such as during the morning hours for a depressed patient whose mood varies, or under conditions of increased stress. Then, when the enormity of his distress fully weighs upon him, he may agree to seek treatment. Or you might emphasize whatever aspect of his condition troubles him the most. "Let's go see if the doctor can help you with your sleeping problem" sounds better than "Let's go see if we can get your mental illness taken care of."

But no matter what tactic you use, always observe two precautions. The first is, never lie to the patient. If you have told your relative that "We are just taking a trip down to look at the river" or "It's time to take you out for your pedicure," and instead he finds himself ensconced in the office of a psychiatrist, you will have lost your rapport with him, and the doctor may never be able to regain his confidence.

The other mistake that you can make is to promise something no one can deliver. If you tell him he will only visit the doctor in his office and promise that he won't be hospitalized, you tie the doctor's hands. With perfect logic your relative can later say, "Well, I did as we agreed and now I'm going home and never coming back." But without bargaining, you can reduce his anxiety about the future by offering more open-ended suggestions such as, "Let's just go to the doctor and see what he recommends. He'll probably help you to feel more comfortable." Or you might try to soften the blow by suggesting that you both need help understanding your problem. Once you get that far, the doctor will know how to present the problem to the patient in a light as reassuring as possible, thereby obtaining his cooperation in treatment.

So now you have arrived in his office—what do you say? He can only practice good medicine if he has good information, so be prepared to help him out with a complete account of your relative's history. If this is particularly long or complex, a written outline including approximate dates, names of hospitals, and other doctors and treatment used (how well did they work?) will help determine diagnosis and treatment. You can also speed the diagnostic process by obtaining records from previous hospitalizations and psychiatrists. These take several weeks to arrive, so plan well in advance if you can. Then all pertinent material will be on hand for the first interview. And take samples of his current medicine—the name "Tofranil" means a lot more to the doctor than even your excellent description of "those little red pills with the funny writing on them."

Encourage your relative to tell the doctor everything—he's no fortune-teller, after all, and needs all the information he can get. People often feel hang-backish about gory details of "shameful" topics like sexual problems, drinking, suicide ideas or attempts, or peculiar ideas such as obsessional thinking and hallucinations. You may have to prompt him or recount some of the lurid details yourself. Much of this is better done privately, out of earshot of the patient, when you can speak freely about his symptoms and your worries. Of course, this means that later *you* should clear out so he can have his turn at bat.

At the end of the session, be sure you understand the doctor's diagnosis, prognosis, and plan for treatment. If you do, you will know much better how to evaluate your relative's response to treatment, what symptoms and side effects to watch for, and how best to reassure him about his progress. Do not be afraid to review anything that is not clear—several times, if necessary—or even to have the doctor write it down. This material is new to you, and no one expects you to understand it all on the first try.

During that first visit, you cannot possibly remember all of the points you have been pondering for the past several weeks or months. And when you leave the doctor's office, your head will probably spin with all the information he has tried to give you, so you may want a second appointment to tidy up the loose ends. Then make a list of the remaining questions, and by the end of that appointment you will have all the information you need.

Once you have become informed, stay that way. People and conditions change, so the facts as you knew them six months ago may not hold true today. If your relative is an outpatient and doing well, you may be able to get all the information you need directly from him, but you should feel free to accompany him to his next appointment if you have a question you must ask the doctor directly. If he is recently out of the hospital, however, you may want to check on his progress more often, perhaps by telephoning his physician. Some relatives feel reluctant to do this, for fear they will intrude on a private relationship or that they will take up too much of the doctor's time. But your value to the doctor and to the patient increases in proportion to what you know, so ask questions when you need to; keeping well informed is both your privilege and your duty. On the other hand, delegate all the telephoning responsibility to one relative—if the doctor talks to Mom, Pop, and all sixteen kids, he will have no time for the patient.

Talking with the doctor also helps you ventilate the worries which you will accumulate. He knows that he will help his patient more if you have confidence in what he is trying to do. So if you worry about lack of progress or any other aspect of the treatment, you must let him know. He is trained to handle upset feelings (even his own) and his ear has been blistered by hotter tongues than yours.

But if things still go poorly, if you worry that he has missed a vital aspect of the case, keep in mind that consulting with another psychiatrist can clear the air for everyone. The patient may benefit from it, and you will feel better afterwards. And the doctor can take it—it has happened to him before.

Once the consultant has seen your relative, ask him to talk over the case with the treating physician. In a difficult case, two heads are better than one, and from their meeting you may obtain a useful consensus. You, too, should meet with the consulting physician, or at least speak with him on the telephone to learn firsthand whether he really agrees with the treatment. If not, talk over his recommendations with the treating physician and try to reach agreement on how to proceed.

But if the two do agree, avoid the temptation to go doctor shopping. When treatment goes badly and your desperation mounts, your natural inclination will be to look around for someone who promises more immediate or total cure, and you will undoubtedly find him. The woods are full of people who promise more than they can produce, who prey upon the hopes and fears of the distressed. So beware of the nonstandard treatment—many a family has squandered its savings chasing a will-o'-the-wisp which offers much, but delivers nothing but further heartbreak. The mother of a manic-depressive man told of her quest for more help at a time her son was being treated for schizophrenia: "We saw one doctor who recommended vitamin therapy, but it didn't work, even though he had a lot of letters behind his name. But then, so does alphabet soup." Reread chapters 14 through 18 to become more familiar with what constitutes acceptable therapy. If you still have questions about a proposed treatment, institution, or individual therapist, check with your local medical society or state psychiatric association.

How frequently should you expect your relative to see the doctor? Of course, this depends a lot on the diagnosis and the patient's condition, but early in treatment you might expect one visit a week as a good average. As symptoms improve and he gets the condition well in hand—perhaps two to four weeks—the doctor will probably decrease the frequency of visits to fortnightly or less, unless more intensive psychotherapy is necessary to resolve problems of living which either have arisen because of the illness or have contributed to it. The timetable will vary considerably with the individual patient, but on the average you should begin to see some results within three or four visits.

Farther down the line in therapy, occasional maintenance visits may be all that are necessary. People attending the lithium clinic (chapter 16) go in only every month or two, and even someone with a severe depression, now well controlled on antidepressants, can usually get along quite well with monthly visits. The doctor will want to see him a time or two even after medicine has been discontinued, and you should encourage this also. He might pick up something in your relative's condition which you have missed. But however frequent the contact, the key to successful maintenance therapy is regular visits with faithful attention on the part of everyone to the possibility of recurring symptoms.

HELPING WITH MEDICINE

By the end of a month or two of treatment, your relative should be well stabilized on his medicine, now carefully adjusted to provide maximum benefits with the fewest side effects possible. In an earlier chapter we mentioned the first law of medicine, "Do no harm." But now is the time to heed the second law, "Don't rock the boat." This means that if your relative feels well, whatever you are doing—keep it up. Do not let him forget, reduce, or otherwise tinker with his medicine until he talks it over with the doctor. Just learning to readjust himself to the workaday world is stress enough right now without imposing the additional burden of a changing chemical equilibrium.

If he was in the hospital when he started his medicine, all he had to do was swallow what the nurses handed him. So for the first few days at home you may find that you may have to remind him about it. He will probably take it with greater regularity and better grace if you can manage a little subtlety in your delivery, perhaps placing the pills on his plate at mealtime instead of interrupting him at odd hours during the day with the command to "swallow this!" (You will both have much better luck if the doctor has prescribed the medicine to be taken once, at most twice, a day— perfectly feasible with almost all psychiatric medications.)

By the end of a hard day, some people have trouble remembering their names, let alone whether or not they have taken all their medicine. You can solve this problem by placing the entire day's supply of pills into a special container each morning. If bedtime rolls around and the bottle still rattles, he knows he has some more swallowing to do. With most medicines he can make up a missed dose later on when he remembers, but you should check with doctor about the particular pills your relative takes to be sure.

If he has been suicidal, you may find yourself in charge of picking up prescriptions and keeping the main medicine supply under lock and key. Other problems might also make it necessary for you to monitor medicine. Some patients become so enamored of the prescription process that they cannot resist experimenting to see how little of the medicine they can get away with. Others, blatantly taking the attitude "If one's good, two are better," with some frequency manage to overdose themselves into the nearest emergency room. Depressives lack the energy to take medicine, schizophrenics don't believe they need it, and manics are far too busy doing six other things to remember. For whatever reason, when the medicine going down differs from what the physician prescribes he cannot know whether what he has tried is good or bad. But if you have kept an eye on your relative's pill-taking and can recognize when he deviates from the doctor's schedule, you can at best get him back on the correct dose, and at least let the doctor know that trouble is afoot.

No one can "fight medicine"—by willing himself to stay depressed, for example. Unlike psychotherapy, drugs work whether the patient wants them to or not. Once he swallows them, they progress inexorably through his system and into his brain, where willy-nilly they will have their effect upon his symptoms. He does not even need to like his psychiatrist if his illness is one treatable with medicines, and if the doctor has prescribed the right one.

A frequently asked question is, What other drugs can he take with those you have prescribed? The answer depends entirely upon the medicine, so you must really ask the doctor each time the problem arises. When your relative consults another doctor (his general physician), he should always mention what medication the psychiatrist has given him. Even if his psychiatric medicines are not causing the symptoms for which he is now seeing his GP, they could affect the type of treatment prescribed for them.

Unless the patient has a specific allergy he can take aspirin, vitamins, and stool bulk expanders (like Metamucil) without fear that they will interfere. He can probably take a long list of other drugs available without prescription as well, but because they occasionally interact harmfully with some psychiatric medicines you should check with the doctor before using remedies such as APC, Empirin, Anacin, nasal sprays and cold remedies, weight control pills, Dramamine and other antinausea preparations, and sleeping pills.

But the drug that patients most often ask about is alcohol. Because it depresses the nervous system, alcohol must be used cautiously by anyone taking psychiatric medicine. If his normal limit is two drinks, one may be all he can tolerate now—more might cause excessive drowsiness which could in turn lead to problems while driving or at work. One drink per day can usually be allowed, although in every individual's case the psychiatrist should be consulted first. And if it comes to a choice between medication and a libation, choose the former. Occasionally, a patient admits he skipped his medicine because he knew he would be drinking, then wonders why he does not feel as well the next day. Enough to make a grown psychiatrist cry!

"Will I have to take drugs forever?" No one likes to regard himself as chronically ill, so this question is also a popular one. The answer depends entirely upon the diagnosis, and because the most common diagnosis is depression, the answer is usually a resounding "No." So you might pass on to your relative, if he asks, the answer psychiatrists try to give their patients: we simply cannot look "forever" into the future, but for now medicine seems to be necessary and should be continued. Most people feel better knowing that anyone has a chance to get off medicine completely at some time in the future, so never tell him that he will have to take pills forever. Every patient can expect to have his medicine lowered to the absolute minimum required to maintain him in good health, so from time to time you should check with the doctor to be sure your relative really needs the full dose he has been taking.

Finally, even the prospect of indefinitely continuing medicine seems less awful when you recall that millions of people with medical illnesses take pills every day, and think nothing of it. Diabetics and heart patients particularly depend upon medicine for their very lives. By this standard, "popping a pill" to keep his thinking straight becomes tolerable.

Your Approach to the Patient

Anyone who wants to help a relative should at least try to understand him. He will probably tell you that you cannot imagine what he is going through, and he will be right. Unless you have been there, you cannot possibly feel the terror and loneliness a patient experiences in the grip of mental illness. But you can recognize his unhappiness, and, even if you cannot feel it emotionally, you can learn to appreciate intellectually the agony he is going through. And with your attempts at understanding and with your support, you can help to lighten the burden he has to carry.

People pick up some peculiar ideas about their relatives' illnesses. One of the commoner misapprehensions is that patients get sick because they want to. Now, you might understandably feel this way, particularly if the illness has persisted for a long time. And, in some psychiatric conditions, patients do seem to derive satisfaction (called *secondary gain*) from the attention they receive when they are sick. But not in primary affective disorder—if you have ever been severely depressed yourself, you will laugh (provided you have improved enough) at the suggestion that these symptoms persist for the pleasure they give. And certainly not in schizophrenia. Schizophrenics would rather be left alone than accept the countless attentions (and medicines) which accompany the diagnosis of mental illness. Even the happy manic who appears to enjoy himself so thoroughly cannot with justice be accused of consciously perpetuating his condition. For one thing, no physiologically normal person could possibly force himself into a manic's frenetic activity for longer than a few minutes without exhausting himself. For another, the manic often feels exquisitely uncomfortable, his abnormal, driven hyperactivity making him fearful, "nervous," or too energetic. Although his behavior may earn him a great deal of attention, it is distinctly of the wrong sort. And deep down, he knows it.

But no matter how wrong-headed this attitude is, with such feelings afoot the family develops striking amounts of hostility towards the patient, fed by the anxiety that he will never recover. If angry feelings toward your relative have troubled you, you have probably also felt guilty—it is not nice, after all, to harbor hostile feelings about someone whom you love, especially when he is sick. Well, you may feel guilty, but you do not have to feel alone. In similar situations, even doctors (even psychiatrists) experience emotions like yours and must learn to cope with them. The trick is to recognize these emotions and to gain control of them, or they will end up controlling you.

But how do you learn to control your guilty, hostile feelings? You start by acknowledging that they exist—you can neither fight an invisible enemy nor can you fight anyone unless you realize you have a problem. Self-awareness has to be the first step in any campaign for self-control. If you have a relative with mental illness, you might stop to ask yourself whether angry feelings have interfered in your relationship with him.

Next, grant yourself the right to have these feelings. We have gone to some trouble in this book to promote your acceptance of the patient's point of view. It would be more than a little hypocritical to deny you the legitimacy of your own emotions. In fact, a lot of the problem is that any normal person would have these feelings, but your guilt causes you to try to suppress them. You are caught in a squeeze play between your instincts and your conscience—a real rock and a hard place.

At the same time, you must learn to differentiate between the wisdom of accepting your feelings and the folly of acting on them. It is perfectly acceptable to wish that Dad would leave home until his illness has been controlled, but it helps neither one of you much to say so. The situation is very like a marriage; occasionally most husbands and wives would just as soon bash one another with a frying pan, but the consequences hold them back. You may wish that your relative would get hold of himself, but unfortunately wishing out loud will not make it come true. Rather than increase his guilt by giving him a piece of your mind, better to unload it on someone else—the doctor, perhaps.

Having read this, your impulse may be to rush right in and tell your relative that you are sorry if your attitude has pained him any. Your best advice: cool it! Confessions usually help us to feel better, at least for a while. But where is the advantage in getting the guilt off your chest, only to load it onto his shoulders? One thing leads to another, and once a family has entered into an orgy of recriminations, it sometimes has trouble stopping the cycle.

Sonny Beech had moved his family repeatedly during the past several years, because he felt depressed by, he thought, first his job, then the weather where they were living. When finally he landed a terrific job in an ideal location and *still* he felt depressed, he sought psychiatric help. As he began treatment, his wife also asked to be seen.

Sandy revealed during several interviews the responsibility she felt to cheer her husband up and the fear that she actually made him worse. As his depression continued unabated, on more than one occasion her fear turned to anger. She told the therapist, "I feel I've tied my life to a sinking log."

Over the years, Sonny had learned he could avoid his wife's complaints by raising a smoke screen. Whenever she tried to tell him how difficult the children had been that day, or explain any of the other problems which families commonly encounter, he would in anguish exclaim that it was all his fault, that his depression and their frequent moves had made their lives miserable. This pattern not only frustrated Sandy's attempts to communicate her feelings, but also denied her husband the self-esteem that goes with actively participating in family problem-solving.

Their psychiatrist attacked vigorously on several fronts. He treated Sonny's depression with high doses of Tofranil. At the same time, he began to see Sandy in psychotherapy, explaining that the depression would not go on forever and that it was not her fault. He encouraged her to ventilate (to him!) the anger and frustration she felt toward her husband. Finally, as his depression slowly diminished, Sonny was able to follow the doctor's advice to stop assuming responsibility for her distressed feelings. Within two months, the family had restabilized at a more effective level of interaction.

In modifying your attitude towards your relative, learning to handle guilt comes first. You cannot interact therapeutically with someone you love if you believe you have made him what he is. To be sure, you may have pooh-poohed his delusions when he first mentioned them instead of listening thoughtfully, but you did not cause the delusions in the first place. If you responded to his continuous crying with anger, not sympathy, you now know that neither of you caused that depression. In the future you will try harder to support him. Because your attitude is so important to helping him, you may even decide upon a psychotherapeutic session or two for yourself—to support the verdict that you stand "not guilty as charged."

Talking with the Patient

Sometimes it makes you uncomfortable, but you have to keep talking with him if you are going to keep living with him. But does this mean that you must learn the fine art of conversation all over again? That you must pussyfoot around, mincing words and measuring thoughts? No—you will find as you go along that he is still human, that he still understands the same language and is still interested in many of the same topics. But he will need special handling in certain areas. Symptoms, for example—we will devote all of chapter 20 to them.

One of the least comfortable topics for you (and most important to him) will be his present illness. If you avoid the subject altogether, he may imagine that he is sicker than he thought, and that you are hiding something from him. So if he wants to talk about his problems, you might as well plunge in and have done with it.

Be positive. You can afford to be—depressions and manias can be cured and schizophrenia improves remarkably with medication. Listen to what your relative has to say. You do not have to accept responsibility for his problem, nor must you solve it for him. All you need to do is listen. The reassurances you offer will be. simple and will largely echo what the psychiatrist has told you. You can with truth say that he will recover or improve, and that slow recovery is in itself no cause for alarm. "Rome wasn't built in a day" pretty well sums up the approach you might take towards the course of his recovery. At the same time, do not encourage him to expect miracles, and avoid making promises which neither you nor the doctor can keep.

So now you are visiting with him, either at the hospital or at home. What do you discuss? This is a question psychiatrists field more often than any other having to do with everyday management. After all, the guilt you feel when your relative becomes ill breeds the conviction that anything you say to him has cosmic significance for his recovery. But just as psychotherapy makes little difference overall in the outcome of your relative's illness (chapter 18), whether you say something or save it probably will not have much long-term effect, either. By carefully choosing your words and the subjects you discuss, however, you can certainly help him to feel more comfortable during the healing process.

You will want to avoid a few topics. Those which are particularly stressful to the patient such as divorce, business (if it is going badly or if he thinks it is), and other unpleasant subjects should be bypassed unless he brings them up first. Your own health is boring to everyone but you, so leave that one out, too. You will have to be careful about asking social questions like, How are you feeling? unless you are prepared to listen to a nonsocial recitation of his problems. It is only common sense to stay away from sensitive issues—politics, religion, and visits from in-laws come immediately to mind. If he reacts badly to these subjects when well, you can be sure his feelings will intensify when he is sick.

If you want to help him feel more comfortable, you may find

yourself having to practice the fine art of conversation monitoring. As a philosopher once put it, "If everyone always spoke his mind, the social situation would be entirely chaotic." Although what you tell him should always be the truth, do not feel compelled to impart every last scrap of information you have gleaned from your reading or from talking with the doctor. Some of it may be speculative at best, some will be better saved until your relative feels calmer and more positive. For example, why tell him that he could soon relapse or that another episode might be waiting months or years down the road—he does not need to hear that while he is still suffering from his *present* episode. You can also put off telling him some of the other facts of life (like the chances his children might be affected) until he has stabilized emotionally.

You will be on safe ground if you let the conversation be guided by his interests, even if they are temporarily limited to what happened in occupational therapy that day, or to the outcome of the ballgame. Try to speak freely and positively, giving unambiguous messages to the patient. Even when he is well, the statement, "You wouldn't care for a picnic, would you?" presents a confusing double message which implies that you are not too keen on picnics yourself. For the mental patient, picking apart the tangled threads of this message is a strain he can well do without.

With a single exception—mania—all mental illnesses produce a bumper crop of low self-esteem. Unable to work effectively or to think clearly, the psychiatric patient quickly runs up a big ego deficit which requires large infusions of self-confidence. Some of this the doctor provides during his regular visits, but because these are relatively brief and (if your relative is an outpatient) infrequent, his self-confidence may have to withstand long dry spells between waterings unless you lend a hand.

For example, you can reassure him that he suffers not from madness but from illness, and that he will soon be feeling better. You can echo the doctor's distinction between *feeling* bad and *being* bad, a difference which mental patients often fail to appreciate. You can remind him of his past successes and express your confidence that he will soon become a productive member of society again. And perhaps most important, you can continually reassure him of his value to you as a friend, of your respect, your admiration, and your love.

TAKING CHARGE

Now, if only you had the patience of Job and the wisdom of Solomon, and if you didn't have a thousand other things to do every day, you could carry all this off without a hitch. But, alas, you are mortal, so you will quickly find that catering to all your relative's emotional needs would tax the talents of a Titan. The job will seem especially unrewarding at first, when the patient is too sick to care and your other relatives are busy making themselves scarce. So if your halo slips once in a while and you find yourself ready to berate him (or to brain him), you can help everyone feel better by taking a well-deserved vacation and putting some distance between you and your problem. This may amount to no more than an afternoon of shopping or a day in the country (leaving someone else in charge if continuous supervision is necessary), but for extended problems you will find longer breaks an absolute must. However long you stay away, you will have to fight the temptation to feel guilty about your absence, especially if it is from a husband or wife. Just remember, vacations are quicker and cheaper than divorces! And you can stop worrying that your relative will think you have abandoned him—he is probably as ready for a vacation as you are.

The psychiatric patient feels helpless, dependent and irresponsible, but you can help erase these feelings and build his self-confidence. At first organize a daily routine simple enough for him to complete without enduring the agony (for *him*) of decision-making. If he is convalescing from a hospitalization or otherwise not working, handcraft projects can help him fill his time with a minimum of responsibility. (When used in the hospital, this same approach is dignified with a title: occupational therapy.)

For any routine to be useful, it must help the patient to *feel* useful. A universal need people have, although its importance is often overlooked, is the desire to feel competent and to be appreciated. So in his daily schedule include chores which are within your relative's capacity to complete—these small successes will help stoke the sputtering flame of self-esteem. But severely ill patients have little in the way of initiative, so you have to start projects for him to finish.

At first, think small. Your relative can probably accompany you on a picnic although he cannot plan one. He can build a model airplane (a little at a time) while failing miserably at balancing the checkbook. You should help him find useful and enjoyable pastimes, and praise his successful accomplishments. You need not comment on the failures—he is well enough aware of them, and the principle that praise works better than criticism applies as well to adults as to children.

You will both be better off if at first you concentrate on what he would like to do, not on what you wish he would do. Holding him to your standards only imposes an additional burden on his already overtaxed self-esteem. The psychiatric patient, like anyone else, can control what he *does* much better than he can how he *feels*. So you can much more usefully induce him to wash the dishes (and feel proud of it) than to smile at a joke. As he improves, he should be made increasingly responsible for what he does ("*You* have to make your bed and clean up your room") but be excused for the way he feels about it (". . . but you don't have to like it").

As he accepts greater responsibility, let him make more of his own decisions—greater freedom of choice is one of the inducements you can offer him for returning to a normal way of life. But the fine line between neglect and overprotection seems a difficult one for many people to walk, according to the testimony of psychiatric patients. Let Sybil Wright, a fifty-five-year-old woman with manic-depressive disease, speak for herself.

> It's a problem to be a mental patient. People are afraid of you when they know you have been unbalanced, and everyone thinks he knows what's best for you. My Mother wants me to stop driving, and my son thinks I shouldn't vote (he's a Democrat). And my daughter, bless her, says I should give up dating and sex. Just because I'm occasionally ill doesn't mean I'm a total ninny!

A clear lesson: let your relative do everything for himself he can. If you are unsure what he can do, let him try, but under your watchful eye. If he thinks it is time he started to drive again, sit with him the first time or two and keep him off the freeway until you are satisfied that his judgment and dexterity are up to the task.

TELLING OTHERS

Whom do you tell and what do you tell them about your relative's illness? This problem is as vexing as any that you will face, probably because there is no single good answer. Families have traditionally kept their mental illnesses more secret than the Manhattan Project, but in recent decades seeing a psychiatrist has been upgraded in some quarters from social stigma to status symbol. Whether you adopt the atomic secret or public forum attitude depends to an extent upon your relative's social and work environment, but in any event the choice should be his. Whenever possible keep a low profile and let him do the telling—he will probably feel much less embarrassed about it than you do.

As to which people should be told, tastes vary. The skeleton in the closet approach is a bit out of date but still prevails in many places. If you and your relative choose to keep the situation to yourselves, that is certainly your prerogative. Unfortunately, people will gossip. An acquaintance of one patient who had taken a sudden leave of absence put it this way: "It couldn't be surgical—that's usually elective. And it's not an ulcer, because people don't hush that up." Triumphantly: "It's got to be in her head!"

Furthermore, the silence routine usually invites speculation that things are worse than they really are, so you might just as well resign yourself to the inevitability of telling something to someone. Whom you tell depends upon their need to know: family, close friends, and the boss at work have a vested interest in the patient and are in a position to help him through the crisis. If they know where he has been and why, it helps them to understand his past behavior and to make allowances for it in the future, perhaps by reducing some of the social and job-related pressure upon him.

What do you tell them? You have to go with what seems comfortable. Overall, you will probably be happiest with what sounds the most plausible. As this is usually the truth, you might start there.

Your problem will be to choose those facts which people need to know, relate them, and keep the rest to yourself. If you matter-of-factly say, "He's being treated by a psychiatrist for depression, and he'll be off work for two or three weeks," no one will be the wiser if you omit the part about the suicide attempt. You should also resist the temptation to include unnecessary details which may prove embarrassing to the patient later—the drinking binge and the nude swimming party, for example.

You may feel tempted to throw up a smoke screen by using one of the popular euphemisms for mental illness. "He's in for exhaustion and tests" has become a polite expression meaning that a VIP has an emotional problem. Whenever a movie star or a politician enters a mental hospital, it is for "exhaustion and tests." "Nervous breakdown" is another totally nonscientific term meaning (roughly) a mental disorder serious enough to interfere with the patient's life. "Nervous strain," "nervous collapse," and a host of other nervousnesses imply more or less the same thing without saying anything. You might as well confess that your relative has a mental disorder and have done with it. Of course, you may want to qualify that statement a bit to satisfy those who are really hungry for news. Thus, "A mental disorder of depression" or "elation" or "hearing things." But you will probably be better off *not* broadcasting the exact diagnosis, even if you have been told it. Terms like schizophrenia and manic-depressive disease have an ominous ring to them, and as likely as not they will be wrong, anyway.

THE JOB

The mental patient probably worries about work as much as anything else. If hospitalized, will he have a job when released? If he does, can he still do it effectively? If his productivity slips while he is being treated as an outpatient, how will his employer react?

Actually, employers often understand more about mental illness than they are usually given credit for. In fact, many prove much more open-minded (perhaps because they have had more experience) than friends and family. Not living with the patient twenty-four hours a day, they view him more objectively. If he has been a good worker, his employer will usually save his job for him. The boss may even be relieved to learn that the reason for decline in his key worker's performance is correctable, and not characterological.

You can help by facilitating the flow of information between your relative and his employer. This may mean nothing more than encouraging him to tell the boss he has been seeing a doctor and taking medicine. But if he has been unable to work at all, you may want to call or visit his employer yourself. He will need the answers to a number of questions beyond "What's wrong?" and "How long will he be sick?" But even if you think you know the answers, your safest reply will be to refer him to the doctor. He knows more about the illness, can give a more informed estimate of prognosis and, because he is used to dealing with employers, may give a more optimistic account than you can. The doctor should be more than happy to speak with your relative's employer—after all, he is being paid to talk as well as to listen. Your job as middle-man between doctor and employer is to make the connection, not to deliver the goods yourself.

When your relative has been unable to work—particularly if he is the family breadwinner—one of the biggest questions in your mind will be, "When can he return to work?" He is probably just as concerned as you are, and may even try to resume working before he is really ready. Far from having to push him back into his accustomed routine, you may have to restrain him from returning to work too soon. Because patients recover at different rates, there can be no reliable rule of thumb as to the best time to return to the job. Whenever possible he should test the water by working limited hours for a few days before plunging back into his full-time responsibilities. If this cannot be arranged, have him return to the job on a date agreed to by his psychiatrist (who may have to issue him a return-to-work slip, anyway).

Depressed patients ultimately return to their previous level of functioning. The same usually applies to manics, who may need a longer convalescence, however. But a few unfortunate patients (some schizophrenics and occasionally a severe manic) will be unable to resume their former work. The apathy which settles in on the schizophrenic after repeated attacks of psychosis places him at such a competitive disadvantage in the job market that he sometimes must content himself with jobs entailing lower responsibility. Some students never return to full-time classes; a skilled tradesman may be reduced to manual labor. These unhappy circumstances are much harder on the family, forced to live on a smaller paycheck, than on the patient, who has also become apathetic about his station in life.

If your relative seems unable to work at his former job, ask the doctor if his trouble is likely to be permanent. If so, you can encourage your relative to try another job—one which does not ask him to exceed his capabilities. To push him beyond his capacity would only increase his anxiety and perhaps further reduce his already impaired performance.

Telling It Like It Isn't

When psychiatric patients apply for new jobs, they often feel uncomfortable and unsure of themselves, particularly if they have been unable to work for some time. And they may have good cause—despite intensive efforts at public education, some employers remain wary of hiring people with a history of mental illness of any type. Many a patient has felt hampered by his own honesty when refused job after job because he has owned up to a history of psychiatric treatment. Therefore, another question commonly asked psychiatrists is, "What should I put down on a job interview form?" The answer depends on the type of job.

Government (civil service) jobs tend not to discriminate against those who have had mental illness, creating less need to equivocate when applying. Besides, the application forms for jobs with governments and the larger corporations usually require the applicant to sign an affidavit that he has told the whole truth, on the penalty of perjury. Under these circumstances, it would be foolish to tell anything else. But even truth can be worded to sound less horrifying. "Saw a psychiatrist for depression, January–March 1975, well since," has a better ring to it than "Shock treatments for psychotic depression." (Applying for insurance policies also demands complete disclosure. Not only do you swear that you have not perjured yourself, but doing so could void your coverage. And who needs to pay for insurance that's no good?)

Smaller employers usually do not put the applicant in a legal half nelson to wring the whole truth from him. But because they are more likely to look askance at a history of mental disease, your relative may want to deny any acquaintance with a psychiatrist when applying for a job. If he is hired, then found out, at worst he would be fired from a job he would not have received in the first place had he told the truth. And if his work has been satisfactory, he will most likely be kept on, regardless.

A woman whose job is in the home, particularly a mother, has a special problem because circumstances often demand that she return to work before she has fully recovered—often immediately following her release from the hospital. At this point, husband and other relatives will have to roll up their sleeves and take care of the work themselves while the patient recuperates further. You can let the Colonel do the cooking, but he'll "chicken out" when it comes to the washing, cleaning, and sewing.

If she has been absent from the home for some time, the children may react to her return by becoming particularly fussy or demanding. You should explain to those old enough to understand that "Mommy has been sick, but she is getting better and will soon be well. For now, let's try to help her as much as we can." For the mother whose family cannot give her all the help she needs, hiring a housekeeper may be temporarily necessary— the hospital or clinic social worker will be able to assist in locating a homemaking service. In some parts of the country, Foster Grandparents may be able to help with the children part-time. And for military wives with husbands stationed overseas the psychiatrist may recommend an emergency leave to bring the serviceman home quickly. You can call the American Red Cross to make these arrangements—they will check with the doctor to be sure he believes such a leave is warranted.

Occasionally, help of a financial sort is available. If your relative carries a disability policy, you should ask your insurance representative whether he qualifies for benefits. If the illness has been caused or precipitated by a job which is covered by Workman's Compensation, he may be eligible for benefits while unemployed. State laws grant disability with varying degrees of liberality, so you will have to check with the state Social Security Administration for further information pertaining to his case. The patient who has recovered from his illness and finds that he no longer has a job may be eligible for unemployment benefits while he once again looks for work; he can apply through his state employment office. And for the family without medical insurance, hard-hit by medical bills, assistance may be available through government-funded Medicaid; inquire through your state welfare office.

If you decide to seek help through any of these channels, remember that there is a danger in using too liberally *any* compensation for not working. After all, the goal of all our therapy is to return the patient to full functioning, so take care that you preserve your relative's incentive for returning to work.

20.
Management II:
Symptoms

What you say to your mentally ill relative depends largely on what he says to you. Whenever possible your conversations with him should be no different from usual—just because he has become ill (and may be in the hospital) does not mean he has been scratched from the human race. But one topic will be of special concern to both of you—the symptoms which brought him to medical attention in the first place.

You usually can discuss symptoms freely and matter-of-factly with your relative and you should do so whenever he seems troubled by them, provided you remember to keep calm. Anxiety and hysteria are as contagious as the plague, and they will handicap you both as surely as a paralysis. But while you are trying to rein in on your own agitation, also avoid minimizing his complaints, pretending that nothing is wrong. You and he both know that something is (perhaps drastically) the matter, and trying to hide that fact with a conversational veneer benefits no one. Like an infection, fear flourishes in the dark; exposing it to light and air promotes the most rapid healing.

To be sure, some symptoms are more frightening than others, and will not go away with a soothing "there, there." Delusions, for example. By definition these false beliefs are fixed in the patient's mind, so you would be wasting your time as well as your credibility to try to persuade him he is wrong. Neither will it help if you reinforce his beliefs by agreeing with him, so without either agreeing or disagreeing, acknowledge the affect behind his fears.

For example, if he complains that the police keep him under surveillance at night, don't deny it or walk him around the block to prove him wrong. You might even meet a policeman on the beat! Let him ventilate his fears at length without contradiction, and then respond sympathetically with, "This must frighten you" or "I'm sure these thoughts upset you a lot." Demonstrating your sympathy and support in this way will earn you his trust and he may be able to confide more to you in the future. Once he has recovered and recognizes the fanciful nature of his delusions, he will remember you as someone who supported him when he was frightened, not as the one who insisted he was wrong.

It seems obvious that you should not let him talk you into acting on his delusions, but sometimes people forget themselves and do just that. You will understand if you have had to live with someone whose delusions refuse to go away, no matter how hard you argue. People like this are often easier to join than to lick, and families will sometimes follow along just to save the peace. But for that they pay a price. One family followed Mom through four changes of residence in as many years to elude the Episcopalians who had tapped the phone line to obtain intelligence about the children, whom they planned to kidnap.

Don't let him act on his delusions either—it can lead to more trouble than either of you needs. A trivial example is the Texan who, à la Evel Knievel, tried to jump his new Cadillac across a twenty-foot irrigation ditch. Another patient allowed "the CIA" to chase him across the country with frequent stops to fight imaginary gun battles in the streets. He was finally hospitalized in Albuquerque when he complained to police officers that a pistol-packing teenie-bopper named Joanne had assaulted him with a machine gun. Your relative's delusions probably will not endanger life and limb, as did Lyonel Child's, but you may have to confiscate his credit cards and checkbook to prevent a one-man run on the bank.

When the delusion is of guilt, you will need to tell him over and over that he has nothing to feel guilty about. This can be a discouraging proposition, inasmuch as you seem to be forever swimming against a tide of self-recriminations. But your reassurances will help him feel better, even if only for a few minutes, and with time (and medicine) that tide will begin to turn. You should try to get your relatives in on the act of propping up his drooping self-esteem. You can all praise him when he accomplishes something, even something trivial, and has done it well. But be sure to pick something *real* to praise—remember, he is only depressed or delusional, not demented, and he will see through your attempts to sandbag his self-esteem.

You can handle hallucinations in another way. When your relative sees or hears things which others cannot, he may become frightened, and eager to be proven wrong. Explain to him that these experiences are like having a dream when awake, and that he will soon awaken. Or tell him frankly that his hallucinations are simply a part of his illness, not something real which he has to fear. Putting what he sees or hears into the context of what is known or normal greatly reduces the terror it holds for him. If he is troubled by illusions, such as misidentifying a crack on the wall as a snake, you can remind him that the doctor has said this sort of experience happens to normal people all the time.

Abnormal speech patterns are hard to change, but you can help some if you have the patience. One thing you should avoid in the case of tangential speech is pointing it out to the patient—if he could understand *that,* he probably would not be talking funny in the first place. Experts have successfully tackled this problem with behavior modification therapy. Each time the patient speaks to his therapist rationally and coherently, rather than with jibberish, he receives a small reward (candy). Hundreds of repetitions later, he has begun to speak more normally. But if you want to try this sort of treatment at home, you will probably spend all your time at it and will be up to your armpits in M&M's. Better to let medicine take care of this one, which it will do with a little time.

Retarded speech should not be forced, either. Although the pace seems excruciating, these patients eventually drag forth their thoughts, and while ill they need your forbearance. With a little time and proper medicine, the retardation will almost magically dissipate. Muteness usually does not last long, either, but while it does you can easily assume that the patient is angry with you. He is not. Either his thoughts conflict so violently that they prevent his speaking, or his inner turmoil has ripped away his ability to formulate thoughts altogether. If you assume he is angry and quit trying to converse with him, he may assume you are mad at *him* and feel worse than ever—and so on. So try to keep up some conversation, even if it only amounts to little more than a monologue. As in baseball, chatter around the infield helps keep up everyone's spirits, chatterer and chatteree.

Am I crazy? Here is a great little question to have thrown at you some morning at breakfast. But over the years it has been a popular item with mental patients. It is hard to answer honestly, yet reassuringly, someone who asks you if he is losing his mind when he has just mentioned that monsters from outer space are turning his brain to jelly. To completely deny the possibility is simply dishonest and may set you up for mistrust later on. But straightforward agreement that he has lost his marbles has little to recommend it, either, in terms of what he is willing to believe and of damage to his self-esteem. You can usually finesse this question with a mild circumlocution, such as, "The doctor says that words like crazy and nervous breakdown have no scientific meaning. He says you've been sick."

If your relative persists in this or any other question where you are really stuck for an answer, go ahead and admit your ignorance. No one expects you to answer every question or solve every problem, so you should feel quite comfortable as you reply "I don't know the answer, but we'll ask the doctor when we see him next time. Let's write it down." People often feel reluctant to toss hot potatoes into the doctor's lap because he is so busy. But the doctor is in business to be busy, and his business is helping you.

DEALING WITH MOODS

Emotions are hard to control—just when you think you have the darn things boxed in, they break out again in a new direction. The doctor has trouble with his patient's moods, too, because they often defy the rules of logic. But in the last two decades, he has learned that they do respond to medication, and that is how doctors usually approach them nowadays. So you can't control your relative's moods, but the way you respond to them still can make a difference—to him in the ways he feels about his moods, and to you in the way you feel about yourself.

The abnormal mood you will most likely have to deal with is depression. If your relative has brief episodes of low mood, lasting only minutes to an hour or so at a time, you can simply reassure everyone (yourself included) that the storm will soon pass. Perhaps a good cry will help to get it out of his system. If his depression is more prolonged or more intense (say, about hurricane velocity), remind him that his medicine should soon grab hold.

Some depressed people feel better with others around. If your relative is one of these, accommodate him with visitors whenever you can. If he improves even temporarily, you will feel better knowing that he feels better. But some people become so depressed that nothing cheers them, even the presence of a best friend. If your relative has felt so severely depressed that the presence of his friends reminds him of how guilty and unworthy he is, do not force the issue—no sense in straining yourself only to make him feel worse. Continue to act matter-of-fact yourself, expressing interest and concern, but not desperation. You can offer Kleenex and comfort, but you cannot force him out of his depression by wishing it away. The desperate relative's stock remedy, telling the depressed patient to "just snap out of it," comes close to a perfect example of wasted effort. He can no more will his way out of a low mood than he could wish himself free of high blood pressure.

The affects of *anger* and *hostility* also crop up frequently in psychiatric patients. If your relative feels overwhelming anger/hostility, he is not thinking clearly. He is being driven by fears and ideas which might seem silly to you, but are real to him. If he barks at you, try to avoid snapping back with biting comments of your own. If you can pass it off without shaming him, you will avoid producing more guilt—hence more anger—and you may be able to cut through the vicious circle which his brain chemistry has started.

At the same time, you have to set limits. If his statements or actions get too far out of line, life becomes intolerable for him and loses some of its lustre for you, as well. If you allow him to say hateful things over and again, he may form a habit which persists even past the termination of his current depressive or psychotic episode. Setting limits will also help keep him from feeling guilty, provided it is done in a way which shows your love and support, and minimizes disapproval. For example, if you tell him, "You're being so disagreeable I can't stand to be with you," you will only promote distrust and further rupture your communications. But you can clear the air and help guide him in a more reasonable direction if you more gently explain, "I know you've been feeling miserable, and I'm sorry, but that kind of talk won't get us anywhere. Let's back up and start again." With a statement like this, you acknowledge the bad feelings and his right to have them. And you express sympathy at the same time that you let him know you expect better behavior in the future.

The other affect frequently encountered is *anxiety*, either caused by depression or existing by itself. In either case anxiety is uncomfortable, even disabling, and if prolonged and intense enough can generalize to those around the patient. There are several things you can do to help reduce the misery your anxious relative feels.

He has enough troubles already with the amount of tension being generated by his own inner machinery, so your best bet is to shut off any additional outside sources. Get him to cut out coffee (substitute the decaffeinated kind if he is addicted), tea, cola drinks, and chocolate. All of these contain caffeine or related substances which in excess can turn any normal person into a quivering bag of coffee nerves—imagine their effect on someone who already feels anxious.

Cigarette smoking can do much the same thing. Nicotine absorbed through the mucous membranes of the lungs initially quiets the nervous system. But within a few minutes this dissipates, leaving a prolonged stimulant effect of the tobacco which signals that it is time for another cigarette. A real addiction has occurred. You probably will not successfully persuade your relative to give up tobacco altogether, but you can help him decrease its effects by limiting the number of cigarettes he smokes each day to a tolerable level, or by suggesting he switch to a more heavily filtered brand, or try a pipe or cigars.

The doctor may have prescribed anxiolytics—Valium, Librium and others as p.r.n. medicines—to be used as necessary. But the typical anxiety attack lasts only a few minutes. By the time drugs could go to work the patient would have recovered anyway. Then all the medicine does is make him sleepy, and just when he needs to call on his energy. So have him take the pills sparingly and only as directed, when the anxiety symptoms become so distressing that nobody can stand it. The drugs are excellent in their place, but whenever possible your relative should try to get along without them.

How? If he is having an old-fashioned anxiety attack with shortness of breath, pounding heart, numbness, weakness, and the fear he will die, you might try the old paper bag trick, for years an emergency room standby. Have him hold a small sack over his nose and mouth while he breathes. This forces him to rebreathe the carbon dioxide he has been blowing off too vigorously with his hyperventilation. Putting the carbon dioxide back into his bloodstream where it belongs brings his body's chemistry back into line, and he feels better almost at once.

Persistent anxiety can be troublesome enough to interfere with sleep, and drive other, more useful, thoughts from your relative's mind. When he complains that he feels "uptight," he is telling the literal truth—anxiety does produce a state of muscle tension that accentuates his feelings of restlessness and discomfort. He literally becomes tense, often with accompanying hand-wringing, pacing, labored breathing, and other signs of agitation. His tight muscles make him feel tense all over.

He can try exercise (we have already recommended jogging) which helps to loosen the muscle tension, thereby making him feel better all over. But calisthenics are not always appropriate (hard to do "jumping jacks" in a car or at the PTA meeting), so you might suggest that he try a popular home remedy which has recently received the blessing of experimental psychology: progressive relaxation. Physicians and psychologists have developed programs which can be pursued either under a doctor's care or as a self-help program. Tape-recorded instructions are available commercially, so you might speak with the doctor to see whether he recommends a program of progressive relaxation.

The method basically is to teach the patient to relax first one portion of his body, then another. It must be done in a quiet room without distractions, usually lying on his back in bed, but with every part of his body supported. He practices concentrating first on one portion of his body—the muscles of his hand, for example, alternately tensing and relaxing them as completely as possible. As he gains control over one part of his body, he works on another, relaxing more and more muscle groups until, after a period of days or weeks, he can at will relax his entire body. In effect, he learns a form of autohypnosis, which he can later practice whenever he feels tension mounting. He may even learn to do it standing up!

Full-blown mania is a symptom which you will be unable to handle yourself. You cannot hold down the manic's soaring spirits, and you cannot control the hyperactivity *unless* you hold him down. And as for the push of speech which washes over you like a tidal wave—you might as well try to sweep back the ocean. You should immediately swim to your physician for help.

In the less severe form of the illness, hypomania, your relative is only mildly overactive. Then you may find yourself having to act as an anchor, constantly dragging him back within bounds of reality. In this affective state, you may make the difference between buying the Pinto he needs and the Lincoln Continental he does not. Simply reminding him of the payments may turn the trick.

Although you need not worry that thwarting his plans will adversely affect his illness (it will not), life will be more comfortable if you follow the basic therapeutic ploy of never refusing something outright, but substituting something else which is acceptable. ("We really can't jet to Jamaica this year, but how about driving to Denver?") If he bridles at your bait-and-switch tactics, then put your foot down with a good, firm "No." Some people fear they will incur the wrath of the patient or make his illness worse, but if you humor him by granting his wishes, you will gain nothing but a flock of creditors.

OTHER MENTAL SYMPTOMS

For two reasons, you can expect him to complain some of poor memory. In the first place, he has an illness which may well cause trouble with concentration, so he just does not pay much attention to his surroundings. Then he is treated with medicines which are notorious for playing fast and loose with memory. (The antidepressants are particularly troublesome this way.) You can give him a notebook and pencil to write things down which he needs to remember, and you can go over the details of those things which he has forgotten, gently, step-by-step if necessary, just as if he were hearing it for the first time. Most important, you can reassure him that this symptom does *not* indicate senility—his memory will recover fully once his illness has responded to treatment.

Particularly in the depths of depression, his *orientation* may suffer, too. It will be especially bothersome if your relative receives ECT. You can help by frequently reminding him of the date, perhaps with a fresh newspaper each morning. If he forgets new faces easily, casually reintroducing recent acquaintances the first few times he sees them will save him the embarrassment of fumbling for names, or worse, not realizing he *should* know them. You can also take pains to discuss current events with him, reviewing what he has missed while his attention has been on other matters (himself, mainly). Be dependable, and help him to keep a regular schedule each day, and his orientation for his surroundings should return as his illness improves.

Loss of interest is another symptom which must be attacked primarily with medication. But while you are waiting for clinical improvement, you can use the daily changes in his interest and energy to help him feel better about himself. For instance, if he shows the type of *diurnal variation* of mood typically seen in severe depression, he will feel worse in the morning and better later in the day. You might get him to work at routine chores in the morning, saving his creative activities for evenings when he feels more like himself. Of course, some patients have their periods of greater activity in the morning—for them you adjust the schedule accordingly.

When his interests slip so far that he does not even take care of his own hygiene and his dress becomes untidy, you will have to take measures which are bold and strong—you cannot pussyfoot around the problem of body odor. If necessary, put him in the shower yourself, hand him his toothbrush already pasted, and pass the bottle (of mouthwash) when he gets dry. Lay out his clothes for him and if you must, pack his dirty duds off to the cleaners— or for burial. If you can keep his hygiene at an acceptable level, you will help him maintain his own self-respect. And you will avoid letting the effects of his mental illness interfere with your own feelings for him.

ALCOHOL

If your relative drinks alcohol, you have a problem, because you must help his doctor decide whether he should drink at all, and if so, how much. Although we have already discussed in some detail (chapter 2) the common symptoms of alcoholism, we should briefly review them. These include personal and interpersonal problems (guilt feelings, fighting, loss of friends, disagreements with family over drinking); difficulties with work (absenteeism, tardiness, loss of job); legal entanglements (traffic accidents or tickets, peace disturbance, criminal activities while drinking); trouble controlling what he drinks (morning drinking, setting rules for himself, sneaking drinks); and health problems (stomach and liver diseases, blackouts, shakes, withdrawal symptoms such as DTs). Trouble in any of these areas suggests the need for further psychiatric consultation, and especially for the avoidance of alcohol altogether.

People often vigorously resist the imputation that they drink too much. "I'm not an alcoholic—I can quit any time!" might be the rallying cry of millions of drinkers who can remain sober for weeks or months on end, but who periodically sacrifice to Bacchus. Many people believe that someone is alcoholic only if he hits the gutter ("But he never missed a day's work in his life") or if he develops DTs ("Why, Aunt Ethel never saw snakes or spiders . . . 'course, she shook a lot"). But from examining many patients, several less obvious patterns of drinking have emerged, all of which spell sickness.

The alcohol-*dependent* drinker relies on it to relieve the stress he collects from everyday life. Never losing control of his drinking or showing gross intoxication, his physical health remains good and his alcoholism may go undetected until hospitalization for an unrelated problem enforces sobriety, and his anxiety overwhelms him. The *compulsive* drinker gulps his liquor and will continue drinking until he loses consciousness or until his funds run out. The *symptomatic* drinker does not even much like alcohol except as a means to relieve the stress of a preexisting psychiatric illness.

The schizophrenic finds he can diminish his hallucinations, the depressive his guilt feelings, and the manic his agitation by treating those symptoms with the only drug readily available—alcohol. The *periodic* drinker remains sober for months at a time, but when he does drink, watch out! He may awaken after a binge, lasting a week or longer, in jail or in a strange town or stranger bed. Some *spouses* of alcoholics claim that they drink only "to keep him company," and never have to rely upon an excuse of their own. Yet they vigorously, though subtly, resist any attempt to get their relative on the water wagon—it might roll off with their excuse for drinking.

It makes little difference whether or not your relative admits he is an alcoholic—if he feels more comfortable (or if you do) with a circumlocution like "problem drinker," why press the issue now? There will be time enough to agree on labels later, after you have seen what a difference a few months of sobriety can bring. Now it is important only that you both agree with the doctor that a problem exists. Then everyone's attention can turn from squabbling over semantics to problem-solving.

If frank alcoholism has been a part of your relative's problem, your only sensible goal is to help him become permanently sober. It has been proven time and again that halfway measures simply do not work. Experiments with "controlled drinking" and promises by the patient to reduce his drinking to social levels are equally doomed to failure and serve only as rationalizations for more of the same behavior. A recent Rand Corporation study which implies that some alcoholics can learn to drink socially has been roundly condemned by nearly every authority in the field—it raises false hopes and provides more excuses for those who would like to go on drinking, but who cannot. To say it again: the alcoholic or symptomatic drinker must give up alcohol completely.

But how? And what can you do to encourage his sobriety? For one thing, if you live with him, you can stop your own drinking and remove all alcohol from the house. You would not keep a cache of heroin in the pantry if he were a junkie, and alcohol is every bit as much an addiction. Having the stuff as handy as his refrigerator only tempts him needlessly.

But by no means should you adopt a "lips that touch liquor will never touch mine" policy. Withholding love and lovemaking has never proven valuable in restructuring human behavior—in fact, it has piled the final straw on more than one already tottering marriage. Experimental psychology has taught us the marked superiority of rewards in shaping behavior, whether of laboratory animals, children, or adults. The lesson seems clear enough: nagging the alcoholic (punishment) should be avoided completely. Instead, use praise or some other reward on those days when the patient remains abstinent.

If he agrees that he has lost control of his drinking, you will want to know about Antabuse. This prescription drug (generic name: disulfiram) affects the enzyme called alcohol dehydrogenase, which is responsible for metabolizing ethyl alcohol. If a patient who regularly takes this drug drinks so much as a beer, he regrets it. He quickly becomes flushed and dizzy; then nausea and vomiting set in. First he fears he is going to die, then he's afraid he won't. He lives, but because the symptoms last for several hours, no more drinking that day. And for 99 percent of the few who try it, no more ever—as long as they take Antabuse. The effect is like a policeman who stands at the patient's elbow, constantly reminding him not to drink.

As is true with most good things, Antabuse has its detractors. Some complain that it is a crutch, that the patient should do it on his own. This statement is half right, half fright. Of course it is a crutch! If you break your leg, you literally use a crutch until you mend. Why should your standards be any different for mental problems and addictions? No one can argue against the ideal of self-discipline and self-help, but if these people could control themselves, they would not be alcoholics in the first place. Catch 22. But with Antabuse, the patient can buy the time he needs to develop control over his drinking problems—and his life.

Antabuse does have one major drawback—before it can work, the patient must swallow it. And this he may be reluctant to do, particularly if, as so often happens, the passing of several months convinces him that he really has no drinking problem after all. Then he forgets to take a tablet here, two there, until soon he has omitted them from his diet entirely. Each Antabuse tablet affects the enzyme for only a few days, so the alcoholic knows he can drink again within a week of his last dose.

The doctor knows it, too, so he may ask you to help your relative remember to take his Antabuse every day. As with any other medicine, you can do this most discreetly by putting the tablet on his plate in the morning rather than handing it to him. This avoids the implication that you are forcing him to take medicine and allows the whole procedure to become a virtually unnoticed habit. If you find yourself in the position of having to enquire whether he has taken his medicine, he may respond with, "What's the matter; don't you trust me?" Then your best response will be the same one your doctor uses: "Of course I trust you—it's your illness I don't trust."

But some people can't be trusted to take their own pills. Those people you will have to check up on pretty carefully. Your doctor should be the one to instigate this—that way, he is to blame, not you, for insisting that your relative chew (it doesn't taste all that bad) his pill in front of you every morning before washing it down with juice.

What about Alcoholics Anonymous (AA) and other organizations for people with alcohol problems? Should he go? With its quasi-religious, group-support approach, AA has helped thousands of men and women give up drinking completely. In larger cities, AA meetings take place every night in different neighborhoods, so every drinker can find a group of people with whom he can feel comfortable without depending on alcohol as a mixer.

But suppose you cannot overcome the "horse to water" factor, and your relative simply refuses to attend AA meetings (or to see a physician, or, in all likelihood, to admit that he has a problem in the first place)? You may just decide to seek some help for yourself. Al-Anon, the auxiliary arm of AA, provides counseling and group therapy for the families of alcohol abusers. Even if (or especially if) you have not been able to change his drinking habits, the supportive guidance you get there should help you organize your own thinking for a happier life for you. Information about AA and Al-Anon can be found by looking under Alcoholics Anonymous in the white pages of your telephone directory.

PHYSICAL SYMPTOMS

Mental illness changes the day-to-day physiology of the body, often producing some most distressing symptoms. Broken sleep frays tempers and fractures human relationships, so you may find yourself in the position of having to help your relative sleep to knit up everyone's raveled sleeves of care. Provide the right bedtime environment: no arguments or exciting movies before sleep, though light reading may help. Try to encourage a regular time for going to bed, darken the room, and try to hold the noise outside to something less than a sonic boom. Although exercising four or five hours before going to sleep will help him relax that night, calisthenics just before bedtime will not (no sense stirring up the body's juices just when it is trying to turn them off). Coffee, Cokes, and chocolate should be avoided after late afternoon, again because of the stimulant they contain.

A light snack may help. That old nostrum of a glass of milk before retiring has recently received some scientific backing. Doctors have learned that one of the ingredients in milk, tryptophane, has sleep-inducing properties. Cereals also contain tryptophane, so a bowl of Wheaties with milk may be all the sleeping medicine your relative needs.

But occasionally home remedies simply do not work, and then the doctor will probably prescribe medicine to help. If your relative needs an antidepressant medicine anyway, one of the tricyclic class like Elavil works satisfactorily in inducing sleep if he takes the entire dose at night. Nine out of ten patients so treated will need no additional "sleeper." When he does need something extra, it should be one of the safer drugs we discussed in chapter 16, and he should first try getting to sleep without it. After a half hour or so of wakefulness, he will feel like tossing in the towel, and he might as well toss down the pill. But be ever alert to discontinue the drug as soon as he no longer needs it.

Waking up in the middle of the night (interval insomnia) is a difficult problem, because it is too late to take a sleeping pill and too early for "breakfast"—the cereal and milk routine. Sleep researchers have learned that the human body and brain operate on ninety minute cycles of electrical and biochemical activity. The would-be sleeper who awakens in the middle of one of these cycles may simply have to wait out the next hour or more until a new cycle begins and he can return to sleep. If so, he might just as well read a book or otherwise profitably occupy himself until sleep becomes inevitable. If he is the sort who tends to fall asleep reading or watching TV, a timer attached to the television or light set to turn off a half hour or so later may prevent another round of interval insomnia later the same night.

Terminal insomnia is the type of sleeplessness most typical of severe depression and one of the most terrifying for the patient. Awakening in dark when all is silent can be a horrible experience, and many psychiatrically ill patients come to dread the darkest hours before the dawn. The best help for this type of problem will be afforded by the medicine your relative takes to treat his underlying psychiatric disorder, but sleeping medicine may be necessary. You can also encourage him not to take naps during the day, thereby cutting through the cycle of sleepless nights/sleepy days, or by installing a small night-light in his room. Then, should he awaken, he will not have to face a physical blackness that matches his mood.

The opposite side of the coin, *hypersomnia,* sometimes troubles people (especially young people) when they become psychiatrically ill. You can help someone who sleeps excessively by encouraging him to eat lighter meals, which will cut down on the post-eating loginess. You can also suggest exercise—jogging, for example —which will pep him up and give him the sense that he can still accomplish things. The trouble with exercise is that to get him to do it, you may find yourself having to set a good example. You may hate it, but your heart will love you for it.

APPETITE AND WEIGHT

For some reason, we cannot stand to see anyone not eating. This tradition probably harks back to the last century when people equated adiposity with prosperity. In addition, each one of us has within him a touch of the Jewish mother who believes the cure for any illness lies in consuming sufficient chicken soup. But the aphorism, You are what you eat, confuses cause with effect—a person's eating habits really reflect the way he feels. Poor appetite in psychiatric patients generally means depression, fear, or anxiety, so the proper approach is not to force-feed the symptom but to treat the underlying disease. This done, the appetite loss generally straightens itself out.

You should regard minor weight loss as an indicator of illness rather than a cause for alarm (most Americans can stand to lose a few pounds anyway, so it may even be the silver lining in the cloud of depression). In general, you should not make a big issue of eating—let him have what he wants when he wants it, as long as he eats something and his physique stays respectable enough to keep the buzzards from circling. But if weight loss continues despite treatment, other measures should be considered. Any patient who has lost enough weight to become really malnourished should be hospitalized until his psychiatric condition can be adequately controlled.

Gain in weight crops up less frequently in major psychiatric illness, although teenagers and young adults suffering from depression are particularly prone to put on pounds. Body weight usually returns to normal once the original psychiatric problem clears. Some of the neuroleptic and antidepressant drugs prescribed by psychiatrists can also produce weight gain, either by altering metabolism or stimulating appetite—no one knows exactly why. Patients sometimes ask for diet pills as the weight problem grows out of hand and they grow out of their slacks, but doctors do not like to prescribe them. The pills themselves can alter mood, which is potentially confusing to the psychiatrist and harmful to the patient. The best treatment for weight gain is exercise—the physical type (your relative might start by pushing himself back from the table before seconds arrive), and the mental type (saying "no" to fattening foods).

Constipation is another problem caused either by illness or medicine, and it usually responds to home remedies. Prune juice and bran cereal are two old standbys that really work—use them, and nothing else may be necessary. Metamucil or some other bulk expander for the stool (it gives the bowel more to work on, using the same principle as roughage) may be tried—one tablespoonful in a glass of water three times a day. If this is not enough, two tablespoonsful of milk of magnesia taken as often as once daily for a short time also helps. Be sure to let the doctor know that constipation is a problem. He may be able to reduce some of the medicines which dry the lining of the intestines and produce constipation in the first place. Antidepressants are particularly bad this way.

Although he can also prescribe more potent laxatives, avoid them if at all possible. Americans worry far too much about their bowel habits, anyway, as anyone who has watched an afternoon of daytime television can attest. Despite all this propaganda, it falls within the boundaries of human experience to live a happy and healthy life without having a bowel movement every single day. Bowels work best when they work by themselves, and laxatives, like any other medicine, should be regarded as a temporary expedient to be discarded as soon as possible.

The problem of sex can be particularly vexing. Mental illness usually plays hob with sexual performance, although occasionally a patient like Gilbert Grand (chapter 2) becomes hypersexual— this presents problems of its own. Depression and schizophrenia usually diminish sexual interest, and this often leaves the patient's partner feeling unfulfilled and frustrated.

When the patient is a woman, this is bad enough—lacking her usual response to her husband, she feels unwifely. For a man it can be a tragedy. His mental illness not only saps his interest but can actually lead to impotence. The ensuing feeling of "loss of manhood" accelerates depression and contributes to the sense that his life has come to an end. The profound anxiety raised by these thoughts overwhelms all other (especially amatory) emotions, so even if an element of lust does poke through the mantle of melancholy, it is quickly overwhelmed by the fear it cannot be consummated.

At this point the frustrated spouse may try to jack up the lackluster performer by laying some scornful words on him, but this stratagem invariably backfires. The wife of one depressed patient sadly reported her experience: "I told him that if he didn't get his act together in the sack, I'd have to do my shopping elsewhere. I didn't really mean it. I just wanted to scare him stiff. But instead it scared him—limp!"

What can you do about sexual difficulties? After reading the above paragraphs the first rule should not surprise you: relax a little. For the patient who has difficulty performing anyway, a mate who snorts and paws the ground is worse than no help. If the patient is your husband, tell him you know he has been so preoccupied that he has not felt much like sex lately. Then hasten to add that you know he will recover soon, and when he does his sexuality will bounce back.

If he has been able to get, but not keep, an erection, he may be feeling so anxious about failure that he cannot succeed. You can offer to go to bed with him "just to relax," wear no night-clothes, and keep yourself closely available, but not demanding. As he realizes he does not *have* to perform, he may relax enough to let nature take its course. If you have chosen a daytime hour when he feels rested and when no one else is at home to distract you, you may find yourself with a dramatic cure on your hands.

Even if your initial success is limited, the spouse who adopts the attitude "We'll worry about sex when you're feeling better—it will all come out all right"—takes the heat off the patient, reduces his anxiety, and gives him the breathing room he needs to become more fully functional later. And by demonstrating your compassion and forbearance, you will also be strengthening the basis of your relationship for the future. Even if the patient cannot perform when the chips (and shades) are down, continue to "keep in touch"—to physically touch him, to caress, to massage physically and with words of love. Now, more than ever, he needs the sense and security of your closeness.

Well and good, you may think, but how long must this state of affairs (sic!) go on? Obviously, no improvement can be expected until the condition causing the sexual problem has been adequately treated. Even then, progress may be slower than you would like. Sex interest sometimes recovers more slowly than the other symptoms associated with depression—perhaps the residual of a habit formed during illness as a reaction to failed attempts at intercourse or to a spouse's pursuant scorn. Whatever the cause, spouses and patients alike, take heart: with reassurance, patience, and a little tincture of time, normal interest in sex will be rekindled. As one satisfied wife from Charleston put it, "Ah kept tellin' him that the South would rise again—and it did!"

21.
Management III:
Hospitalization

When you come right down to it, hardly anybody *wants* to go to a hospital, particularly one for psychiatric patients. Just mentioning "mental hospital" evokes visions of stark, stone walls interrupted by miniscule, barred windows from which inmates dolefully peer. Considering the prevalence of this stereotype, it is not surprising that many people at first agree with the sentiment expressed by one entering patient, "You'd have to be *crazy* to want to come here."

Fortunately, none of the common misconceptions about mental hospitals comes close to the mark, and all would be laughable if they were not so widely believed. Most of today's psychiatric wards are recently built, modern, attractive units, often located in a general hospital. They were designed with acutely ill psychiatric patients in mind, patients who require splints for their psyches more than bandages for their bodies. It makes good sense to have these people where they will receive care specially tailored to fit their needs. Although it might embarrass you less to admit your psychiatrically ill relative to a general medical ward, it makes no more sense than sending him to obstetrics if he has had a heart attack. In this day of medical superspecialization, encourage him to benefit from all the expert help he can get.

When to Hospitalize

We have already touched (occasionally hammered) upon some of the indications for hospitalization. Suicidal behavior—attempts,

297

threats, and/or ideas—is the single most important reason, but hospitalization may also be necessary for control of other sorts of behavior. Although psychiatric patients uncommonly become assaultive, particularly in proportion to the number of suicide attempts they make; when violence does occur it usually mandates hospitalization. While even rarer, homicidal ideas like those entertained by Lyonel Child present another powerful indication for detention. Many teenagers (and not a few adults) who habitually run away from home may need similar placement for purposes of evaluation or treatment.

The average diagnostic evaluation can be done in the office. It usually takes no more than one, occasionally two, interviews with a psychiatrist. But some people need more than the usual outpatient evaluation. Uncle Jack's headaches may require special neurological tests. His teenage nephew may need several days of observation before the psychiatrist can decide whether his apparently psychotic behavior has been fabricated or not. Taking a depressed patient out of his home setting may help the doctor decide whether his illness was caused by the stress of his environment— these so-called reactive depressions should then improve without medicine. Some patients enter the hospital to begin ECT or some of the more complicated types of drug therapy (chapter 14). Still others, severely deluded, lack insight that they have anything wrong with them, and simply refuse to accept the treatment they need unless it can be given in a structured, supervised setting.

Of course, we could also draw up an impressive list of reasons for *not* entering the hospital. Routine work-ups and examinations can be done quickly and adequately on an outpatient basis, and at far less cost. (Occasionally a patient will ask to be hospitalized so medical insurance will pay for his work-up. This places a heavy drain on our health care and financial resources, and should be vigorously discouraged—left unchecked it would quickly lead to massive deterioration in quality of care.)

Depression, mania, alcoholism, and schizophrenia are the most common reasons for hospitalization, but persons with mild cases can usually be treated adequately as outpatients, particularly if friends or family assist with management. Although some patients with diagnoses other than these may also legitimately be admitted, the vast majority of hospitalizable patients have one of the big four conditions. In a number of psychiatric conditions hospitalization simply does no good; it actually harms others, as in the case of the hysteric patient who chronically seeks attention by being sick.

Entering a psychiatric hospital is a reasonable option only for diagnosis or active treatment. It is not the place to send Grandma for chronic care when she reaches her dotage, nor should you regard it as a hotel where you can get away for a rest. "Active treatment" means the medical and physical procedures we have discussed in chapters 14–17, therapy which has been proven to produce improvement more quickly or more completely than the passing of time alone. It has been (and in some parts of the country, remains) fashionable to hospitalize patients solely for daily psychotherapy, a process sometimes lasting many months or even years. But because it has been well demonstrated that psychotherapy alone does not improve upon the natural history of schizophrenia or of affective disorder, this practice can no longer be condoned.

GETTING ADMITTED

In chapter 6 we discussed the different types of hospitals, and you may want to review that section now. In descending order of importance, here are some of the attributes you should look for in a good psychiatric hospital:

1. Your doctor goes there. This is the *sine qua non* of good psychiatric treatment, because the doctor sets the standard for care. Without its director, the finest orchestra in the world may not play well enough for you to distinguish Beethoven from boogie-woogie.

2. How good is the staff? Not only must there be *enough* people (average: four staff hours per patient per day) to give each patient the individual attention he needs, but each staff member should be intelligent and sensitive, capable of understanding and soothing the pain your relative feels.

3. How close to home? Visits from the family help the patient retain contact with his normal surroundings. They also help the physician to better understand the problems at home. You will enjoy each other's company more if you do not have to travel all day to get there.

4. Quality of the facility. To be sure, modern buildings with well-appointed rooms do not improve the quality of care, but they can increase your relative's comfort while he stays there. Diversions to relieve the tedium of hospitalization should include sports activities, field trips outside the hospital, occupational and recreational therapy, and group therapy.

Although your doctor can provide you with some of this information, try to visit the institution under consideration before your relative enters.

The actual process of admitting him is easy—provided he wants to go. But the situation becomes sticky if he is frightened or apprehensive, or if he downright refuses to go. A couple of generations ago these things were handled simply; when Uncle Jake lapsed into his semiannual stupor, you rang up the sheriff, who would drive out and haul him away. Nowadays we are much more concerned with patients' rights and due process of law, so it now requires more than your casual opinion that "old Jake needs to be locked up again." With some thought and tact on your part, the case of the reluctant relative usually can be handled with finesse, rather than resorting to those strong-arm tactics which sometimes lead to further resentment and resistance to treatment.

The greatest resistance to entering the hospital often comes not from the patient, who may be so miserable that its security and solitude look good to him, but from his family. Relatives worry inordinately about the disgrace ("What will the neighbors say?"), or more commonly about the supposed psychological harm ("That place will just make him worse!"). The psychiatrist knows few situations more frustrating than trying to treat a seriously ill patient who, though agreeable to hospitalization, finds himself tugged in the opposite direction by a well-meaning but misguided relative. There has never been any evidence that brief (a few weeks) hospitalizations are at all harmful; in fact, this step can be not only helpful, but lifesaving. If you feel uncomfortable about hospitalizing your relative, talk it over with the doctor—request a consultation if you still feel dissatisfied. After that, if you still cannot support this step, step out of the way so your relative can receive the help he needs.

But suppose you agree with the doctor, and it is the patient who hesitates. Then your service to him can be much more active. Urge him to act now upon the doctor's suggestion—too many lives have been lost by temporizing, "waiting to see if he won't get better in the next few days." A severely psychotic or depressed patient often cannot even decide what clothes to put on, so don't expect him to think clearly about anything as important as what sort of help he needs. He really needs someone to take over and make his decisions for him, and if you and his other relatives present a united front supporting the doctor's recommendations, he will probably capitulate and enter the hospital. Present the decision to him as one which has already been made, as if he has no choice in the matter (even though, strictly speaking, he does—he is simply in no condition to make it rationally). Then follow through firmly, guiding him—by the arm, if necessary—through the admissions procedure.

You should avoid tricking him into the hospital. This problem surfaces with the teenager whose parents, fearing he will refuse admission, explain that they are taking him out for pizza. When instead he ends up in a strange bed on a locked ward, the outraged patient often requires sedatives and restraints. The good intentions which paved the way to this sort of predicament do little to cement family relationships, either during hospitalization or afterwards. Even if his taste for pizza survives, it may be a long time before the patient can again stomach his parents. And the anger he feels at their apparent duplicity will probably generalize to his jailers—the psychiatrist and staff who keep him in the hospital—thereby making him doubly difficult, if not impossible, to work with.

With the teenager, the firm approach works best. Until their children are eighteen years old, parents still legally control them and can sign them into a hospital. Presenting this step as a no-choice situation will usually get the job done without inviting massive recriminations later on.

Commitment

But all the tact and soft-soap in the world will not entice some would-be patients into the hospital. Psychotics who fear they will be harmed or who believe nothing is wrong with them resent the implication that they need care and resist any attempts to force it upon them. These few patients—a small minority of all hospitalized patients—must then be detained involuntarily so they can receive the help they so desperately need. Such an involuntary hospitalization is called a commitment.

The laws of most states provide for some sort of involuntary stay. This usually involves an informal judicial hearing, requested by petition from a relative, friend, a doctor, or a policeman. It alleges that mental illness has so disabled the patient that he cannot properly care for himself, or that he is dangerous to himself or to other people. Lyonel Child was clearly committable because of the danger he presented to the community. Had Lois Downing attempted to sign herself out of the hospital once she awakened from her nearly fatal carbon monoxide poisoning, she could have been detained, too. Gilbert Grand threatened no one's life, but his behavior so incapacitated him for everyday life that most psychiatrists would agree to certify him for commitment.

Most states only require that any two physicians (obstetricians or pathologists will do) agree that commitment is necessary, a practice stemming from days gone by when psychiatrists were as rare as surfboards in St. Louis. The patient may contest the commitment order (although he is usually too sick to do so), may engage an attorney to defend him, and call psychiatric witnesses of his own.

But more often the need for hospitalization arises so acutely that waiting for the ordinarily leisurely commitment could result in harm to the patient (or to someone else). To handle these crises, most states allow an emergency medical certification whereby a physician, upon interviewing the patient, can sign a paper ordering him detained at a psychiatric holding facility such as a state, veterans, or private hospital for a limited time (two to thirty days, depending on the state). Although any physician can sign this type of medical hold, psychiatrists are most familiar with the indications for its execution, which are essentially the same as for the more formal commitment. Once the patient has been admitted, he cannot be detained past the brief evaluation period unless his doctor presents evidence supporting a regular court commitment.

How do you initiate these legal maneuvers? Your best start usually is to speak with your relative's own psychiatrist. He knows your state's laws and your relative's state of mind. If he decides that commitment or emergency certification is necessary, he will be able to help your family through this difficult time. If no private psychiatrist is available, you can apply through your county or state mental health center, where psychiatrists and counselors can answer your questions and advise you on how to proceed.

Once the arrangements for admission have been made, you should take your relative to the hospital as quickly as possible (no point in dallying now—unlike wine, these problems do not improve with age). It is a good idea to take along another person to help control him if he becomes acutely upset or agitated. If he is powerful, you may need a small army of neighbors, and if the situation warrants, the police or sheriff's department may be needed. Peace officers often deal with acutely ill mental patients so they know how to do it, but by law they can only help if the patient clearly needs acute care. Should your relative become violent, obviously out of control (for example, intoxicated so he could harm himself), or deeply depressed to the point of suicide, the police can take him to the closest mental health facility for evaluation.

All of this sounds pretty terrible. To the casual reader, dragooning people off the streets and whisking them away to hospitals in police cars seems more like terrorism than treatment. To fully understand these situations virtually requires personal acquaintance with the dread you feel when someone you love becomes bent on self-destruction, or loses the ability to think rationally, or even to care for himself. Some psychiatrists volubly insist upon the right of anyone to pursue his destiny as he sees fit so long as he does not interfere with the rights of another, even if he kills himself in the process. That's kismet! Dr. Thomas Szasz has repeatedly written that mental illness is not sickness at all, merely behavior used by the individual to cope with stress. He believes that civil commitment is unjust and should not be used even to save a life.

If your relative has been seriously depressed and suicidal, or if he has been disrupting his own and everyone else's lives with paranoid ideas, then you know something about mental illness of which Dr. Szasz appears ignorant—the intolerably destructive effects of deviant behavior. And because you are deeply concerned about your relative, you will probably go the extra mile to insist that he receive help when he needs it. Fulfilling obligations like this is just one of the often painful ways that people have of caring for one another. The willingness to temporarily circumvent another's wishes should be viewed as an outgrowth of the love and responsibility relatives feel for one another.

Because treatment has improved so remarkably in the past few years, most commitments of manic-depressives and schizophrenics now can be brief. Many patients improve so rapidly that a few days after emergency certification they ask to become voluntary patients, a request which will usually be granted. Those who continue to resist treatment are protected by a number of legal safeguards. In recent court decisions, committed patients have been guaranteed the right to active treatment rather than passive custodial care; periodically a review board must reconsider their cases. But all the legal machinary in the world cannot replace the safety afforded by a well-trained psychiatrist who, when your relative must be involuntarily hospitalized, can accurately diagnose his illness and quickly begin effective therapy.

If you are like most people, you worry that your relative will be angry that you insisted upon hospitalization, even when he obviously needs care. Because he now appears so adamantly opposed to seeing a psychiatrist, you presume that he will always remain so, and that he will forever blame you for forcing him into treatment he neither likes nor wants. Actually, the reverse is more often true. After the screaming and shouting have quieted and the patient has recovered, he will be grateful that someone cared enough to take the courageous step which restored his health, and perhaps saved his life. Recovered from his depression, one patient put it this way: "You doctors ought to have the option of taking people into a back room and knocking them on the head to make them listen."

In the Hospital

The type of treatment any patient, voluntary or not, receives once he has been admitted depends, not surprisingly, on the doctor and on the hospital, and how the two interact. One advantage to the hospital is that the doctor can see his patient every day—then he can more quickly adjust or change medicines than he could otherwise. He will support the patient psychotherapeutically, and together they will try to resolve problems which may either result from or contribute to the illness. He will also have a chance to talk with you, so you can discover together what changes you might make at home to help the patient once he has been discharged. The social worker can help with problems like job and financial counseling, or with such mundane, but vital, tasks as finding a place to stay.

The physician may call in a psychologist to assist in two areas: testing to clarify diagnosis, and psychotherapy. The latter often takes the form of group therapy—your relative sits down with a group leader and other patients who discuss their problems and try to benefit from each other's experiences and solutions. Many a patient has expressed his gratitude for a session which taught him that others have had problems similar to his—and survived.

One of the advantages of the psychiatric hospital over a general medical ward lies in the quality of the staff. The psychiatric nurse has been specially trained to deal with mental patients, and her job encompasses far more than dishing out pills. She knows that an important part of nursing is talking with her patient to calm his fears, reassuring him that someone understands and cares. Her experience with the emotionally distressed helps her to evaluate the subtleties of behavior and expression by which a person can communicate his state of mind more clearly than he can speak it. Her observations of behavior may be particularly valuable for the patient who puts on a happy face for his doctor, or whose clinical state changes from one time of day to the next (diurnal variation)—the doctor who sees his depressed patient only in the evening, when he is feeling better, may not otherwise appreciate the severity of his disease.

Nurses and their aides may be asked to pay special attention when your relative is first admitted or any time he seems likely to harm himself or run away. An attendant may be assigned to stay with him at all times, a precaution variously called "one to one," "special observation," "close watch," or "suicide precautions." If the danger seems excessive, either doctor or nurse may transfer the patient to the Intensive Care Unit (ICU)—a euphemism meaning a closed and especially secure environment. This may be nothing more than a locked room with a window in the door, but larger psychiatric hospitals usually have an entire ward where more severely ill patients can be safely housed until they improve sufficiently to be transferred to an open unit.

Some people become quite concerned when a relative must enter this type of high-security environment—they imagine him locked in a padded cell or a rubber room and worry that he will be terribly unhappy there. This puts the cart before the horse. If he must spend time in the ICU, it is *because* he has been so unhappy that he needs careful observation to assure his safety. Most patients require intensive care for only a few days, or a week or two at most, until treatment takes effect.

Occupational and recreational therapy (OT and RT) are two specialized forms of therapy which most patients receive during hospitalization. OT is more than simply filling in time by making things—it helps the patient regain his self-esteem by feeling the accomplishment of creating. Because occupational therapists are trained to judge the level at which a patient can perform, they prescribe tasks which challenge him, yet which he can complete.

RT encompasses quite a diversity of activity, and the more diverse the better. Physical exercise (jogging, calisthenics, basketball or individual sports like tennis) may help him get back into fighting trim and feel better about himself. And those who have improved sufficiently can enjoy a variety of social activities, among them field trips, dances, sing-alongs and parties (no need to feel guilty about putting your relative into a good mental hospital—it may seem like a vacation).

VISITING

No matter how good the activities and USO shows were, the troops always preferred news from home. The same holds true for patients in the hospital. The doctor will encourage you to see your relative as soon as he can benefit from it. You should visit him as regularly and frequently as your time, his schedule, and the doctor will allow. Life in a mental hospital can be pretty unreal, and your visits help him to regain and maintain contact with the real world. Your presence continually reminds him of something he already knows, but which in his misery he may have forgotten: that you love him.

Visiting may have to be limited to husband or wife until the patient feels mentally strong enough to receive his larger circle of friends. Then, try to hold the number of visitors to two or three at a time—a mental patient is hard-pressed to host a party, and mob scenes bother other patients and disrupt the hospital routine. That routine, by the way, will usually specify visiting hours. But if your schedule prevents you from visiting during these rather limited times, ask the doctor to allow you extra visits. He can usually arrange it.

At first keep visits brief—perhaps no longer than a few minutes to bring needed articles from home and to converse briefly on neutral topics. But later on, when your relative has improved and you both feel more confident, you can bring news from home and discuss issues of greater substance. Try to avoid lecturing him; telling him to "snap out of it" is tempting, but futile. Casting blame upon him or others, or taking blame upon yourself will only aggravate the situation which has caused him to come to the hospital in the first place. So wait to start combing through the snarls and tangles of your lives—resolving problems like these requires a healthy, active mind, not one so troubled that it needs mental hospitalization.

LENGTH OF HOSPITALIZATION

How long should your relative stay in the hospital? As briefly as possible, consistent with adequate improvement. The longer he is out of circulation, the harder he will have to work to readjust himself to the real world.

Because active, effective treatment has only recently appeared on the scene, many psychiatrists practicing today can recall the time when the words "mental illness" could spell a life sentence, and hospitalizations were measured in months and years, not days and weeks. Maybe this is why some psychiatrists still maintain a too-leisurely attitude toward length of stay. Some regard four to six week incarcerations as "short stays" despite evidence that modern medicines and techniques can treat and release the vast majority of patients in a month or less.

Most antidepressants require five days or more to become effective, so depressed patients usually must stay at least a week, and more commonly ten days to three weeks. The patient who needs ECT will have to remain longer, occasionally up to five weeks, but they are decidedly in the minority. The average manic can expect to stay two to four weeks, and it often takes a month or more to bring a schizophrenic into good control. Alcoholics can be dried out in a week or ten days, after which they should be discharged—several studies have proven that longer hospitalization does nothing to improve their prognosis. (Of course, if depression complicates alcoholism, a longer admission may be needed to straighten out this aspect of the problem.)

Recent studies show that for *any* of the important psychiatric illnesses, retaining the patient in the hospital past the time when his acute depression has lifted or his psychosis has resolved contributes nothing to his health. Staying past the point where the patient could get along satisfactorily at home may have quite the opposite effect, encouraging some patients to give up control or to become infantilized, a process sometimes called *hospitalism*. The doctor should try to steer your relative on a safe course between the reefs of early release and the shoals of excessive hospitalization. Careful physicians keep their patients in the hospital until they seem about ready for release, then hold them a day or two extra as a precaution against relapse. You can think of this extra time as a sort of insurance policy.

For many reasons a patient may want to leave the hospital before he is really ready. Because he feels frightened or anxious he may say, "The atmosphere here is making me worse," "We can't afford it," or "I'm bored." Actually, the last of these *can* serve as an indicator of readiness for discharge. Newly admitted patients often regard the hospital as a sanctuary from the cares of the world, but as they improve they chafe at confinement and become bored with beading moccasins. When your relative begins to express this feeling of boredom and requests discharge, he may be about ready for it.   .

The other reasons for wanting to leave are usually less valid, though they are often trotted out as excuses by patients who want to get out anyway. If your relative seeks early release, find out from the doctor whether the remainder of this hospitalization is absolutely essential (to finish a course of ECT, to prevent suicide, the medicine has not yet taken effect), or merely desirable ("It would be nice to have an extra day or two to make sure he won't relapse"). Then you will know how vigorously to support the recommendation to stay. Try to ignore the standard complaints he may use to gain your sympathy. Old favorites include "The nurses are mean to me" (they are probably trying to encourage him to do things for himself, or refusing to let him have sharp objects), "The food here is terrible" (nothing tastes good when you are sick), and "It freaks me out to be with these sick people" (he is probably doing a job on them, too).

Patients who are so severely ill that they *must* not leave can be detained involuntarily on a commitment. But occasionally a less severely ill patient who nevertheless *should* be in the hospital for further evaualtion decides to leave against medical advice (AMA). Because he is not psychotic, legally he cannot be detained. But because he is not ready for release, his physician must ask him to sign an AMA form absolving doctor and hospital of responsibility.

AMA discharges are a real problem. They waste your money and everybody's time, and as often as not they later lead right back to the hospital—with the patient usually sicker than before. If your relative plans to leave against advice, you should first speak with his doctor to learn as much as you can about the plans for future treatment, prognosis, and possible consequences of early departure. Then you will be in a position to make the most effective argument for staying. Whatever their state of mind, people usually want to please their families, so if you and his other relatives unite in your determination to help him, you may yet persuade him to stay.

If he insists on leaving, be sure the doctor prescribes him medicine to take home, and that he has an office appointment within a few days. Even though he has disobeyed medical advice, the doctor will still want him to receive the best possible follow-up care. Outpatient treatment may yet succeed with him, but if it fails perhaps the relationship now established will be trusting enough that your relative will later return to the hospital for definitive care.

When your relative begins to feel better, his doctor may want to try a visit home. How he functions back in his normal surroundings can provide a useful measure of his improvement. His first pass may be for only an hour or two—no sense in risking relapse by asking too much right away. If he survives the shock of this quick dip in the real world, later he can try the total immersion of an overnight pass. When this also proves successful, he will be nearly ready to discharge.

That happy day will have come when: (1) his symptoms have been eliminated or considerably decreased; (2) his medicine dose is stable; (3) he can look after himself or has someone to take care of him; (4) he has a stable, comfortable place to live; and (5) adequate follow-up care has been arranged. Once these criteria have been met, further hospitalization will not help and he should leave.

After Hospitalization

When the day of discharge finally comes, your relative will still not be completely recovered. (If he is, he may have been hospitalized too long.) So, like someone recovering from a heart attack, he must be slowly reintegrated into his old life, and you will have to do the integrating. Besides looking after his medicine and providing for his general physical care, you may have to assume some of his normal responsibilities for a time. You should be prepared to drive him about if he feels shaky behind the wheel, remind him to pay bills, and help him keep appointments. These are only a few of the day-to-day activities most of us take for granted, but which the newly released psychiatric patient may find difficult. Anyone who has been out of circulation for a while needs time to catch up on the news and build up his strength. When he returns to work, he might do better on half days at first, rather than jumping straight back into his normal routine.

At home, you should try to maintain a relaxed atmosphere—it helps foster sympathetic relationships. An established routine (preferably his own) will put him back on his feet more quickly. Although he will probably be able to stand the ordinary stresses of daily life, a peaceful, cheerful environment will help smooth the way for a speedy convalescence. With a little practice you will learn to walk the fine line between being oversolicitous and undersensitive, coming at last to treat your relative as he should be treated—which is, naturally.

Patients who see their doctors after discharge from hospital do better than those who do not. So it stands to reason that good follow-up care is important to maintain your relative's newly regained emotional stability. The same doctor who cared for him in the hospital should see him as an outpatient as well, but this is not always possible, particularly if he was treated in a government or university-type hospital. Then you should take some steps to assure good continuity of care.

Anyone is more likely to keep an appointment if he knows who it is with. So before discharge, try to have him meet the physician who will follow him as an outpatient—you can ask the inpatient physician or social worker to arrange this. If his follow-up care will be provided some distance from the hospital, such as by an outlying mental health center or a family practitioner, you might request the inpatient physician (who you hope is not also an impatient physician) to send a letter outlining the proposed postdischarge program. Hand the letter directly to the new doctor—although discharge summaries are usually sent to follow-up physicians, they have a way of getting stuck in the hospital steno pool for weeks on end, far beyond the time they are most needed.

The first follow-up visit should come within a week or ten days of discharge. Intervals much longer than this leave too much room for problems to develop. Depending on the nature of the original illness, the doctor will probably schedule subsequent visits for intervals of anywhere from a week to a month, although if new problems have cropped up even more frequent visits may be indicated. As improvement continues, the interval between visits will increase proportionately. During this phase of treatment, you should always have available the doctor's telephone number, and feel free to use it. If things do go sour it can happen in a hurry, but prompt attention at the onset of recurrence can often bring the situation quickly under control, avoiding further hospitalization.

RELAPSE AND CHRONICITY

No one likes to think about illness relapsing, particularly with hospitalization still a fresh memory. But symptoms sometimes recur, a fact with which we must live and with which you can deal effectively if you prepare yourself.

When your relative is discharged, his doctor should let you know what sort of symptoms could spell recurrence—if he forgets, ask! Subsequent attacks will usually resemble the first one (with the obvious exception of the manic-depressive patient, who may go from a high to a low, or vice versa). Not only can you expect the same symptoms to occur again, but they will probably even fall into the same pattern. If your depressed relative's early symptoms were loss of interest in his bowling league followed by insomnia, recurrence of these symptoms should alert you that another episode may be on the way.

Nearly all manics eventually develop depression, and about 25 percent of depressed patients will also have a mania. So if your relative has had one condition you should learn to recognize the symptoms of the other (chapters 7 and 8). Because of the biphasic or triphasic nature of manic-depressive disease, he is more likely to proceed to the opposite extreme just after recovery from one phase of bipolar disease.

These precautions notwithstanding, you need not fear recurrent symptoms—just be alert for them. You have already come through the really frightening phase of mental illness—the agony of knowing something is terribly wrong, but not understanding it or knowing what to do about it, and fearing that nothing *can* be done.

With the uncertainty of that first episode now behind you, your anxiety level should drop enough that you can stop fearing the future and start planning for the present. The prospect of relapse leading to chronic hospitalization is the fear which haunts many patients and their relatives. Actually, chronic illness occurs in a minority of the psychiatric patients we have discussed in this book. Medicines can now reach nearly all, no matter how seriously ill, and with proper treatment few require long-term hospitalization. Schizophrenic deterioration, in which patients regress so severely that they cannot work, care for themselves, or even talk sensibly, has become virtually a thing of the past. This dread outcome, formerly a common endstage of schizophrenia, was caused in large part by the isolation and neglect once prevalent in our large, government-operated institutions. Over the last forty years, better laws and a developing awareness that mental patients need more than just food and a place to sleep have virtually eradicated both cause and effect.

Away from Home

Despite everyone's best efforts, some patients cannot (or will not) return home. Sometimes there is just no room at the inn, but more often a personality clash with other members of the household stirs the home brew until nobody can stand it. Still other patients need more supervision or care than the family can provide. Whatever the reason, a little searching will reveal several alternatives to the cold-war atmosphere of relatives mutually co-existing under one roof.

Of all the possibilities, your relative will probably favor independent living—a house or an apartment of his own, either alone or with a roommate. This choice can be good or bad depending upon his degree of recovery, need for supervision, and especially on his previous track record with independent living. Realistically, if he has been continuously ill for years, has had several hospitalizations, and has relapsed following each one because he failed to take medicine, he is less than a first-class candidate for independent living. But there is no reason why even a long-standing psychiatric illness, once fully controlled, should prevent anyone from living as he wishes. In our anxiety to protect, we sometimes overprotect the patient who, though long incapacitated by illness, at last improves to the point where he can look out for himself.

Some people temporarily (or longer) cannot live alone but need less supervision than continuous hospitalization provides. They can choose among several degrees of care.

After-care facilities may be called halfway houses or board and care facilities, but they provide the same basic function: some of the supervision provided by hospitals at a fraction of the cost. Although all of these facilities provide room and board, some structured activities, and a degree of supervision, the quality of their service varies as widely as their locations. If you are considering this type of placement, obtain a list of those available near you and visit them all. Smaller facilities, often quartered in private homes, may accept only males or females, but those licensed for a larger capacity (including the halfway houses) usually accept both sexes. Because licensing laws vary from state to state, the type of facility available will also depend upon where you live. Your psychiatric social worker can best inform you about your options.

Special Help

A number of agencies and private organizations provide advice, support, and material help for mental patients struggling to regain and retain their health. Meeting patients who have experienced (and conquered) similar problems can be more supportive than almost any other activity, hence the popularity of groups like Recovery, Inc., and We Care. You can find local chapters in the white pages of the telephone directory. Another special interest group, Alcoholics Anonymous, through the years has helped millions control their drinking habits. Those whose mental illnesses are complicated with alcoholism may also find help here. A word of caution: the AA philosophy discourages using drugs in any form. This includes not only tranquilizers but Antabuse and antidepressants as well. Here is an area where the psychiatric patient must sometimes take the AA program with a grain of salt.

The importance of being able to work constructively can hardly be overemphasized. Everyone needs a sense of competence and usefulness to substantiate good feelings about himself, and no one needs this type of support more than a recently recovered psychiatric patient. Although most people return to their former occupations once released from the hospital, a few cannot. For them, job retraining may be necessary. Vocational rehabilitation can provide counseling and testing services to determine what type of work is most appropriate for your relative. Once his needs and capabilities have been evaluated, he can be referred to one of the retraining programs in your area. You can find out about these programs through the hospital Social Service department or by calling your state employment office or mental health center.

Postscript

Where is psychiatry going? No one asks rhetorical questions unless he thinks he knows the answers, and I confess that I consider myself no less prescient than the next psychiatrist. But the future of our profession is dyadic, not unitary, holding prospects for practitioner and patient which, though of course intertwined, are quite different. So we had better consider them one at a time.

The prospects for any group of patients lie in prevention. Unfortunately, we cannot now prevent any mental illness in the sense we can prevent rheumatic fever by treating with penicillin the strep throat that precedes it. Prevention of this sort—heading it off at the pass before it strikes—requires thoroughly understanding its causes, and we know far too little of the antecedents of manic-depressive disease and schizophrenia. The one causative factor we can identify, inheritance, cannot now be controlled except by the decision of one's parents not to have children. And by the time that need becomes apparent, it is of course already too late. Whatever portion of psychiatric illness the environment contributes will surely prove more manipulable, but we do not yet know how to do that, either.

There is a second way to prevent illness, and this is available even now. That is the prevention of further episodes of illness once a patient has become ill for the first time. Here is a more practical method—it does not try to prevent new cases completely, only to reduce the patient's down time once he has been identified as ill. With drugs like lithium the physician can control the course of illness, rather than sitting helplessly by to await each new attack. A giant step indeed, one nearly worthy of an epithet which has been applied to it, "the third revolution in psychiatry."

Pleasant thought, though hyperbolic; revolutions need more cannons than one, and soldiers who know how to use them.

The third type of prevention consists of limiting the harmful effects of an illness once it has appeared. This is the rationale behind all the medicines and psychotherapy we use. That is also why you have read this book—to learn what you can do to help limit the distress caused by illness in your own family. This sort of prevention holds the greatest promise for benefits in the immediate future, and it provides your point of attack upon the problems confronting you.

The psychiatrist has a future, too, but rather different from his patient's. With the development over the last few years of new treatment methods and strategies, it has become increasingly important that those who care for patients learn to appraise scientifically the value of the methods they employ. I believe that the future of psychiatrists lies in a willingness to adopt this "tough-minded" approach.

Unfortunately, far too few psychiatrists now insist on controlled data in evaluating treatment methods, and fewer still use rigorous diagnostic criteria in the day-to-day practice of their profession. Those who do are sometimes called antihumanitarian, and schools which teach healthy skepticism, antitherapeutic. But if we lack the willingness to objectively evaluate what we are doing, we will never learn to match up the most accurate diagnosis with optimal treatment. And how therapeutic, how humanitarian is that?

The "new" therapies advanced for the treatment of psychiatric or psychological problems are really nothing more than variations on a few old themes, the most prevalent of which has been psychotherapy. Primal scream therapy, transactional analysis, and erhard seminar training (est) are among the more recent "discoveries" touted as helping people learn to feel better.

Now, I have no basic quarrel with anyone who wants to soften up the often stringy fiber of life. If you can find something to help you get along better with other people (or with yourself), to give you the courage to get married (or divorced), to ask the boss for a raise (or, if you are the boss, to refuse the same request from your employee without feeling guilty), then do it—within reason, of course. Transcendental meditation, encounter groups, psychoanalysis, group therapy—any of these may help you chart a successful voyage of self-discovery. So, if you are inclined to go exploring, cast off!

But too often patients, relatives, and therapists alike fail to distinguish between problems of living and real mental illness. Apply this year's therapeutic nuance indiscriminately to illnesses which are as old as mankind, and the method often loses its charm.

It may even become harmful. An occasional psychotic patient decompensates under the stress of an encounter session; now and then someone kills himself while the therapist treats his theory of disease instead of his patient. But this trickle of tragedies is engulfed in the torrent of patients who waste their time on useless mental gymnastics as faddish pseudo-therapy displaces potentially helpful treatment. It is the hundreds of thousands of people who suffer needlessly because of psychiatrists' ignorance or inexpertise whom I consider to represent the true outrage of psychiatry.

Not that the more conventional atrocities have been misrepresented. Subjecting anyone to a lobotomy against his will should be unthinkable, yet even quite recently such infamies have been not only thought, but enacted. No patient confined to a mental hospital should be denied voting rights, nor should he be held without treatment or judgment, nor should his mail be opened against his wishes; yet these infringements occurred routinely until the last decade or two, when attorneys and activists went to work to force psychiatrists and hospital superintendents to mind their constitutional p's and q's. That every patient has a right to legal counsel will be acknowledged by any psychiatrist in his right mind, a list of whom would unfortunately be more exclusive than one might wish.

Not everything is rosy on the legal front, either, as lobbyists and legislators jostle for position at the head of the line to limit some patients' rights to effective treatment. The example of lobotomy and its successor, the cingulectomy, is too well known to do more than mention. Clearly, these procedures are drastic last resorts which should not be used for any but the worst cases of depression and obsessive-compulsive disease, patients who do not respond to any other treatment. Yet legal busybodies, egged on by know-nothing psychiatrists, seek to limit your relative's right to psychosurgery, even if he wants it and if it represents his only hope for survival.

Other legislation has recently been proposed in California which would absolutely prohibit anyone under the age of eighteen from receiving ECT—even if nothing else could relieve a suicidal depression. And if still another group of fuzzy-thinking libertarians has its way, some day your relative will have the right to kill himself if depressed, and there won't be a thing you can do to prevent it.

Throughout this book I have been occasionally critical of my fellow psychiatrists. This is no more than they often deserve. I have read most of the popular books by and about patients who have been abused to one degree or another by members of my profession. I find most of these accounts frightening, depressing, embarrassing, poignant—and believable. Any psychiatrist with a consulting practice could add new cases every month: the depressed student whose too-low dose of antidepressant lost him two years of school; the depressed woman whose psychiatrist told her, "You're just spoiled," despite her five manic-depressive relatives; the psychotic sixteen-year-old whose psychiatrist refused to prescribe adequate drugs because he did not believe in them. Despite their number and their blatancy, these failures of treatment rarely surface on the public consciousness, probably because diagnostic concepts have been hard enough to be grasped by psychiatrists, let alone the general public.

These egregious errors of diagnosis and treatment involve the illnesses of schizophrenia and affective disorder, the oldest and best-recognized of psychiatric conditions. At the turn of the century and earlier, they made up the bulk of the patients seen by alienists, as we were known then. Some today argue that these are the only two conditions psychiatrists should treat, that neurologists, psychologists, and counselors can competently care for the others. In any case, I do not believe it asks too much for anyone who calls himself a psychiatrist to have a working knowledge of contemporary treatment methods in manic-depressive disease and schizophrenia. These illnesses are just too important to leave to the whim of individual prejudice. Just as the internist must keep up with the latest in antibiotic therapy, psychiatrists should be held to current standards of scientific diagnosis and treatment.

I believe the slipshod psychiatry of today will encounter in the future two sorts of limitations, the effects of which will be to force practitioners into the mainstream of sound psychiatric practice. The first of these coercive factors, third party pay, has already begun to affect the quality of care. With each passing year, a greater proportion of medical care is financed by someone other than the patient. In the early 1970s, at least 50 percent of all general psychiatric patients were at least partly covered by private insurance programs or by various government agencies (Medicare, Medicaid, and CHAMPUS). Usually these agencies footed well over half the bill.

The huge sums spent by insurors entitle them to some assurance that the services they buy are worth having. The move toward professional standards review organizations (PSROs) has already begun in an effort to force physicians to police the quality of care given by colleagues. In seeking to define what the standards of care should be, many of these review organizations have adopted criteria for diagnosis strikingly similar to those discussed in chapters 7 through 10.

Will uniformity thus imposed be enough to ensure quality care? I doubt it. Most psychiatrists even today are trained to emphasize the understanding of interpersonal dynamics (the soft-headed approach), often at the expense of hard-headed values like criteria for diagnosis and follow-up studies to evaluate effectiveness of treatment. Retraining tens of thousands of physicians whose minds are already made up would be a Herculean (if not impossible) and certainly thankless task, but an essential one if all practitioners are to continue to have equal access to all patients.

The alternative I find both likely and unlikeable—the division of our profession into yet another subspecialty: diagnostic psychiatry. The specially trained and licensed diagnostic psychiatrist would consult in difficult cases at the request of the insuror, perhaps a few days after a patient is admitted to a psychiatric hospital. He would see that a scientific diagnosis has been made, that it has led to appropriate treatment, and that (if reevaluation is ever required) the patient is not kept in the hospital too long. Non-compliance with diagnostic standards would result in refusal to pay the hospital or doctor—a big stick, indeed.

Depending on your outlook, this proposal may sound like either Big Brother or simply a big bother. But the concept represents more than simple utopianism—we already have ample precedent for such a step. For a year and a half, California required three consultations before a patient could even receive a course of ECT, a law enacted to protect patients from unnecessary treatment. But the legislature failed to require the consultants to have any particular expertise in the use of ECT, let alone any commitment to the use of scientific diagnosis. Numerous cases arose in which the impaneled "experts" either were philosophically opposed to ECT under any circumstances or simply rubber-stamped the treatment proposal of colleagues who returned the courtesy. This arrangement, whereby the doctors all are paid but the patients receive no benefit, is less boon than it is boondoggle, and it is not what I had in mind. But it does provide a precedent for the type of coercive measure I believe will ultimately be adopted.

Third party payers like Blue Cross are already getting into the act, requiring consultation before elective surgery. Not surprisingly, they have found some proposed operations to be even more elective than the patients thought—in fact, totally unnecessary. Insurance companies and governments alike now require hospitals to establish utilization and review committees to assure that no patient is confined longer, examined more often, or treated more than necessary. Small beginnings, perhaps, but they represent the foundation for much closer supervision of psychiatry in the future. Unpleasant news for psychiatrists, but we have no cause for complaint; we have brought it on ourselves.

The general thesis of this book implies another consequence for psychiatrists in the near future, and that has to do with malpractice. Up to now we have escaped this furor relatively unscathed. We are infrequently sued; damages are awarded more rarely still. And our insurance premiums have been modest, at least compared with those of other medical specialists. When a psychiatrist is hauled before the bar, it is usually for problems related to ECT, drug reactions, or general negligence. To my knowledge, not one has ever been successfully sued for failing to make a proper diagnosis, probably because so few people can understand what psychiatrists are talking about, anyway—diagnostic concepts have simply been too fuzzy to test in court.

But the advances in diagnosis made during the past three decades will change that. Psychiatrists—or families, or lawyers—need no longer depend, as once we all did, on subjective opinions, hunches, or psychological tests of questionable validity. Instead, using objective criteria based upon scientific data obtained from thousands of other patients, anyone can state, often with authority, whether or not a patient has been diagnosed correctly. And when legitimate questions remain, it should at least be evident whether the diagnosis was made carefully.

Right now the old style of diagnosis and therapy enjoys a wide following; it is still taught in many medical schools and residency programs. But psychiatric journals are increasingly given over to articles on scientific psychiatry, and even the popular press occasionally suggests that for most patients other approaches exist besides "the couch." It will take but a few years—about a decade, I would guess—for people to come to expect proper care from a psychiatrist, just as they would from any other physician, and to infer negligence when it is not forthcoming. Then will begin the unhappy parade of patients and families seeking in court the satisfaction they should have found in the clinic. And there, I believe, they will not be disappointed.

A great pity, but it doesn't have to be this way. Doctors are human and make mistakes. The complete psychiatrist, being at least as human as other doctors, does not always know the answers, no matter how well trained he is. Sometimes he barely understands the questions. But he does know the result he wants, and that is help for your relative and happiness for your family. To this end he will practice the science of medicine as artfully as he can, but he must be guided in what he does by his relationship with you. And you must work to make this relationship increasingly a trusting, thinking, and helping one if you would be your brother's keeper.

Glossary

These terms are defined as they have been used in this book. Many have more general meanings as well.

affect: the feeling or emotion behind a thought; the way a person appears to be feeling; often used interchangeably with mood.

mood

affective disorder: a prolonged (more than a few days) disturbance of affect, usually too sad or too happy.

akathisia: restless inability to sit still which sometimes develops as a side effect of neuroleptic drugs.

alcoholism: prolonged (two years or more) excessive drinking leading to problems (social, work, legal, financial, or health) for the drinker.

ambivalence: the state of having two (usually opposite) feelings about something or someone.

antidepressant: any drug or other treatment used to treat depression.

antisocial personality: a chronic personality disorder beginning in youth, characterized by lack of conscience, impulsivity, inability to live by society's rules, and (often) criminality. Synonyms include *sociopathy* and *psychopathy*.

anxiety: an emotional state of tension or apprehension; often accompanies depression.

anxiety neurosis: nonpsychotic illness characterized by attacks of anxiety accompanied by pounding heart, difficulty breathing, weakness, and other bodily symptoms.

anxiolytic: reducing anxiety; a class of drugs, also called minor tranquilizers, used to treat anxiety.

association: the way in which one thought is joined logically to the next.

autism: egocentric thinking of a subjective nature in which reality is distorted; includes daydreams, delusions, fantasies, and hallucinations.

barbiturates: sedative drugs used to calm agitated or anxious patients. Highly lethal and potentially addicting, they have been superseded in modern psychiatric practice by anxiolytics and neuroleptics (q.v.).

bipolar: type of affective disorder in which the patient has both manias and depressions; used interchangeably with manic-depressive disease.

blackout: alcohol-induced amnesia for events which occur while the person is drinking; often symptomatic of alcoholism.

blocking: sudden stoppage of speech, often in midthought; often symptomatic of schizophrenia.

breakdown: nonscientific word denoting psychiatric illness or nervousness.

catatonic: subtype of schizophrenia characterized by disorders of motion. Typically, these patients posture, maintain positions into which they are placed, grimace, are mute.

chromosome: "strings" of genetic material (genes) contained in the cells of every living organism. People have twenty-three pairs of chromosomes.

cingulectomy: one of the newer brain-cutting operations (psychosurgery) which have replaced the more destructive lobotomy.

cohort: group of people who have something in common, e.g., year of birth.

compulsion: the urge to perform an act over and over despite one's desire to resist; usually occurs as a part of obsessive-compulsive disease.

concordance: the similarity of a twin pair for a trait or illness; opposite of discordance.

controlled study: testing a theory by comparing two or more groups with each other. In one of these groups a particular condition (such as treatment with active drug) is present, whereas in the others (the control group), it is not. The control group counters the possibility that the experimental results might have occurred by chance.

cyclothymic: personality type in which the mood alternates between mild highs and lows; less severe than manic-depressive disease.

delirium: temporary loss of orientation, memory, and ability to solve problems, often accompanied by hallucinations. Due usually to effect of toxins on the brain.

delusion: a fixed, false belief. A patient's conviction that his relatives are working for the Nazis is a delusion—provided they aren't.

dementia: (usually permanent) loss of ability to think, remember, and solve problems, due to changes in brain structure or metabolism.

dementia praecox: antiquated term for schizophrenia.

depression: mental state of low mood, sometimes occurring in reaction to life stress (reactive depression), but often occurring as a primary illness without known precipitant. See affective disorder.

diagnosis: the physician's evaluation of a disease or problem, formulated to help him predict course of illness, outcome, best treatment, and other facts about the patient.

discordance: when only one member of a twin pair has a particular trait or illness; opposite of concordance.

dopa: neurotransmitter thought to be implicated in schizophrenia.

double-bind: a statement which requests someone to do two contradictory things, so he is wrong no matter which he chooses; alleged by some to be a cause of schizophrenia.

dystonia: abnormal muscle tension; may occur as a sudden cramping due to neuroleptic drugs.

ECT: electroconvulsive therapy. Electrically induced seizure effective in treatment of severe depression.

ego: the conscious self; psychoanalytic term referring to that part of the psychic apparatus that mediates between the person and reality.

empirical: something which has been learned by observation. An empirical treatment is one for which there seems no rationale, but it works anyway.

endogenous: coming from within. Used to describe depression for which there seems no obvious cause (primary depressions).

enzyme: a biochemical which helps speed up chemical reactions in the body.

epidemiology: the study of disease in populations. An epidemiologist hopes to learn how to control illness by identifying its cause from patterns of occurrence in populations.

etiology: cause.

euphoria: abnormally happy or optimistic mood; typical of mania.

flight of ideas: type of loose association in which thought jumps from one topic to another in an understandable fashion (the connection between thoughts is apparent).

four A's:　　　　　a mnemonic for the four symptoms which some psychiatrists consider most typical of schizophrenia (autism, ambivalence, loose associations, and disturbance of affect).

gene:　　　　　a unit of genetic information which either acting alone or with other genes determines the appearance of inherited characteristics.

grief reaction:　　　　reactive depression caused by loss (usually death) of a loved one.

hallucination:　　　a false sensory perception in which the individual sees, hears, tastes, smells, or feels something which is actually not there.

hebephrenic:　　　subtype of schizophrenia characterized by disturbance of affect (silly or flat) and loose associations (tangential speech).

hypersomnia:　　　excessive sleeping.

hypnotic:　　　drug whose main function is to induce sleep.

hypomania:　　　abnormally high mood and excited behavior which has not reached psychotic proportions; less than full-blown mania.

hysteria:　　　chronic nonpsychotic illness occurring predominately in women, characterized by excitability and the tendency to complain of many physical and emotional symptoms.

id:　　　psychoanalytic term referring to that part of the personality harboring one's instincts and drives.

illusion:　　　misinterpretation of an actual sensory stimulus.

incidence:　　　the number of new cases (as of an illness) which are detected in a particular period of time; cf. prevalence.

insight:　　　self-understanding, particularly of the fact that one is ill.

insomnia: difficulty sleeping. May be initial (trouble getting to sleep), interval (waking during the night), or terminal (awakening early in the morning, unable to get back to sleep).

judgment: the ability to make an appropriate decision in a given situation.

labile affect: excessive variation in mood.

libido: in psychoanalytic terms, energy of the sex drive.

loose associations: disturbance of the coherence of thoughts; often used synonymously with tangentiality.

mania: abnormal affective state of elevated mood with hyperactivity, push of speech, flight of ideas, and (often) delusional grandiosity.

MAOI: monoamine oxidase inhibitor; a class of antidepressant drugs effective in certain types of depression.

mental status: the level of functioning of all aspects of the mind.

milligram (mg): 1/1000 of a gram: an aspirin tablet contains 300 milligrams of drug.

mood: a person's subjective emotional state; often used synonymously with affect.

multifactorial: having several causes. In multifactorial inheritance, more than two genes of equal potency produce the clinical picture.

natural history: the duration and outcome of an illness left untreated to run its course.

negativism: behavior opposite to that requested; seen in catatonic schizophrenics and normal two-year-olds.

neuroleptic: a class of drugs which has both calming and antipsychotic properties; formerly called major tranquilizers.

neurosis:	ill-defined psychiatric condition or illness in which the patient has symptoms and is uncomfortable, but knows something is wrong; that is, he is not psychotic. Also used as an insulting adjective to describe patients, mothers-in-law, and other psychiatrists.
neurotransmitter:	any chemical used by the body to pass messages from one nerve to another.
norepinephrine (NE):	the neurotransmitter thought to be responsible for maintaining mood; also called noradrenalin.
organic brain syndrome (OBS):	temporarily or permanently diminished capacity to think, learn, reason, or remember due to chemical or physical changes within the brain. May be either a delirium or a dementia (q.v.).
obsession:	an unwanted thought which keeps recurring despite efforts to resist it.
obsessive-compulsive disease:	a nonpsychotic illness in which the patient is troubled by obsessions and compulsions.
orientation:	the portion of the mental status exam which evaluates the patient's awareness of where he is, who he is, who other people are, and the date.
orthostatic hypotension:	drop in blood pressure due to change in position (usually standing up). This produces dizziness.
paranoid:	delusions of persecution; subtype of schizophrenia characterized by auditory hallucinations and delusions of persecution.
phobia:	unreasonable fear of something.
placebo:	inactive treatment given for its psychological value in improving symptoms; e.g., sugar pills.
premorbid personality:	a patient's personality characteristics before he became psychiatrically ill.
prevalence:	the number of cases (as of an illness) existing at any given time; cf. incidence.

primary: an illness which occurs chronologically before other illnesses or conditions, as in primary affective disorder.

proband: the first case of an illness or condition identified in a family; index case.

prognosis: an estimate of how well a patient will do in the future.

pseudoneurotic: a term used to label certain patients whom some psychiatrists believe have schizophrenia. Most do not.

pseudoparkinsonism: neuroleptic-induced tremor and stiffness of muscles which resembles naturally occurring Parkinson's disease.

psychiatrist: a medical doctor who specializes in treating mental and emotional disorders.

psychoanalyst: a psychiatrist who subscribes to the psychological causation of mental illness, and who treats it with long-term, insight-directed psychotherapy.

psychologist: a specialist (he may or may not have a doctorate but is not a medical doctor) in the study of the workings of the mind. He may do testing or psychotherapy, but cannot prescribe medication.

psychopath: older synonym for antisocial personality (q.v.).

psychosis: severe mental disorder in which the patient has lost touch with reality (has hallucinations or delusions). It is not an illness itself, but a description which can apply to patients with many different psychiatric illnesses.

psychosurgery: any of several brain-cutting operations occasionally used to treat otherwise intractable depressions or obsessive-compulsive disease.

push of speech: rapid speech, often hard to interrupt, typically seen in mania, where it is associated with flight of ideas (q.v.).

rapport:	a sense of liking or good feeling between two individuals.
schizoaffective:	a psychotic illness combining features of schizophrenia with those of affective disorder (either depression or mania). It is officially classified with the schizophrenias, but is more often due to affective disorder.
schizophrenia:	a usually chronic psychosis characterized by delusions, hallucinations, tangential speech, and abnormalities of affect.
schizophreniform:	a psychosis which looks like schizophrenia and may turn out to be schizophrenia, but does not meet strict diagnostic criteria. Many of these patients are called schizoaffective by their psychiatrists.
secondary:	an illness occurring subsequent in time to another psychiatric illness; a secondary affective disorder would be depression occurring in an alcoholic, hysteric, antisocial personality, etc.
sedative:	any drug that quiets or calms an excited patient.
sensorium:	consciousness; that portion of the mental status examination which covers the patient's orientation, ability to calculate, to reason, to remember, and his fund of general information.
side effect:	any unwanted result of treatment.
sociopath:	synonym for antisocial personality (q.v.).
succinyl choline:	muscle-paralyzing drug used in ECT to reduce the intensity of the electrically induced seizure.
suicide:	intentionally killing oneself.
superego:	psychoanalytic term meaning the conscience.
symptom:	anything a person feels that indicates he is ill.
tangentiality:	type of loose association in which one thought bears no understandable connection to the previous one.

tranquilizer: a drug used to calm anxious or agitated patients. Major tranquilizer is a term used synonymously with neuroleptics (q.v.), which have antipsychotic properties as well. Minor tranquilizers are anxiolytics.

tricyclic: the most commonly used class of antidepressant drugs.

undifferentiated schizophrenia: term commonly used to label schizophrenic patients who show such a mixture of symptoms that a more specific subtype diagnosis cannot be made.

unipolar: type of affective disorder in which only depression occurs.

X-linkage: type of genetic transmission in which an illness or trait is carried on the X chromosome. Therefore, mothers can transmit it to children of either sex, but fathers can pass it on only to their daughters.

Suggested Readings

Beers, Clifford W. *A Mind that Found Itself*. Garden City, N.Y.: Doubleday and Company 1960. Autobiography of a manic-depressive man who spent time in the early years of this century in an institution. Good insight into what it is like from one who has been there.

Cammer, Leonard. *Up from Depression*. New York: Pocket Books, 1971. More advice and help for relatives of the depressed.

Choron, Jacques. *Suicide*. New York: Charles Scribner's Sons, 1972. History, philosophy, and data on the "easy way out."

Fieve, Ronald R. *Moodswing: The Third Revolution in Psychiatry*. New York: Morrow, 1975. Good discussion of bipolar disease, with emphasis on treatment with lithium.

Freedman, Alfred M.; Kaplan, Harold I.; and Sadock, Benjamin J. *Comprehensive Textbook of Psychiatry—II*. Baltimore: Williams and Wilkins, 1975. Two volumes on every imaginable topic in psychiatry. If you really want to get into the subject, here is the place to go.

Goodwin, Donald W., and Guze, Samuel B. *Psychiatric Diagnosis*. 2nd Ed. New York: Oxford University Press, 1979. Best brief discussion of the well-defined psychiatric diagnostic categories. Written for physicians, but understandable by laypersons.

Kline, Nathan S. *From Sad to Glad*. New York: Ballantine Books, 1975. Authoritative discussion of biological aspects of depression by one of the original drug researchers.

Knauth, Percy. *A Season in Hell*. New York: Harper and Row, 1975. Excellent contemporary description of what it is like to have a depression, written by someone who is there.

Snyder, Solomon H. *Madness and the Brain*. New York: McGraw-Hill, 1974. Erudite discussion of schizophrenia, primarily from the biological point of view. Long on theory, short on advice.

Index